D1058966

Well Said!

Well Said!

PRESENTATIONS AND CONVERSATIONS
THAT GET RESULTS

Darlene Price

⁴AMACOM

American Management Association
New York • Atlanta • Brussels • Chicago • Mexico City • San Francisco
Shanghai • Tokyo • Toronto • Washington, D.C.

Bulk discounts available. For details visit:
www.amacombooks.org/go/specialsales
Or contact special sales:
Phone: 800-250-5308
E-mail: specialsls@amanet.org

This publication is designed to provide accurate and authoritative information in regard to the subject matter covered. It is sold with the understanding that the publisher is not engaged in rendering legal, accounting, or other professional service. If legal advice or other expert assistance is required, the services of a competent professional person should be sought.

Although this book does not always specifically identify trademarked terms, AMACOM uses them for editorial purposes only, with no intention of trademark violation.

Library of Congress Cataloging-in-Publication Data

Price, Darlene.
   Well said! : presentations and conversations that get results / Darlene Price.
      p.   cm.
   Includes index.
   ISBN 978-0-8144-1787-4 (hardcover)
   1. Business presentations.   2. Public speaking.   I. Title.

   HF5718.22.P75   2012
   658.4'52—dc23

                                                              2012015319

About AMA
American Management Association (www.amanet.org) is a world leader in talent development, advancing the skills of individuals to drive business success. Our mission is to support the goals of individuals and organizations through a complete range of products and services, including classroom and virtual seminars, webcasts, webinars, podcasts, conferences, corporate and government solutions, business books, and research. AMA's approach to improving performance combines experiential learning—learning through doing—with opportunities for ongoing professional growth at every step of one's career journey.

Printing number

10   9   8   7   6   5   4   3   2   1

Dedication

This book is dedicated to the thousands of coaching participants in client organizations who have put these presentation and communication principles into practice. They've shown up for coaching prepared, persistent, and passionate—willing to practice the basics, eager to master the finer points. At work, at home, in the community, and the larger world, these individuals have cultivated the courage and the talent to speak up, speak out, and make a difference. Thank you for your commitment to excellence.

Contents

SECTION III:
Mastering a Confident, Dynamic Delivery Style

SECTION IV:
Seizing Every Opportunity to Persuade Decision Makers

Preface

You have something important to say—something of value that others need to hear. Even though other people in your organization may speak on the same topic, present the same product, and use the same visuals, you sell the message in a unique way. *Your* personal style, experience, observations, trials, successes, and stories engage and persuade listeners in a way that no one else can. As Eleanor Roosevelt reminds us, "When your message benefits others, you not only have a right to speak, you have an obligation to speak."

It is easy to shy away from this challenge. In fact, many presenters do. With the communication and presentation technology available today, you can detach from your audience and your message and let colorful slides, slick graphics, and impersonal videos do the talking for you. Please don't misunderstand: visual aids are an important element to an effective presentation. The key point to remember, however, is that *you* are your best visual aid. *You* are the message. *You* sell the message. This book shows you how.

THIS BOOK WILL ADVANCE YOUR CAREER

As your career advances, you will have more and more opportunities to present and persuade—to stand up in front of a group of decision makers and influence their thinking. Whether it's five people gathered around a table, twenty leaders in a boardroom, or five hundred attendees in a conference center, you need to become practiced and proficient in the skills that count—the skills that enable you to carry off your presentation with style, confidence, credibility, and persuasion; the skills necessary to get you noticed, remembered, promoted—and most important, the skills that allow you to be your natural unique self at your very best.

Like you, this book is unique—a far cry from any cookie-cutter approach. You will learn principles and techniques that are based on the author's collective trial-and-error experience, which spans over twenty years of speaking face-to-face to thousands of audiences all over the world. You will discover what works and what doesn't. You will learn how to persuade people to invest in you, your product, and your company by being yourself—naturally and exceptionally. When you communicate with people on a human level—when you share not only products and solutions but above all, yourself—you connect with them and make them feel important. And if I've learned one thing, it's that people buy from people they like.

THIS BOOK WILL INCREASE YOUR BUSINESS

Why is presentation and communication proficiency so important? Information and technology alone do not sell. People do. More than ever before, there is demand in today's high-tech automated world for what some call "high touch." There is no decline in the need of face-to-face impact. If anything, it is on the rise. In fact, a survey of American executives found that the most sought-after skill in the workplace today is the ability to verbally present clearly, confidently, and concisely. When you demonstrate effective presentation skills, decision makers listen to you, customers buy from you, and employers promote you. This book gives you the essential steps for presentation skills that pay off.

THIS BOOK WILL BUILD YOUR CONFIDENCE

A presenter's confidence is the cornerstone of a great presentation or powerful conversation. By using the field-tested techniques, exercises, guidelines, and checklists presented in this book, you will overcome the initial anxiety associated with public speaking. You will become comfortable—even enthusiastic—about presenting yourself and your message with clarity, credibility, and confidence.

Well Said!

Laying the Groundwork for Getting Results

CHAPTER 1

The Most Important Element of All

> You've got to start with the customer experience and work back toward the technology, not the other way around.
>
> —STEVE JOBS

When I conduct executive-level presentation coaching programs aimed at persuading tough decision makers, I often begin by waving a crisp $100 bill around the room and asking the participants, "Who would like to win this?" Several hands shoot up in the air, folks sit up a little straighter in their chairs, and all eyes are fixed on the green oval portrait of Benjamin Franklin. Once I have their attention, I continue, "In the next thirty seconds, you'll win $100 if you can answer this question correctly: What is the most important element of every presentation?" I set a thirty-second timer for all to see. The competitive outgoing types immediately shout out their answers: "Body language!" "Voice tone!" "Professional image!"

"All good guesses," I reply, "and critical elements to success, but not the *most* important." The guesses continue. "The opening?" "The close?" "The content?" The timer is ticking. I urge them on. "Think about it," I say. "Of all the elements that make up a successful presentation, what is most important of all?" They look befuddled. "Humor?" "Good visual aids?" "Oh I know! It's the presenter's level of expertise!" I nod my head, but they sense my disappointment. The last few take a stab. "Preparation?" "Storytelling?" "Props?" The thirty-second timer buzzes and I return the bill to my wallet. The correct answer? The audience.

Believe it or not, in the hundreds of presentation coaching programs I have conducted over the course of twenty years, fewer than ten people have won that $100 bill. Why? Self-focus versus audience focus. According to my audience surveys, which also number in the hundreds, failing to speak from the audience's perspective is the most common strategic mistake presenters make. The audience responses indicate that it's the primary reason a sale is not made, a budget not approved, a proposal not agreed to, a request denied. The presenter fails to align with the audience and speak from the decision makers' point of view.

Under normal circumstances, most of us probably strive to maintain a sense of compassion and understanding toward others. We know the importance of listening and empathy when building a healthy relationship. We know that to truly connect we have to see things from the other person's perspective. Unfortunately, when it comes to delivering a high-stakes presentation where our reputation, level of success, and possibly even our job is on the line, our individualistic desire to survive and thrive dominates. All of a sudden, in front of a group of decision makers, including our boss, the company's senior leadership, plus our customers, we become self-focused. We want to look good, sound smart, and be perceived as confident, credible, and in control. We want to make a great impression, win the order, close the deal, earn their trust, get the vote, or gain the funding.

There is nothing wrong with wanting these outcomes. The key is to realize that these payoffs are the consequences of an audience-focused presentation. They are not the main goals. If we become too self-focused we design and deliver a presentation from our own perspective, not our audience's. We choose the content we want to talk about; create the slides that feature our favorite points; present the data we think makes us look smart. But the primary goal of a presentation is to persuade the audience by speaking from *their* perspective. The most effective and most influential presenters I work with, from entry-level sales professionals to chief officers of major corporations, begin the presentation process by asking, "Who is my audience?"

By getting to know your audience first, addressing what is important to them, and solving their issues, I promise you will win much more than a $100 bill. From your boss and coworkers, you will win respect, recognition, and career advancement. From your customers and prospects, you will win trust, confidence, and most likely their business. So what does this look like?

Talk to a man about himself and he will listen for hours.

—BENJAMIN DISRAELI

KNOW YOUR AUDIENCE: LEARNING ABOUT DECISION MAKERS

Judy, an award-winning chief information officer of a large hospital, is a master at knowing her audience. As a CIO, she is responsible for managing a highly complex computer network that keeps everything running smoothly, from ordering medical supplies to ensuring patient safety. One of Judy's software vendors (a client of mine) asked her if she would be willing to give a presentation and product demonstration to one of their prospects, another large hospital, which was considering investing in the same software. The deal was worth more than $10 million to my client, and the senior account executive had his entire year's quota riding on this one opportunity. I was invited to work with Judy on the preparation process.

When the big day came, it was obvious Judy and her team had done their homework. She and the senior account executive had interviewed members of the prospect's team over the telephone and discovered their specific business challenges and key objectives. In Judy's opening speech, she looked directly at the visiting chief executive officer and his staff, called them by name, thanked them for coming, and warmly welcomed them. She revealed a flip chart sheet labeled "Your Wish List." It was composed of the prospect team's top ten problems, which they hoped the software could solve. Judy clarified and verified the wish list with the group, added a couple of more last-minute requests, and said, "Now that we've confirmed exactly what's important to you, we can ensure a tailored presentation that meets your specific needs. Let's get started."

Throughout the day of presentations and product demonstrations, Judy and her team of presenters referred back to this list. They showed how every feature and function of the software solved an issue on the wish list and helped the prospect attain their objectives. It's no wonder that at the end of the day, the visiting CEO stood up to thank everyone and said, "This is the best hospital tour I've ever experienced. Every question and issue we came with has been addressed. You've proved the value of the software and it delivers exactly what we're looking for. I see no reason to keep us from moving forward with the purchase." He turned to the senior account executive and said, "What's the next step?"

Bingo! Judy and my client got exactly what they wanted by giving the audience what they wanted. This principle of reciprocity is known as the Golden Rule of Presenting.

When is your next presentation? To ensure you achieve the outcome you want, take the time to get to know your audience. Use the following ten questions, as Judy and her team did, to analyze your audience and address what is most important to them.

TEN CRITICAL QUESTIONS TO ASK ABOUT YOUR AUDIENCE

1. *Who are they?* Connecting with your audience means understanding them on a professional and personal level. Know their names, roles, titles, responsibilities, and day-to-day work activities. Find out the basic demographics such as their age range, education level, professional experience, economic status, cultural influences, race/ethnicity, and political leanings. What is the gender ratio, men to women? Will the decision maker(s) be in the room? Do these individuals have the authority to buy your solution or approve your proposal? If possible, take the time to find out some personal information. Do the attendees get along and like one another? What do they have in common? Are there any avid sports fans in the group? What are their special interests and hobbies? Are they parents and/or grandparents?

2. *What are their expectations and why are they here?* Find out what your audience expects to gain by attending your presentation. What are their individual motivations? Are they willing and eager participants, or is their attendance mandatory? How interested will they be in what you are talking about? Considering audience expectations is a vital part of crafting a persuasive presentation. If your audience members arrive needing and wanting one thing, and you as the presenter deliver something different, regardless of how good you are, it's likely that they'll be disappointed.

Marty, the vice president and general counsel for a major online retailer, was asked to present to the company's board and executive committee on the topic of privacy. A customer was suing the company due to an alleged breach of privacy, so in their minds it was a burning topic. These individuals had canceled plans, delayed trips, and moved appointments to attend the meeting. Marty, wanting to promote his own agenda at the meeting, began by saying, "I know many of you are eager to hear about privacy, and we'll cover that later in the presentation if time permits, but I would like to spend most of this hour reviewing our contracting policies." There was almost a riot. The chairperson spoke up at once and insisted Marty stick to the issue the audience was there to discuss. In a very public and embarrassing way, Marty learned to stick to the topic and meet the audience's expectations.

3. *What are their main issues and challenges?* Discover what keeps them awake at night and causes them headaches, hassle, and frustration. Be able to pinpoint the problems that are causing them financial loss, decreased customer satisfaction, low morale, and operational inefficiencies. What do they need to be more successful, meet their business metrics, and fulfill their goals? As the Native American proverb goes, "Walk a mile in their moccasins." Show them you understand their unique situation and empathize with their problems. In the words of Martin Luther King Jr., "Life's most persistent and urgent question is, 'What are you doing for others?'"

4. *How does your message solve their problem?* There is an old adage that says every audience is tuned to the same radio station: WIIFM, which stands for "What's In It For Me?" What are you doing for the people in your audience? Be able to state confidently how the audience benefits from your message. What purpose does it serve in terms of helping them? Now that you know the audience's main issues, be sure you can show them how your product or idea resolves their concerns and makes life easier for them. This satisfies the other two questions the audience is asking: "So what? Who cares?" Do not expect the audience to figure out the benefits for themselves, regardless of how obvious the advantages seem to you. Clearly and overtly articulate how your solution will help them.

5. *What do you want them to do?* What is the call to action? The purpose of presenting is to persuade. Ideally, your talk will influence people to act in response to your message. Otherwise, why make the effort? Ask yourself: "At the end of this presentation, I want my audience to _____." Fill in the blank with your single clear-cut objective beginning with an action verb. For example: "At the end of this presentation, I want my audience to:

- ➤ Recommend my product to decision makers
- ➤ Request a detailed product demonstration
- ➤ Buy my product
- ➤ Approve the budget

➤ Fund my project

➤ Vote "yes"

Remember Dorothy in *The Wizard of Oz?* Even though the book is more than two hundred pages long and the movie lasts nearly two hours and features a cast of colorful characters, Dorothy is striving for one single overriding objective: to go home; to get back to Kansas. Every scene, conversation, song, and dance is motivated by that single clear-cut objective. What is your Kansas? Think about the single most desired action you want your listeners to take away after they hear your message. By doing so, you reap mighty dividends. Not only will you be able to direct your listeners' thinking and craft the content accordingly, but you will also be able to state a clear call to action at the conclusion of your presentation and achieve a measurable outcome.

6. *What is the single most important idea you want to communicate to this audience?* Richard Rodgers and Oscar Hammerstein II, the well-known American songwriting duo, perfected this technique. They created a string of popular Broadway musicals in the 1940s and 1950s. Legend has it that before they began composing, they asked themselves, "Which tune do we want them whistling when they leave the theater?" This decision determined which scenes featured the song, which character sang it, and how often the audience heard it. I recently attended a production of *The Sound of Music*, and sure enough, I hummed "Climb Ev'ry Mountain" all the way home. What phrase, idea, or proposition do you want your audience to remember after your presentation?

I once prepared a computer manufacturer's CEO for his keynote address to 1,500 salespeople. He emphatically stated that the main "tune" he wanted them all whistling as they left the conference was, "Build customers for life." He wanted his sales force to believe it was the company's mission and their job to deliver outstanding customer service. We composed the presentation around this theme. His speaking points, slides, stories, and statistics all pointed to this main idea. It's no surprise that when I interviewed dozens of salespeople afterward and asked, "What's the main idea you took away from your CEO's speech?" every reply included, "Build customers for life."

7. *How much does your audience already know?* Be sure to find out how much they know about your topic so you can gauge your content accordingly. The amount of details and type of content you include in your

presentation should depend on your audience's knowledge level. A presentation describing the effects of a new heart medication requires far less detail when your audience is made up of patients as opposed to cardiac surgeons. The key issues to consider are the audience's level of familiarity and comprehension. With that in mind, ask yourself two questions:

How familiar is my audience with the topic of my presentation?

Is my audience likely to understand my terms and concepts, or should I plan on explaining them?

You don't want to talk over your audience's head, and you don't want to talk down to them, either.

8. *What are your audience's attitudes about you, the topic, and the environment?* Several years ago, I coached two corporate presidents, Anne and Larry, from separate and unrelated companies, in the very same week. Both leaders were delivering presentations that were seemingly the same: a thirty-minute, all-employee state-of-the-corporation address, delivered live at their headquarters and broadcast via the Internet to remote offices. Anne's company had a stellar year. The firm gave out unexpected bonuses; they were featured in multiple trade publications as a "Most Admired Company." And, based on employee satisfaction surveys, they were rated as one of the best companies to work for in the state. Anne was respected and adored by a grateful workforce. No surprise, when she walked on stage, the applauding fans rose to their feet. Larry, on the other hand, faced an entirely different situation. His company had posted a devastating multimillion-dollar loss in the previous quarter. He'd laid off hundreds of employees, and rumors were flying that more "head-whacking" was to come. Remaining managers had taken a pay cut, and disgruntled employees were blogging negative comments. As you can imagine, Larry's audience had an entirely different attitude about him, his topic, and the overall corporate environment than did Anne's.

As you prepare, ask yourself about the likely attitudes of the people in your audience. Are they likely to be supporters and advocates of your ideas who are positively disposed to you and your message? Are they opposed to your ideas? Are they undecided, neutral, uncaring? What emotions, biases, prejudices, and opinions do they hold toward you and your topic?

9. *What are their personality types?* Yvonne, the senior vice president of marketing for a national cosmetics company, was furious when she called me for help. The day before, she had attempted to present her new business

strategy to her CEO. He interrupted her after five minutes. "I have no idea what you're trying to say," he told her. "When you figure it out, let me know." He excused her and asked his assistant to call in the next presenter. Unfortunately, Yvonne forgot to consider her listener's personality. Yvonne's CEO is a fast-paced, quick-thinking, high-driver type who wants to hear the crux of the message in the first five minutes. Yet, Yvonne mistakenly prepared a painstaking presentation with down-in-the-weeds details and a methodical step-by-step process. In the first five minutes, she was still plowing through numbers in the first column of her ten-page spreadsheet. We may argue with the CEO's lack of manners, sensitivity, and tact, but his job is to produce results for the company and to ensure his time is spent on revenue-generating outcomes. When presenting to this dominant, direct, and decisive personality type, you as the presenter must be prepared to speak in a clear, concise, and convincing manner, asserting your conclusions and recommendations up front.

On the contrary, you may have other decision makers in your audience who are detail-oriented, methodical thinkers who want to hear about your process and logic. The point is to know to whom you are speaking—and know it ahead of time. The fast-paced, risk-taking executive receives information differently than does a fact-oriented, quality-minded engineer, scientist, or technologist. Are your listeners serious minded, or do they laugh easily? Are they talkative, outgoing, and energetic, or quiet, reserved, and somber? As you are getting to know your audience, think about the different types of personalities in the room. What behavioral traits and learning styles best describe them? The answers to these questions will determine what you say, how much you say, and the order in which you say it. This insight is invaluable later in the process as we develop a logical structure and develop persuasive content.

10. *What objections or questions might this audience have?* What would cause this audience to oppose your topic or proposal? What issues might cause a delay or denial of your request? What issues must be overcome to achieve your goal? By identifying the obstacles ahead of time, you will be prepared to show your audience that their concerns are not as formidable as they might have thought. Once you have identified the obstacles to your success, you can muster the arguments necessary to overcome them. No matter how excellent your product, proposal, or recommendation may be, audience members almost always raise objections, have questions, or demand additional information.

Mike, the chief operating officer of a large computer system manufacturer, was preparing to present to a group of unhappy customers. As I helped him prepare for the possible questions and objections the audience might have, we carefully rehearsed honest and appropriate answers. After a couple of hours, Mike paused. "This is certainly not fun, but very necessary," he said. "I guess it's true—real leaders face the music even when they don't like the tune." Mike did his homework ahead of time and found out the key issues affecting his customers. He then took the time to formulate and practice effective answers. Only then was he able to craft a thoughtful, audience-focused message that addressed his audience's key concerns and ultimately salvaged their business.

What issues or concerns could keep your audience from adopting your message and carrying out your call to action? Maybe they fear the change you're recommending and dread the adjustments it requires. Perhaps they are uncertain about which vendor to choose or whether they can afford your solution. Maybe they are skeptical and doubt your company's ability to deliver. Whatever the reason, your success as a persuasive and confident presenter will depend on your ability to anticipate your audience's questions and objections—your ability to face the music of the audience—even when you don't like the tune. Equally important to predicting their reasons for resistance will be developing the skills to overcome these objections and answer their questions with finesse and confidence. We will cover those specific techniques in Chapter 12.

HOW TO GATHER INFORMATION ABOUT YOUR AUDIENCE

As you analyze your audience using the ten critical questions, there are multiple resources to help fill in the blanks. Take out your magnifying glass, light your pipe, play the role of Sherlock Holmes, and conduct a full investigation. Here are a few ways to gather critical information about your audience.

> ➤ Speak to the attendees several days or weeks before the presentation. Schedule a call and ask them what they would like to gain from the presentation. Ask what they're expecting. This interaction provides firsthand feedback, allows you to establish a personal connection in

advance, and enables you to customize your presentation to meet their needs.

➤ Send out a questionnaire or survey. If you cannot personally speak with the attendees, consider sending a quick five- or ten-question survey that can be completed in ten minutes.

➤ Speak to their managers or senior leaders. I always find it helpful to ask the boss what he or she wants and needs their people to gain from the presentation.

➤ Talk with the audience's coworkers or people inside the organization. Insights from fellow employees will help you get a feel for the overall attitude, atmosphere, and environment.

➤ Read the latest articles relating to your audience's industry, company, or interests. Gather as much current information as possible about their values, mission statement, and performance data. Be sure to read their marketing materials, annual reports, newsletters, brochures, product spec sheets, or other related collateral material. Browse the company website and relevant industry websites.

➤ Visit their facility, store, or office. Nothing impresses an audience more than a presenter who has done his or her homework, especially when that entails gaining firsthand experience and taking the time to see their company in action.

➤ Study their competition. If you are delivering a sales presentation, be sure to know the companies and products that your prospect audience considers to be their main rivals.

➤ Converse and mingle with participants as they enter the room. Ideally, you should arrive and set up early enough to be fully available to participants as they walk in. Use this time to gather last-minute information from audience members that you can weave into your presentation, such as their names, relevant stories, humorous examples, special requests, learning goals, and schedule adjustments.

➤ Use an Internet search engine to investigate the key decision makers who will attend your presentation.

➤ Ask questions during the presentation to gather on-the-spot feedback. In a later chapter we will look at various audience interaction techniques, one of which is asking the audience questions during the presentation.

TOP LOGISTICAL AND ENVIRONMENTAL QUESTIONS

Success is the sum of details. —HARVEY S. FIRESTONE

In addition to the ten critical questions that lay the groundwork for your audience analysis, you will also need to know the answers to a number of logistical questions to ensure that your presentation runs smoothly. Prior to your presentation, as you talk with the organization's leaders and/or employees, see how much you can learn about the following:

➤ Who will be introducing you? Are you introducing yourself?

➤ How many audience members will be present?

➤ Will people be joining you remotely via the telephone or Internet?

➤ How much time do you have for your presentation, including Q&A?

➤ What is the time slot of your presentation?

➤ What is your placement on the agenda (first, middle, last)?

➤ What agenda items, speakers, and topics precede and follow you?

➤ Where is the presentation location/venue?

➤ What is the earliest you may access the room for setup, walk-through, and rehearsal?

➤ What is the room setup and seating arrangement? Can they be changed?

➤ Will you stand or remain seated to present? What are other presenters planning to do?

➤ Are you giving a team presentation with other presenters or are you solo?

➤ What audiovisual equipment will you need? Laptop, screen, projector, microphone?

➤ If you use a microphone, is it a handheld, lapel, or stationary model?

➤ Are you expected to use a lectern? If so, can you leave the lectern and move around the stage and room to better connect with the audience?

➤ What kind of lighting is in the room? Are the slides still visible with the lights on?

➤ Is there a meeting theme, occasion, or special event tied to your presentation?

➤ What is the expected attire for the attendees? For the presenter(s)? Is it formal, business, business casual, casual?

➤ Will food or beverages be served before, during, or after your presentation?

➤ Will special VIPs, senior executives, dignitaries, guests, or the press be present?

➤ After your closing, do you introduce another speaker, or close the entire program/event?

Getting to know your audience is much like building a relationship with anyone else: the more you know about them and the more time you invest in learning what is important to them, the more likely you are to establish rapport and create a meaningful connection. The bedrock of a great presentation is showing your audience you know them. So, if you are ever in a workshop and the facilitator offers $100 for the correct answer to the question "What is the most important element of every presentation?" you can be the first to call out, "The audience!"

CHAPTER 1: EXECUTIVE SUMMARY

➤ The audience is the most important element of every presentation.

➤ Answer these ten questions to prepare for a persuasive presentation:

1. Who is my audience?
2. What are their expectations and why are they here?
3. What are their main issues and challenges related to my topic?
4. How does my message address or solve their issues? How does it help them?
5. What do you want them to do as a result of hearing your message?
6. What is the single most important idea you want to communicate to this audience?
7. How much does your audience already know?
8. What are your audience's attitudes about you, the topic, and the environment?
9. What are their personality types?
10. What objections or questions might this audience have?

➤ As you complete your "homework" by learning more about your audience, find out everything you can about the venue, how you'll be introduced, what the audience already knows, the objections you could face, and the single most important idea you will want to communicate.

CHAPTER 2

How to Persuade a Decision Maker

> Be sincere, be brief, be seated.
>
> —FRANKLIN D. ROOSEVELT

Imagine you and your colleagues are sitting in a business meeting when suddenly you smell smoke. It's that smoldering stench that only comes from a fire. Sure enough, smoke begins to ooze slowly under the door. You can see fear fill the faces of everyone. Do you sit tight and wait for help? Do you open the door and risk a rush of flames? Should you jump out the window (from the fifth floor)? To your relief, a fire marshal enters the room to help.

By the way, he's an award-winning firefighter with three decades of experience. In fact, he teaches at the local fire department and serves as a mentor to new volunteers. His workshops and lectures on safety draw big crowds and everyone agrees he's a local hero. He knows so much about the subject it's sometimes tough for him to decide what to say.

Now back to the fire and your personal safety. Given this fire marshal's extensive background, depth and breadth of subject matter expertise, and impressive reputation, what would you like him to talk about when he enters the room (just as you're beginning to cough from smoke inhalation and the temperature is rising)? Consider the following list of speaking points in his impressive repertoire. Please circle the one(s) you would like him to say. And remember, the building is on fire.

A. Allow me to show you the proper way to install a fire alarm.

B. It's time now to review your company's fire prevention policies.

C. The fossil record of fire first appears in land-based flora in the Middle Ordovician period.

D. There's a fire on the first floor. Please listen carefully.

E. Today we'll discuss the biggest fires in history.

F. Scholars attribute the first use of controlled fire to Homo erectus 400,000 years ago.

G. The nearest fire escape is down the hall, second door on the left, marked with a red X.

H. Let's watch a step-by-step video on how to extinguish a fire.

I. Two million fires are reported every year in the United States.

J. For your safety, be sure to comply with the following procedures . . .

Chances are you chose D, G, and J. Why? Because they are the only ones on the list that are relevant to your situation and will help you survive. Despite the fact that the fire marshal is an eloquent, intelligent speaker and passionately lectures on the other seven subjects, frankly you are only interested in three of them. The reason is self-interest. As explained in Chapter 1, you are tuned to radio station WIIFM—What's In It For Me? Can you imagine how inappropriate, bizarre, and off-base it would seem for the fire marshal to enter your smoke-filled room and begin lecturing about anything other than your safety and an evacuation route?

WHAT DO DECISION MAKERS REALLY WANT TO KNOW?

Decision makers feel exactly the same way. They too are tuned to WIIFM. As senior managers and leaders in the corporation, they are putting out fires every day. Metaphorically speaking, they live in smoke-filled rooms. When you, the fire marshal, arrive to say something helpful to them—in a face-to-face conversation, a formal presentation, a teleconference, or webinar—they only want to hear D, G, and J. They want you to answer the questions, "Where is the fire?" "What is the evacuation route?" "Briefly, what procedures do we follow to get there?"

Persuasion is everywhere in human interactions. From the caring efforts of a mother convincing her feisty five-year-old to eat his vegetables to the overt attempts of advertisers trying to sell us a new car, people and businesses seek to influence others. The situations vary, but eventually there comes a time when you are after just one thing: compliance. You need to direct another person's behavior toward a specific course of action or a point of view; you want them to do what *you* want.

This skill is critical in presenting to decision makers. Whether your goal is to sell, inform, motivate, train, entertain, or build goodwill, it's your ability to persuade an audience that ultimately determines your degree of success or failure. When you finish speaking, you want the decision maker to say "yes" to your point of view.

To be successful at affecting the beliefs and actions of others, you must not only understand what motivates people to act, but also how to use that knowledge to your advantage. As Aristotle wrote, "The fool tells me his reasons; the wise man persuades me with my own."

What Persuasion Is Not

Persuasion is neither coercion nor intimidation—far from it. People may be forced to do something, but they cannot be forced to believe something. The history books are full of failed marriages forced between two royal families. The same is true of a speaker who tries to marry a message to an audience when there is no emotional commitment. It is a mismatch that ends up in divorce. The audience's minds pack their bags and leave, and the speaker is still standing up there, rambling on. Audience members must be persuaded in ways that are agreeable to them; they must choose on their own volition to see it your way.

Persuasion is not data-dumping, hauling a truckload of information from one place to another, and unloading it on an audience. People get buried under the weight of too much information. Good data is important, but good demeanor is crucial. While facts, figures, statistics, charts, and graphs do lend support to your message, they do not sell your message. Remember, people buy from people they like.

What Persuasion Is

Persuasion is the ability to convince another person to adopt the idea, attitude, or action you are recommending; to make the decision you want them to make. As Aristotle pointed out, it involves using the listener's reasoning and understanding, not necessarily your own. The wisest presenters use the logic and reasons that are important to the audience in order to reach a mutual agreement.

While sociologists and psychologists have developed dozens of models and theories to suggest the reasons for why people behave in the ways that they do, the simple fact is that they respond based on self-interest. Since audience members are self-interested people, you can bet they are asking themselves one primary question about your presentation: "What's in it for me?"

THE FOUR Ps OF PERSUASION

As a general rule, people are motivated to act based on four reasons, or four key payoffs. Think of them as the Four Ps of Persuasion:

- ➤ Profit
- ➤ Pleasure
- ➤ Power
- ➤ Prestige

Profit

If your product or message enables decision makers to save or make money, if it adds to the bottom line in any way, be sure to stress that benefit to your audience. You will see ears and eyes perk up immediately. Profits are to a business what oil is to an engine, the driving force behind successful operation. In the end, this is the measure of every decision maker. Does your proposal or product help decision makers gain income, earnings, revenue, efficiencies, return on investment, or productivity? Does it reduce costs and expenses? If so, repeatedly reinforce this payoff throughout your presentation or conversation. Profit is a primary motivator for most decision makers. If possible, don't simply say, "and this solution will increase efficiencies by 30 percent." Instead, add to that phrase a quantifiable dollar amount such as, "and in your case, this equates to two million dollars annually to your bottom line."

The other side of the profit coin is loss. Fear of loss is also a motivator. You may want to show decision makers what it will cost them if they don't adopt your proposal. Or emphasize how you will help them avoid loss and circumvent overspending.

Pleasure

Is there anything about your proposal, product, or service that can help the decision maker achieve a desired outcome with less effort involved? Simply put, most decision makers want to "work smarter, not harder." They want you to help them achieve their goals in the fastest way possible. In your presentation or conversation, be sure to tell your audience how your product or service will save time and improve their lives. But don't stop at, "cuts time in half." How might your listeners use the extra time? "Spend more time with family?" "Produce 30 percent more widgets?" Ask yourself these questions to pinpoint the pleasure aspect of your message:

- ▶ How does my proposal help this group of decision makers achieve their goals with less effort?
- ▶ How can I make them feel good about buying my product or saying *yes* to my recommendation?
- ▶ How does my solution make life easier for this decision maker?
- ▶ Are they getting something rewarding from the experience, e.g., does your product help the environment, or is a portion of sales supporting a charity?

Whether your solution is user-friendly, saves time, decreases hassle, is easy to use, offers fun, increases satisfaction, boosts morale, or provides intrinsic rewards, tell the listener how her life will be improved as a result of doing what you are suggesting. What do your pleasure-seeking decision makers gain by choosing you over someone else? Be sure to emphasize the payoff of pleasure.

Power

One of the main tasks of corporate decision makers is to shape their environment. This takes intelligent power; the act of successfully controlling resources and mitigating risks to achieve one's desired outcomes. I have heard many senior leaders use phrases such as:

- ▶ "Within a year, we're going to *own* this market. So get out there and *crush* the competition."
- ▶ "Our goal is to *dominate* this space and *take over* as the number one leader in the industry."

Notice the language of these leaders. Their action verbs all imply power, authority, and supremacy. Your message will be even more persuasive when you appeal to their need to feel powerful. How does your solution help your audience dominate the industry, increase market share, or conquer the competition? How does it increase their strength and authority? Does it help them control resources such as time, money, and people? Does your solution put them in charge and help them mitigate risk? Does it give them command over weak spots, vulnerabilities, or potentially negative outcomes?

In his 1651 book *Leviathan,* English philosopher Thomas Hobbes defines power as one's "present means, to obtain some future apparent good." Determine how your message provides a "means" of power to help your audience achieve the outcome they want.

Prestige

In the seventeenth century, scientist and philosopher Blaise Pascal once noted that "The charm of fame is so great that we like every object to which it is attached." Prestige is the level of distinction and prominence at which a person or company is regarded by key stakeholders. It involves one's reputation and implies status, recognition, and even exclusivity. How does your product or message help decision makers improve their standing among others, or their company's reputation among customers, prospects, and partners? Will it help listeners outrank their competition? If so, be sure to use the prestige motivator. Tell them how your solution "ensures they will receive the recognition they deserve" or "creates goodwill in the community," or "guarantees they'll earn kudos from their customers" or "be viewed as a hero." Subtly show your listeners that your solution will make them look good and will optimize others' perception of them.

Influencing the beliefs and actions of others is the foundation of an effective presentation to a decision maker. Your role as a presenter is to lead the listener down a logical path toward a desirable course of action or point of view by appealing to his or her interests and reasons. The Four Ps of Persuasion will help you convince your audience to see it your way.

DECISION MAKERS' BIGGEST COMPLAINTS ABOUT PRESENTERS

Several years ago, a number of my clients asked me to develop a course that taught rising high-potential managers how to present effectively to an executive-level audience of decision makers. Apparently there had been consistent complaints among senior leadership that managers didn't know how to present to a higher-level audience. It occurred to me that before I doled out a single piece of advice to these managers, I should go straight to the source of the complaint. I asked 237 senior leaders in Fortune 100 companies, "What qualities do you dislike most in speakers who present to you?" According to the survey, it seems that decision makers are quick to forgive some mistakes that happen by chance, such as technical difficulty, environmental issues, even the speaker's nervousness. But, according to these executive respondents, there are other mistakes that are serious enough in their minds to jeopardize a speaker's credibility, limit his or her career advancement, and significantly decrease the ability to persuade. Here are the ten biggest complaints ranked in order of importance. The speaker:

1. *Gives too much information (TMI).* This is the number one pet peeve because it wastes an irreplaceable resource: time. In the few minutes they have with you, decision makers are looking for answers, direction, solutions—not details, process, and in-depth analysis. Plus, TMI goes against the grain of most high-level decision makers. Remember the personality type: results-oriented drivers who want immediate outcomes; they like to make quick decisions; they want to hear the bottom line up front. When a speaker mistakenly presents a "data dump" to a senior-level audience, those decision makers will usually interrupt, leave, disengage, or become hostile.

2. *Rambles on.* One chief officer in the survey described rambling as "lengthy and confusing speech." Another deemed it an "inconsequential conversation." The cause of rambling is most often a lack of preparation. Rather than organizing the message into a clear opening, body, and close with prioritized points (most important to least important), the speaker simply strings together a series of thoughts with no rhyme or reason, often failing to take the audience into consideration.

3. *Fails to tie the message to the audience's key business drivers.* Many senior leaders told me that the ineffective managers/presenters about whom they complained were "just disseminators of information." They would disappointingly arrive to the meeting and read a spreadsheet, give a report, or narrate a slide show. The respondents made it very clear they wanted presenters to be *interpreters* of the data, not just disseminators; intelligent people who could directly relate the message to the audience tuned to WIIFM.

4. *Lacks confidence and enthusiasm.* Before decision makers can believe, they have to see that *you* believe. Presenters who seem timid, hesitant, or listless tend to be perceived as insecure, uncommitted, and boring. With decision makers, a presenter who comes across as self-assured, energetic, and passionate about the topic scores a lot of points.

5. *Hasn't done any homework.* This complaint came from decision makers who experienced a presenter's lack of valid support and quantitative measurements.

6. *Doesn't anticipate audience questions and objections.* Decision makers look for an important skill known as contingency planning. They want to see that you, a rising leader in the corporation, can predict and prepare for Q&A and impromptu think-on-your-feet situations.

7. *Fails to ask for what the speaker needs from the decision maker.* In response to this particular complaint, the president of a major telecommunications company told me, "I'm the one person in the entire company who can give these people what they need to drive their business, and yet they sit here and present for an hour and don't ask me. I want them to tell me what they need to be successful . . . is it more FTEs (full-time employees); a larger budget; face time with me to discuss key issues? Just ask."

8. *Responds defensively to decision makers' feedback.* Eleanor Roosevelt once said, "No one can make you feel inferior without your consent." Keep that adage in mind as you present and converse effectively with decision makers. After all, we know they can sometimes ask questions and raise objections in a tone that sounds abrupt, discourteous, and even offensive. But according to the survey responses, they don't necessarily mean to come across this way—it's just their hard-charging, results-oriented nature. That means when you as the presenter feel attacked, you ideally remain upbeat, courteous, and positive. Avoid taking their pushback personally. It's their job to find the holes in arguments and prove it's a sound proposal before accepting it.

9. *Lacks an executive image.* Despite the popularity and prevalence of the business casual dress code, when it comes time to meet with executives and present to the decision makers in the company, look your best. Remember, you want to dress one notch above the best-dressed person in the audience as a show of respect.

10. *"Doesn't teach me anything new."* The executive vice president of one of the world's largest consumer electronic companies put it this way:

"If someone is in my office presenting, and he or she doesn't teach me anything new about my business—something I don't already know—why am I paying them?" He went on to say that he relies on his team to "teach" him what's going on in the business and keep him abreast of critical issues.

EFFECTIVE INFLUENCING: THE THREE Cs OF HIGH-IMPACT CONVERSATIONS

Once these senior leaders had been surveyed and interviewed, and their top complaints were clearly communicated, the course I was commissioned to design practically wrote itself: "Effective Influencing: The Three Cs of High-Impact Conversations." These senior leaders shared with me that the three top communication qualities they deem most promotable and persuasive are:

1. Clarity
2. Conciseness
3. Credibility

First, be clear. Create a message that is easy to follow and understand. Use good structure including an opening, body, and close. This shows your listener you are prepared and avoids the rambling and ambiguity that obscures your message. In Chapter 4, you'll discover the details of how to craft a presentation that convinces decision makers.

Second, be concise. Once you are organized and prepared with a logical outline, be sure to use as few words as possible to give the necessary information. Also, prioritize your points in order of importance to the audience and get to the bottom line quickly. As one CEO adamantly stated, "Give me the big picture first—I want to hear the whole gist of the story up front in five minutes or less."

Third, be credible. Make it easy for decision makers to believe you. Show them you've done your homework and understand their business challenges by tying your solution to their problems. Also, look and sound the part: use effective body language and voice to exude confidence, and convey executive presence through professional dress and appearance. We'll explore these keys to success in greater detail in Chapter 8. By avoiding the top complaints of decision makers and optimizing the Three Cs, you're well on your way to inspiring trust in the minds of your listeners and delivering a confident, convincing message.

ARISTOTLE'S THREE MODES OF PERSUASION: ETHOS, PATHOS, AND LOGOS

As we conclude the chapter on understanding how decision makers are persuaded, there's one more critical concept to cover to ensure we're fully equipped to influence our listeners: Aristotle's three modes of persuasion, known as *Ethos*, *Pathos*, and *Logos*. In W. Rhys Roberts's translation of Aristotle's *Rhetoric* (Princeton: Princeton University Press, 1984), we read:

> Of the modes of persuasion furnished by the spoken word there are three kinds. . . . Persuasion is achieved by the speaker's personal character when the speech is so spoken as to make us think him credible. . . . Secondly, persuasion may come through the hearers, when the speech stirs their emotions. . . . Thirdly, persuasion is effected through the speech itself when we have proved a truth or an apparent truth by means of the persuasive arguments suitable to the case in question.

Ethos

In Aristotle's framework, the Greek word *Ethos* refers to the credibility of the speaker, or ethical appeal. It means your first path to persuasion involves your character, conviction, and credentials. We tend to believe people whom we respect. Decision makers want to know you are someone worth listening to; an authority on the subject; someone who is likable, respectable, trustworthy, and qualified. You can help establish ethos during the opening of your presentation when you provide a brief self-introduction.

Pathos

The mode of Pathos, or emotional appeal, persuades your audience by engaging their emotions. Though the Greek word itself means "suffering" or "experience," for our purposes we interpret it as an appeal to the decision makers' sympathies, hopes, and imagination. The most effective way of conveying pathos is through narrative or story, which can turn a complex abstract matter into an imagined experience—palpable and present. For example, tell a relevant, brief personal story; describe a customer situation; craft an applicable analogy; give an example; show a photo; use tasteful humor; or employ a prop. Also, strive to be a likable person, warm and friendly, prepared and interested in the audience's well-being. You want to engage both the emotional and imaginative aspects of the listener's psyche. As one psychologist told me, "Persuasion requires engaging the listener's head *and* heart; appealing to both facts *and* feelings."

Logos

The mode of Logos ("logical") means persuading the audience by appealing to their sense of reason and judgment. It refers to the internal consistency of your message, including the clarity and conciseness of the claim, the soundness and common sense of its reasons, and the effectiveness of its supporting evidence. Most often, the logical appeal comes in the form of concrete proof, such as relevant data, facts, statistics, product specifications, and quantitative evidence.

To optimize your ability to influence decision makers, be sure to include all three of Aristotle's three modes of persuasion. This ancient master of persuasion reminds us to combine the use of two types of convincing evidence: fact-based logical material (Logos) *and* feelings-based emotional material (Pathos). By doing so, we appeal to our decision maker's head and heart and significantly increase our chances of getting the result we want.

CHAPTER 2: EXECUTIVE SUMMARY

- ➤ Follow the fire marshal exercise: Present only information that is relevant and important to the audience
- ➤ Use the Four Ps of Persuasion: Profit, Pleasure, Power, and Prestige.
- ➤ Avoid the top ten complaints from decision makers about presenters:

1. Gives too much information.
2. Rambles on.
3. Fails to tie the message to the audience's key business drivers.
4. Lacks confidence and enthusiasm.
5. Hasn't done any homework.
6. Doesn't anticipate audience questions and objections.
7. Fails to ask for what the speaker needs from the decision maker.
8. Responds defensively to decision makers' feedback.
9. Lacks an executive image.

10. "Doesn't teach me anything new."

➤ Practice the Three Cs to convince decision makers: Be clear, concise, and credible.

➤ Leverage Aristotle's three modes of persuasion: Ethos, Pathos, and Logos.

CHAPTER 3

Establishing Credibility

> What can give us surer knowledge than our senses? With what else can we better distinguish true from false?
>
> —LUCRETIUS

Let's conduct a thought experiment in the power of perception. Pretend for a moment that today is your birthday. You would like to take the day off, but true to the trooper you are, you ventured into the office and have spent most of your special day attending important meetings.

You haven't told anyone that it's your birthday, but sometimes managers keep track of such things on their calendars, so you are keeping a watchful eye just in case your colleagues are planning to surprise you. After making it through lunch with no birthday surprises, you are in the middle of your third meeting of the day when suddenly the conference room door swings open and in walks your manager with a big, beautiful birthday cake glowing with candles, and a nicely wrapped package. A smile grows across your face from ear to ear, as you pleasantly welcome the attention. It's your favorite kind of cake too, chocolate fudge. You can almost taste it as your manager approaches, plus you can't wait to see what's in the package. Then suddenly he passes you and keeps walking to the end of the conference table. "What's going on?" you wonder.

"Happy Birthday, Alison!" your manager says to one of your colleagues at the end of the room. "Her birthday was over the weekend." There is applause from your coworkers and Alison beams brightly, soaking in the admiration.

"Thank you," she says.

As everyone sings "Happy Birthday," you are perplexed. You didn't know Alison's birthday was so close to yours, and you are disappointed that your birthday has been forgotten.

There is a big blowing-out-the-candles ceremony, followed by everyone complimenting Alison on her stellar contributions to the team. Then, Alison delightedly digs through the balloons, bows, and brightly colored paper to discover her gift.

"Great!" exclaims Alison, examining her present. "It's a presentation remote—I've been wanting one of these! Plus a book on effective presentation skills. Wow, thank you very much!"

Just when you're feeling totally forgotten and frankly annoyed by all this attention Alison is getting, especially since her birthday was this past weekend and not today, your manager says to you, "Oh yeah, I think you have a birthday too sometime this month, don't you?" You nod affirmatively. "Well, the cake can be for both of you. Uh, hold on a minute, I'll be right back." The manager disappears, there's a spattering of polite applause for you from one or two people, and everyone else shovels cake into their mouths.

The manager returns in a couple of minutes and says, "I almost forgot." He quickly hands you a wrinkled brown paper bag and says, "Happy Birthday." He has another meeting, so he swipes a piece of cake, excuses himself, and leaves the room. You open the bag and sure enough, it's the exact same gift Alison received: a top-of-the-line presentation remote and presentation skills book. Alison is still beaming at the end of the table but you're not feeling so swell. In fact, how would you feel if this happened to you? You ended up sharing a cake with Alison; you received exactly the same gift; and the same greeting: "Happy Birthday." But it wasn't the same, was it? Let's unpack the experience and determine why Alison is happy and you're not.

There was no enthusiasm and no excitement for your birthday. Alison received warm and fuzzy attention, while you were overlooked and treated indifferently. Your manager put no time, thought, or extra preparation into your special day and didn't surprise you at all. The greeting may have been said, though in a lackluster voice tone, but no one sang "Happy Birthday" to you; no one took time to compliment you; no one asked you to blow out birthday candles. In fact, the whole thing seemed like an afterthought. To add insult to injury, Alison's present was attractively wrapped—it actually looked like a birthday present, while yours was haphazardly tossed in a left-over lunch sack. So in a nutshell, the presentation to Alison included:

- ➤ More time, thought, and preparation
- ➤ More attractive wrapping
- ➤ More personalization and recognition
- ➤ More attention and focus on Alison
- ➤ More warmth and enthusiasm from the manager
- ➤ More involvement with your colleagues

PERCEPTION DETERMINES CHOICE

The reason for taking you through this imaginary birthday experiment? When you are presenting to a decision maker, whatever you're selling may be something very similar to what your competition is selling. With two similar (if not identical) products or services to choose from, what is it that convinces someone to choose you versus the competition? Internally within your company, what is it that persuades a decision maker to promote you rather than a colleague? That decision often comes down to how you present your product or service and how you sell yourself. If the decision maker sees more preparation, more time, more thought, more customization, more attention, and more enthusiasm coming from you, you are more likely to win and gain the outcome you want.

As an audience member yourself, what do you think is the number one trait all audience members want to see in a presenter? If you think about it for a moment, I think you'll agree: "Enthusiasm." Enthusiasm is the outward expression of sincerity, and sincerity is an inner quality that one radiates.

There is more to persuading decision makers than your PowerPoint presentation or even your product demo; it's about you and how you convey the message. You need to gift-wrap every presentation you make. To illustrate, let's turn things around for a moment and think about the times when you are a decision-maker, i.e., when you shop. Which produce do you want from the grocery store? Fruit that's bruised and old-looking or fresh-from-the-farm, firm, and plump? What restaurant do you want to try for dinner tonight? The one with the broken neon sign in the window and no cars in the parking lot, or the one where people are enjoying their food out front on the little patio under umbrellas and pretty lighted trees? Which car would you like to buy when visiting the car dealership? The one that has a small dent in the fender and hasn't been washed, or the shiny one where you can see your reflection in the paint? I think you get the point. In these examples, we haven't yet tasted the fruit, or tried the restaurant food, or taken the car for a test drive, yet we made assumptions, which led to choices, all based on our perception. Perception determines the choices you make.

When you are presenting to decision makers, before they get to know you, before they meet your team, before they see your demo, before you get your foot in the door and are in the running, you have to start by creating a positive perception. As just demonstrated, people buy based on perception. In fact, perception is often more important than facts or reality, because for most people, their perception *is* their reality. Perhaps that's why nineteenth-century German philosopher Friedrich Nietzsche asserted, "All credibility, all evidence of truth comes only from the senses."

THREE FACTORS OF PERCEPTION: VISUAL, VOCAL/VERBAL, RELATIONAL

To Nietzsche's point, the decision makers in your audience use three senses to evaluate you and your credibility: sight, hearing, and touch. That is, their perception of you is formed by how they *see* you, *hear* you, and *feel* about you. I call these the Visual, Vocal/Verbal, and Relational Factors of perception.

First, the Visual Factor considers how the audience sees you. The goal is to hone your body language, dress, appearance, grooming, executive presence, the room setup, and environment. You need to be intentional and conscientious about everything the decision makers see in order to craft a positive perception through their eyes.

Next is the Vocal/Verbal Factor—how your audience hears you. The objective in this area is to enhance your voice tone, vocal variety, and use of persuasive words and phrases while applying persuasive logic to your presentation structure. The goal: Every word and phrase you say reinforces the audience's perception of you as authoritative, intelligent, and well prepared.

The third sense, touch, is the basis of the Relational Factor. It refers to how the audience feels about you. Do you and your message "touch" them in a meaningful and positive way? This factor includes physical touch (giving a confident handshake, for example) as well as emotional touch (such as developing rapport and creating a positive connection with the audience). Your audience focus, customized message, friendly demeanor, humor, and attention to detail create trust and emotional appeal.

Throughout this book, these three factors of perception—Visual, Vocal/Verbal, and Relational—serve as an overarching framework. In fact, every tip and technique you read about and apply is designed to optimize how your audience sees you, hears you, and feels about you. By keeping in mind these three pillars and gauging your success accordingly, you'll have all the bases covered. It also ensures that you master the most important adage of all when it comes to persuading an audience: "It's all about connection, not perfection!"

CONNECTION, NOT PERFECTION!

When you think of a really great speaker, someone you truly admire and enjoy listening to, who comes to mind? Perhaps he is a boss, coworker, or friend. Maybe it's a politician, clergyperson, or captain of industry. As you picture this speaker in your mind, and envision him holding an audience captive, think of a few words or phrases to describe his style. Why do you like him? What does he do or say that inspires and motivates you? How does he do it? If you'd like, take a moment and jot down a few of the qualities that make this person such a successful communicator and speaker.

Some of your descriptors may include words such as *enthusiastic, authentic, sincere, confident, informative, helpful, funny, entertaining, inspiring, motivating, positive, prepared, interesting, audience-centric, a good storyteller.* At some level you felt a personal connection with this speaker—he engaged you, taught you something you didn't know, held your attention, roused your curiosity, caused you to think, made you laugh, challenged you in a positive way, helped you see the future in a brighter way. What a wonderful and gifted speaker!

Now, I'm going to take a guess that the following words and phrases do *not* appear on your list: flawless; displays correctness and accuracy in every detail; meets exact and precise standards; conforms absolutely to a specified measurement of conduct; and strictly adheres to proper procedures. According to most dictionaries, that's the essence of "perfection." But it sounds pretty boring! May we conclude therefore that effective presenting is not about "perfection"? As you know and have just described, it's about connection.

But here's the dilemma: If asked, "Do you want to deliver a perfect presentation or an imperfect one?" I think all of us would opt for perfect. But in reality, a perfect presenter or presentation does not exist. And yet we, in our desire to achieve the ideal, hold ourselves to this unachievable and frustrating standard.

It reminds me of King Sisyphus from Greek mythology. As punishment for his misdeeds, King Sisyphus was made to roll a huge boulder up a steep hill. Before he could reach the top, however, the massive stone would always roll back down, forcing him to begin again. He was consigned to a maddening eternity of useless efforts and unending frustration. Thus it came to pass that pointless and impossible activities are sometimes described as Sisyphean.

Week after week, I work with first-time clients who approach presenting as a Sisyphean effort. They attempt to write the perfect script, and they expect to recite it perfectly word for word. They labor hours to create the perfect slides, and expect to cover every single bullet point, perfectly. They develop the perfect agenda and pack every second with perfectly researched content. They push, push, push this heavy stone up the hill. When rehearsing, if they miss a word, skip a point, or make a mistake in any way, you can almost hear the boulder come crashing back down the hill. Frustrated and upset with themselves, they start again, and again. It's painful to watch.

Linda, an executive vice president for one of the world's largest investment banking firms, was one such client. She wanted to practice a critical presentation she was scheduled to deliver in two weeks to an audience of potential investors. No doubt, her content was dense and complex, covering topics like asset management, mergers and acquisitions, future market direction, and business diversity. She had one hour on the conference agenda to convince listeners that her firm was the right choice. Knowing she had to fill sixty minutes, cover fifty-two slides her boss had given her, and seal a multimillion-dollar deal was a bit overwhelming.

Nevertheless, Linda began rehearsing. Staring at the screen, trying to remember her script, carefully belaboring every point, she would pause, back up, say a phrase again, stumble over her words, lose her train of thought, and start over. Twenty minutes into the hour-long practice session, Linda hadn't reached the fifth slide. She was becoming more and more noticeably upset. That's when I turned off the video camera and said, "That's okay, Linda— this is hard work. Let's take a break and just talk for a moment. Since we're going to be working together, I'd really like to get to know you a little better. Can you tell me about your family? You mentioned earlier you attended your daughter Tiffany's first ballet recital over the weekend. I'd love to hear more about that." What Linda didn't know is that I secretly turned the camera on again and recorded every word she said, every movement she made. When she finished the story, I said, "There's something I'd like to show you." On the monitor, I first showed Linda her "performance" of pushing the boulder up the hill, trying so hard to perfectly deliver her business content without making a single mistake. She said, "Oh, @#$%. Please, turn it off." As you can imagine, her body was stiff, her face devoid of expression, her voice tone was flat, her eyes were unsettled, her hands were clenched tightly, and her speech was hesitant.

Then I quickly switched to the video of Linda telling the story of her daughter's ballet recital. It was thrilling to watch Linda as she watched herself. Tears came to her eyes as she saw this seemingly rigid, monotonous presenter transform into an enthusiastic dynamic speaker with charisma. She saw herself gleefully laugh out loud as she described her "tomboy Tiffany in a tutu." Her eyes sparkled as she described her child's personality. Linda's body relaxed and became animated as she imitated a plié; her voice was filled with passion and her speech was natural and conversational. Once again, she said, "Oh, @#$%," but this time for a different reason. "Wow," she said, "what a difference. How do I become *that* person on stage instead of the other one?"

Linda's question is at the very heart of effective presenting. The goal—despite the internal and external pressure—is to be yourself, at your very best: natural, expressive, spontaneous, and authentic. Whenever communicating with another human being becomes about perfection—about measuring up, performing, impressing rather than about connecting—it rarely goes well. As it did for Sisyphus, the heavy stone ends up rolling back down the hill and sometimes takes us down in the process.

The good news is, Linda left the stone behind. She stopped perfecting and started connecting. As a result she figured out how to be *that* person and gave a stellar presentation at the conference. She opened with a brief personal story about why she worked for this company and believed in it. She provided customer testimonials—in fact, she arranged for two customers to join her on stage and briefly share their perspectives. She cut more than half the slides, yet still covered all the necessary content and topics. She addressed tough issues without belaboring the point. Finally, she closed with a video of the company president sharing his philosophy of partnership and commitment. There was plenty of time remaining for Linda to answer questions and address the issues most important to the audience. In fact, Linda's audience was so engaged, the session extended thirty minutes into the lunch break.

Now let's be honest. During her presentation, did Linda make a few mistakes, stumble on some words, leave out a point or two, and occasionally say "um"? Did she lose her place, have to refer to her notes a time or two, even take a sip of water to gather her thoughts? Yes—because she's human. But more important, did the decision makers in the audience know, or even care? Absolutely not. The only real mistake is thinking that these slip-ups equal failure. Of course, it's essential that we are well prepared, know our material, and present the facts; however, knowledge alone is insufficient. Linda set aside perfectionism, focused on her audience's needs, and laid the groundwork for trust, rapport, and a long-lasting relationship.

If we focus on the audience, not ourselves, whether in a one-on-one conversation or a packed conference center, we'll deliver a crowd-pleasing, even praiseworthy, presentation every time. That's because success is ultimately about connection, not perfection.

And by the way, the investors chose Linda's firm as their bank and she went home with the largest order of her career.

CHAPTER 3: EXECUTIVE SUMMARY

➤ "Gift wrap" your presentation.

➤ Eliminate "brown paper bag" impressions.

➤ Decision makers often accept or reject your proposal based on their perception of you.

➤ Optimize the three factors of perception: Visual, Vocal/Verbal, and Relational.

➤ Remember, it's about connection, not perfection!

Developing Persuasive Content

CHAPTER 4

Crafting Your Presentation

> Tell the audience what you're going to say, say it; then tell them what you've said.
>
> —DALE CARNEGIE

You have probably heard that Dale Carnegie quote before. What you might not realize is that this simple three-step process for organizing your presentation is actually a streamlined version of Aristotle's ideas on giving persuasive speeches. It's a rhetorical structure that has convinced audiences made up of emperors and senators, kings and queens, judges and juries, customers and prospects, business leaders and decision makers across the millennia. There are at least three reasons this bromide has been around for centuries:

1. It keeps you, the presenter, focused and on track as you prepare and deliver your presentation.

2. It makes your audience feel more comfortable and secure because they will know where you are headed.

3. It helps your audience remember what you say. When you tell people what they are about to hear, tell them, then tell them what they just heard, they are much more likely to retain the message and act on it.

ORGANIZING YOUR PRESENTATION WITH PERSUASIVE LOGIC AND STRUCTURE

As a speech coach, I have surveyed thousands of audience members across five continents and twenty industries. When I ask about their top ten most desired characteristics of an effective presenter, the word "organized" appears on more than 90 percent of the respondents' lists. As a general rule, people are more comfortable when a certain amount of order is present.

Jim is the newly appointed president of customer operations for a leading government software company. One of his top salespeople had worked for months to get a meeting with the mayor and city officials of a major metropolitan area. The city had an outdated infrastructure, which meant costs were out of control, taxes were going up, and the officials' elected positions were at stake. They needed help and Jim had the perfect solution, making it a fantastic opportunity for Jim, his company, the city government, and taxpayers. If there was ever a time for a well-organized persuasive presentation that followed Carnegie's "tell them" principle, this was it. Unfortunately, Jim had the audience on the edge of their seats, but for the wrong reason. According to Jim's boss, it was actually because they were trying to muster enough nerve to leave! Within ten minutes, the mayor stepped out to take a call while the city manager checked her e-mail. Within five more minutes, the city's chief engineering officer was typing away on his laptop; the head of IT yawned; and three city council members carried on a private conversation. It should be no surprise, then, that the meeting was over forty-five minutes before Jim had intended. It reminds me of the adage, "It is better to leave your audience before your audience leaves you."

The city government officials chose another vendor. As a result of this lost opportunity, the software company's CEO asked me to work with Jim. He told me Jim was a brilliant leader who had earned the respect of his people; that no one knew the business better than Jim; and the company could not afford to lose him. "His only problem," said the CEO, "is that he has a bad habit of winging it."

We have all endured those "winged" presentations. We have all been on the edge of our seats, wanting to leave. The presenter fails to give us a road map to follow; there is no purpose or central theme; no reason or incentive to listen; no memorable points or key takeaways; no humor or involvement; no compelling close or call to action. Instead, the presenter aimlessly rambles through unrelated ideas and laboriously pontificates on the topic from his own perspective. This style yields a bored audience and a jeopardized career.

As I worked with Jim, I discovered he had several reasons for skipping the critical step of structure. Jim felt he didn't have to prepare because of the depth and breadth of his knowledge. Plus, he said he was much more comfortable when he just said whatever came to mind. He viewed structure and organization as a time-consuming, labor-intensive chore unworthy of the effort. And he felt that an outline prevented him from being spontaneous and cramped his natural style.

On the contrary, structure does not prevent spontaneity and flexibility. Those qualities are paramount to a skillful persuasive presenter. The point is to have enough structure for the audience to feel comfortable and for you to appear focused and prepared, while remaining adaptable, flexible, and instinctive.

The good news is that Jim had another opportunity to present one month later to an even bigger prospect, a city government twice the size of the first. He wanted to succeed this time and was willing to put forth the effort of preparation. Pretty soon, Jim saw how easy and quick it is to organize a message using the simple formula presented in this chapter. He realized he could honor his own natural style *and* be organized at the same time.

Much to his boss's delight, Jim nailed the presentation and came home with one of the largest orders of his career.

HOW TO DEVELOP AN EFFECTIVE OPENING, BODY, AND CLOSE

A persuasive presentation consists of three sections, delivered in this order:

I. **The Opening** (tell them what you are going to tell them)
II. **The Body** (tell them)
III. **The Close** (tell them what you told them)

Let's look at each section in more detail and learn how this structure not only helped Jim persuade a tough group of city officials, but also provides an easy-to-follow framework for you *and* your audience.

Develop the Opening

Tell them what you are going to tell them. Before diving into the main crux of the presentation, set the stage by providing your audience with a well-organized opening consisting of three key elements:

- Introduction
- Attention-getter
- Executive preview

A powerful introduction

In one minute or less, your introduction should warmly welcome your audience and thank them for their attendance. Quickly establish your credibility and enthusiasm, and clearly state the purpose of the presentation. Granted, few of us enjoy talking about ourselves, but if the people in the room do not know you or are not familiar with your credentials, it is important to *briefly* position yourself as an experienced authority on the subject. In addition, it is a bonus if you can tell the audience why you are glad to be there and excited to share the message with them. Consider the following guidelines when developing the introduction of your opening.

- Offer a warm welcome and thank-you to establish rapport and show appreciation.
- Give a brief self-introduction to establish your credibility and experience.
- State the purpose of your presentation to provide focus for the audience and tell them exactly how they will benefit from your message.

Here is Jim's new and improved one-minute-or-less introduction, which follows the preceding outline.

- Good morning everyone, and welcome. Thank you for the opportunity to visit with you here at the Columbus City Hall. It's a privilege to spend time with you.
- My name is Jim Smith, president of customer operations for Acme. By way of background, I've been in the government software business for twenty-three years including leadership roles in engineering, IT, sales, and operations. During that time, I've personally managed

software implementations for more than 100 cities in the United States. But what's more important, and the reason I'm excited to be here today, is because I've seen those cities benefit as a result of Acme's solutions: Collectively, their documented total of increased efficiencies exceeds $200 million within the first year of using Acme solutions.

➤ That brings us to the purpose of today's presentation: to show you how the City of Columbus can significantly reduce cost, improve labor efficiencies, and increase citizen satisfaction by partnering with Acme.

A compelling attention-getter

In 1962 *Time* magazine called David Ogilvy "the most sought-after wizard in today's advertising industry." He once said, "You have only 30 seconds in a TV commercial. People screen out a lot of commercials because they open with something dull. When you advertise fire-extinguishers, open with the fire."

There is a lesson in that for those of us who present. We need to open with "fire!" The attention-getter grabs attention and holds the audience's interest. It is a magnetic tool that hooks your audience and keeps them watching—or listening. The following list features my top twenty favorite attention-getters.

1. Startle them with a surprising statistic or fact related to their industry or your topic.
2. Refer to a newsworthy event or current headline.
3. Ask a rhetorical thought-provoking question followed by a pause.
4. Ask a question and invite audience responses.
5. Conduct a survey and ask them to raise their hands.
6. Recite a relevant quotation.
7. Tell a brief personal story.
8. Use an analogy, metaphor, or anecdote.
9. Ask the audience to imagine a scenario.
10. Give an interesting or creative definition of a key word.
11. Use a prop or creative visual aid.
12. Recount a historic event that relates to your topic.

13. Use humor, which may include an amusing personal story, funny saying, witty example, short cartoon, or clean joke.

14. Perform a magic trick and relate it to your topic.

15. Show a photo.

16. Use an audiovisual aid such as an audio or video clip.

17. Compliment the audience on special awards, achievements, or recognitions.

18. Conduct a quiz, game, activity, or exercise.

19. Motivate by showing them a progress report such as before-and-after results.

20. Use the mirror technique. That is, reflect back to the audience an intimate understanding of who they are as it relates to your topic. Show them you know them by immediately stating several facts about them, such as listing their key business issues, performance numbers, or corporate values.

Jim combined two attention-getters. First, he showed three shocking statistics that mirrored his audience's business challenges. Then, segueing from his introduction, Jim immediately advanced to the slide shown in Figure 4-1, which appeared on the screen.

Figure 4-1

6,000

$150,000

20%

He paused for a moment, then announced:

➤ Last week, in our meeting with Sue Bell and other members of the Street and Traffic Maintenance Division, we learned that her department alone is spending approximately 6,000 additional hours annually in project management, just trying to organize the daily tasks of their road crews. That's roughly $150,000 your city is spending in

unnecessary labor costs. And, as a result of these process inefficiencies, roads are not being repaired or built as quickly as the public
would like, and your citizen satisfaction rating dropped by a sharp 20
percent last year. The good news is, Acme's award-winning work
management tool, called "RoadDirector," can quickly and easily
solve these issues by significantly reducing labor costs and increasing
the efficiency of both your staff members and road crews. The result
will be more productive workers, a healthier bottom line, and happier
residents.

This audience-focused attention-getter launched Jim into a compelling
presentation that had the decision makers on the edge of their seats—this
time for the right reason: acute interest. He grabbed their attention by immediately addressing the most important thing to them—themselves! The
audience felt Jim cared enough about them to do his homework and learn
about their key business challenges. Not only that, but within the first two
minutes of his presentation, Jim assured them his solution has solved similar issues for other city governments (to the tune of $200 million), and he
could do the same for them.

Any effective attention-getter grabs the audience's interest, sets the stage
for a persuasive presentation, and makes the presenter look like a real pro.

A strong executive preview

The executive preview shows your decision-making audience that you are
organized and prepared with a well-thought-out plan. They immediately see
that you are going to lead them down a logical path and not waste their time.
The preview is where you "Tell them what you're going to tell them."

This technique is used very successfully in the entertainment industry.
Recall the last time you were in a movie theater. You are snuggled into your
seat, popcorn in hand, lights down, and all eyes on the screen in rapt attention. Does the movie begin right away? No. What precedes the feature presentation? Previews of coming attractions. And, based on those previews, you
may say to yourself, "Oh, I want to see that one!" In a moment of anticipation while your attention was captured, they sold you another movie ticket
based on a preview.

Similarly, your executive preview offers in advance a few clinching clips
of what is to follow in your full-length feature presentation. It consists of a

few sentences that state the purpose, points, and benefits that lie ahead for the audience—in essence, what's in it for them to listen attentively.

The following guidelines for the preview help prepare the audience for what they are about to hear:

- Provide a road map or agenda and explain how the presentation is organized in order to accomplish the previously stated purpose. This entails highlighting the key points you will be covering. Consider Jim's example:

  - Let's take a look at our agenda.

    1. First, you'll discover the findings from Acme's recent Benefits Realization Study, which reveals the main deficiencies in your current process.
    2. Second, you'll see how an *integrated* solution can deliver measurable results in cost reduction, labor efficiency, and citizen satisfaction.
    3. And third, you'll hear why Acme is the leader in the industry and our recommended next steps.

- Mention any logistical issues, if necessary, such as confirming the time length of the presentation; how you wish to handle Q&A (whether you will take questions during or after the presentation); whether you will provide handouts or copies of the slides afterward.

  - We have one hour allotted for this meeting. Does that still work with everyone's schedule? [Audience nods yes.] In respect of your valuable time, my presentation will only last twenty minutes. Please feel free to ask questions or offer comments throughout. This will leave us the remainder of the hour to discuss what's most important to you. In addition, you'll receive copies of these slides plus the Benefits Realization Study at the end of the presentation. Are there questions or comments before we move forward?

- Make a transition statement that leads into the body of your presentation.

  - Okay, let's move into key point number one and review the findings from the recent Benefits Realization Study.

Develop the Body

Tell them. Now, it is time to develop the crux of your message, the body. The body of your presentation consists of three key elements:

➤ Key points

➤ Supporting material

➤ Transition statements

Select three key points

Ray, the CEO of one of the nation's largest retail clothing chains, had a problem with how his regional store managers presented to him. He said to me, "Every quarter they arrive at my office to present a one-hour operating forecast, and I have no idea what they're trying to tell me." When I did some research, I discovered these regional store managers felt overwhelmed with massive amounts of data involving their stores' performance. They had a difficult time narrowing the focus, selecting the appropriate material, and summarizing three months of retail activity across dozens of stores into one hour.

I asked the CEO to specify exactly what he wanted from his managers, so that we could set clear expectations for them. He said, "Tell them to imagine three buckets, and only three. Label each bucket with a big idea. Put data related to that big idea in the bucket. If it doesn't relate, leave it out."

I thought to myself, "Okay, he only wants to hear three key points and no more. I get it." But still needing a little more input I asked, "What type of information would you like them to put in the bucket?"

He quickly replied, "If it doesn't make money or cost money, don't put it in the bucket—I don't need to hear about it." I communicated this message to his team and we prepared and rehearsed accordingly. Imagine Ray's delight when every senior leader presented their next quarterly presentation using "three buckets" titled Sales Volume, Sales Projections, Sales Strategy. They narrowed their content to include only the data that related to revenue or expense; they spent ten concise, compelling minutes on each "bucket"; then, they had thirty minutes left for the CEO's questions and discussion.

Follow the "Rule of Three." Ray, whether he knows it or not, is actually using a proven communication technique called the Rule of Three. Much like his regional managers, you may have scads of information you feel you need to cover. It's fair to ask, "Why not four points, five, seven, even ten?" What if you have many valid points to communicate during your presentation? Why limit it to three? Because adhering to the Rule of Three works. It's an age-old principle in communicating that suggests when things come in a pattern of three, they are inherently more satisfying, easier to remember, even funnier.

The ancient three-word Latin phrase *omne trium perfectum* means everything that comes in threes is perfect, or, every set of three is complete. The Rule of Three reflects the natural way in which people mentally follow and store information. It's a learning method that begins in childhood. We receive information in threes with the ABCs, Reading/wRriting/aRrithmetic, and numerous children's stories: The Three Blind Mice, Three Little Pigs, Three Billy Goats Gruff, Goldilocks and the Three Bears.

The Rule of Three is the basis of comedic timing. A series of three is often used to create a progression in which the tension is created, then built up, built up even more, and finally released. Most every joke has three parts or characters, with the third serving as the punch line.

A well-known example of the Rule of Three in written political rhetoric is the U.S. Declaration of Independence appeal to "life, liberty and the pursuit of happiness." In Abraham Lincoln's Gettysburg Address, he argues for a "government of the people, by the people, for the people." The Rule of Three is a prominent technique used in oratory and writing.

Most American names come in three parts: first, middle, and last. Our calendar is broken into morning, noon, and night. Standard mealtimes are breakfast, lunch, and dinner, which we eat using a knife, spoon, and fork.

Most important for our purposes, the Rule of Three helps your audience remember your key points. Rather than presenting an array of numerous ideas that randomly swirl in your listeners' minds, the Rule of Three crystallizes your message into the three most important points you want to make. It demonstrates the adage "less is more." The more you tell people, the less they will remember. The less you tell them, the more they will remember.

My own audience studies and surveys indicate that twenty-four hours after your presentation, your audience will remember, at best, only 10 percent of what you said. Make sure that 10 percent is composed of your three big ideas. Then, label three buckets with those big ideas and put everything related to each big idea in its bucket. If something doesn't relate to a big idea, don't put it in the bucket. Just leave it out.

Select audience-focused key points. The following questions help you select the three most important key points:

➤ What points would specifically pique my audience's interests and address their needs?

➤ What points will best support my objective and call to action?

➤ What points do I want this audience to remember most?

Use a logical sequence to label key points. After you've identified the three points, it's time to sequence them in a logical order that makes sense to the audience and is easy to remember. Consider the following methods:

➤ *Problem/solution:* As you'll recall from the beginning of this section, Jim opted to sequence his three key points using the problem/solution format.

1. Reveal deficiencies in the current process.
2. Discover how integration delivers cost reduction, labor efficiency, and citizen satisfaction.
3. Learn why Acme is the industry leader plus learn about recommended next steps.

➤ *Top three benefits:* Sam, a top account manager for a major supply chain company, had been knocking on his prospect's door for six months. When he finally cinched a thirty-minute appointment with the chief operating officer, he was ready. Sam had conducted a thorough analysis of his audience and learned the CIO's top three pain points: a lack of productivity and efficiency due to antiquated technology; skyrocketing expenses due to poor processes; and, consequently, an embarrassing drop in customer satisfaction ratings. Sam knew his solutions could solve the CIO's issues. Even though Sam has seventy-three products in his solution suite, twenty optional add-on services, an impressive half-hour corporate overview including the company history, dozens of slides on supply chain methodology, and an impressive list of clients spanning twelve industries, this seasoned presenter asked himself, "What is most important to my audience?" Here are Sam's three key points:

1. Increase your operational efficiency.
2. Lower your total cost of ownership.
3. Improve your customer satisfaction.

Sam spent about five minutes in each "bucket" briefly describing how he understood the CIO's business and could help solve the company's main challenges. He concluded his presentation in fifteen minutes with another fifteen remaining for discussion and Q&A. It was no surprise that the CIO asked Sam and his team of experts to return the following week for a half-day demo, which eventually led to his winning the CIO's business.

➤ *Step-by-step:* Robert, the president of a major real estate company, was invited to speak to a group of prospective first-time homebuyers. Despite the myriad details involved in the process of buying a house, he narrowed the scope to address only the most relevant important points for this audience. He titled his presentation, "Three Simple Steps to Take Before Buying a Home."

Step 1. Order your credit reports.

Step 2. Gather your financial documents.

Step 3. Create a budget.

➤ *Acronym:* Jill, a senior vice president of product marketing, is a highly sought-after presenter in her company due to her proven track record of turning prospects into buyers at trade shows. Even though her software is a complex enterprise collaboration tool with hundreds of features, she has organized her product's key advantages around a simple acronym. Prospective buyers immediately understand how they WIN through her solution's three main features:

1. **W**orkgroup solutions
2. **I**nternet access solutions
3. **N**etworking solutions

➤ *Least important to most important:* Joe, the chief safety engineer for a heavy equipment manufacturing company, was inundated with employees' on-the-job mishaps and hospitalizations due to careless behavior, which had cost the company $3 million the previous year. His chief executive officer told him he needed to persuade the workforce to follow proper safety procedures, or Joe's job was at stake. He used the technique of least important to most important to organize his three key points, as shown here.

By following proper safety procedures, you will:

➤ Keep your job (least important)

➤ Prevent personal injury (more important)

➤ Save your life (most important)

➤ *General to specific:* Kevin, a senior vice president of sales, presented at his company's national sales meeting to a hard-working sales force. The salespeople were eager to hear about the year's performance, because that would determine the amount of their bonus checks. He opted to begin with broad overall company results and build anticipation by progressively moving toward specific personal results. By the time he reached the third point and asked, "So now would you like to hear what these results mean to you?" all the members of the sales team were on their feet applauding. His key points were organized from general to specific:

1. Company results (general)
2. Departmental results (more specific)
3. Individual employee results (very specific)

➤ *Spatial relationship or geographic:* In the case of presenting performance figures or year-end results, you might present them by region:

➤ Eastern
➤ Central
➤ Western

➤ *Chronological order or historic:* Paul, a chairman of the board in the telecommunications industry, favors this method of organization. He instructs all those reporting to him to organize their speaking points using this simple flow:

➤ Past (last quarter's results)
➤ Present (this quarter's results)
➤ Future (next quarter's forecast)

➤ *Alliteration:* Donna, the president of a large management-consulting firm, presents to corporate executives on how to improve their operational and workplace performance. She has organized her key points into the "The Three Ps of Performance":

➤ People
➤ Process
➤ Products

➤ *Combination of techniques:* You may also combine techniques for added impact. Consider the following example, which uses both step-by-step and acronym. The Watson-Glaser Critical Thinking Appraisal, which was developed in 1925, is a tool widely used for developing future leaders. Condensing hundreds of books and pile-high data on cognitive psychology, this tool organizes the complex topic of critical thinking into an easy-to-remember three-step acronym known as the "RED" model:

Step 1: **R**ecognize assumptions.

Step 2: **E**valuate arguments.

Step 3: **D**raw conclusions.

Because listeners will not remember all of your presentation, ask yourself, "What do I *most* want my audience to remember from my message? Which tune do I want them whistling when they leave the theater?" Then, based on those answers, select and sequence your key points in an easy-to-follow, easy-to-remember method.

Add supporting material to your three key points

Have you ever watched one of those courtroom dramas where the lawyer spends the last ten minutes of the show persuading the judge and jury to see it her way? As an attorney, she presents evidence that substantiates her case. As an effective presenter, you do the same thing in front of your jury: the audience of decision makers. The proof you offer them will determine whether they agree or disagree, buy or reject, act or ignore.

Evidence—essential for a powerful presentation—comes in two types: qualitative and quantitative. There are feelings and facts; abstract and concrete; heart and head. As you may know from personal experience, a consumer's first response to a television commercial is based on how they *feel* about it. If they feel positively toward the product, then they listen for facts and findings to validate their feelings.

A persuasive presenter seeks first to connect on an emotional level by eliciting positive feelings from her listeners; then she offers concrete evidence to confirm those feelings. The key to persuasive supporting material is to balance feelings and facts, emotion and logic, head and heart, as illustrated in Figure 4-2.

Figure 4-2

Qualitative Material (Feelings-based)	Quantitative Material (Facts-based)
Customer testimonials	Statistics
Audience participation	Cost analysis
Personal stories and examples	Financial reports
Quotations	Market research
Humor	Product specifications
Photos	Demographics
Anecdotes	Spreadsheets

Where can you find supporting material? The list is almost endless, but here are several information-rich sources that may offer you convincing supporting material:

- ► The Internet: search engines and online research sites
- ► Your own personal experience, education, observations, and insights
- ► Your organization's intranet, files, videos, and libraries
- ► Media reports and documentaries
- ► Annual reports
- ► Budgets and financial reports
- ► Newspapers
- ► Newsletters
- ► White papers
- ► Collateral marketing material
- ► Catalogs and product spec sheets
- ► Audio and video programs
- ► Books
- ► Interviews/surveys
- ► Libraries
- ► Dictionary
- ► Trade magazines applicable to your subject

Apply the ACT Test. You have so much information, yet so little time. How do you select which information to use in your presentation? Put each piece of supporting evidence to the test—the "ACT" test. Weigh its value in terms of your **A**udience, **C**ontent, and **T**ime allotment. Ask yourself these questions:

➤ *Audience:* How does this piece of information help my audience? Does it specifically address their needs? Does it state or imply a benefit to them? Is it stimulating and thought-provoking?

➤ *Content:* Does this piece of supporting material arouse my audience's interest? Is it specifically and directly relevant to a key point? How well does it support or prove the point? Does it elicit emotion or offer concrete evidence? How will it help me reach my objective and urge the audience to say "yes" to my call to action? Is it "must-know" material or just "nice-to-know"?

➤ *Time:* Do you have time to include this piece of supporting material? Keeping in mind all the other material you must present, plus audience interaction and the Q&A session, can this piece of information be delivered within the allotted time? Can you make it concise and simple to understand? Remember, less is more.

Include transition statements between key points

The third element of the presentation body is transition statements between key points. Transitions make a significant critical contribution to the success of a presentation.

Imagine this scenario. You are driving along in your car at about forty-five miles an hour when suddenly the driver of the car in front of you comes to a dead stop in the middle of the road and then proceeds to turn left without signaling. You would have appreciated some advance notice of his decision, right? And depending on the distance between your car and his, you might notify him of his inconsideration via your horn. If audience members had horns, a few of them would probably want to use them every time a presenter fails to "signal" a change in direction.

Like a turn signal, a transition between key points notifies the listener that you are about to change the course of direction. It leads your audience from one key point to the next by briefly summarizing what you have just said and introducing what you are going to say next. Here are a few examples of transitions—or signals.

> ➤ Now that we've taken a look at the Benefits Realization Study and uncovered some of the deficiencies in the current process, let's move to key point number two and see how an integrated solution can solve these issues and deliver measurable savings.

> ➤ We've talked about how job safety is good for business and how it prevents injury to our employees; now let's move on to the third and most important point: how it can save your life.

Transitions can be as simple as a single sentence or phrase. Yet they are important signals that alert your listeners that the message is progressing and shifting gears. You, as the presenter, know when you are making a change—leaving one point and moving on to the next. But your audience does not. Without clearly stated transitions, you can be halfway into your next point before the audience perceives a change, which causes them to miss out on vital information. Building transitions into your presentation and effectively using one between each key point makes you, the presenter, appear organized and in control. Your audience will appreciate your guiding them from one point to the next and keeping them on track.

Develop the Close

Tell them what you told them. Finally, it's time to conclude your presentation with a powerful persuasive close that consists of three key elements:

1. Summary
2. Call to action
3. Appreciation

Following the body of your presentation comes a compelling, convincing close. First, summarize the key points and benefits of your message. Next, tell your audience exactly what you want them to do in response to your message. And finally, thank them for their time and attention. Let's look at each element in more detail.

Tips for developing a successful summary

Begin your summary by saying, "In conclusion," or "In summary." This sends a signal to the audience that the presentation is coming to an end and heightens their attention level. Next, briefly summarize the key points and benefits you have presented. This is the final chance in your presentation to reiterate what's in it for them. Be sure to include the key takeaway you want the audience to remember.

In addition, you want to launch the close as you did the opening, by capturing attention and provoking thought. Therefore, you should refer to the attention-getter you used in the opening. For example, if you opened with a shocking statistic, refer back to it. Or, if you opened with a quote, story, or illustration, allude to it. This approach places bookends on your presentation and ties the presentation together with persuasive logic. Consider the following guidelines when developing the summary section of your close.

- ➤ Briefly recap your presentation's key points and benefits.
- ➤ Refer back to your opening attention-getter to bookend your presentation.
- ➤ Repeat the one thing—the key takeaway—that you want your listeners to remember.

Tips for a convincing call to action

Will they place the order? Do they agree with your point of view? Are they convinced they should do what you are recommending? You will never know unless you ask them—better yet, strongly urge them. A call to action tells the audience exactly what you want them to do. The closing is where your presentation should produce results. It leaves no doubt about what you want your audience to do with the information you have presented.

The call to action is the twin sibling of your single clear-cut objective. Remember, in the first step of audience analysis, you completed this statement: "At the end of this presentation, I want my audience to_____." Here is your chance to go for it. Sample call-to-action beginnings may include:

- ➤ "I encourage you to . . ."
- ➤ "I urge you to give your unanimous approval to . . ."
- ➤ "I ask that you . . ."
- ➤ "I request your . . ."
- ➤ "I implore you to heed the safety measures just discussed . . ."

Show appreciation

Audience members give you, the presenter, one of their most valuable resources: time. For several minutes (usually an hour or more) they offer you their attention, thought, and consideration. Tell them you are grateful for the opportunity; not only is it good manners, but it is good business. Everyone likes to feel appreciated.

People also prize recognition. If appropriate, publicly recognize and credit people in the audience who helped make the presentation possible—perhaps the person who invited you to speak or helped with setup. Acknowledge volunteers—anyone who offered assistance, or anyone who deserves recognition for an outstanding achievement relevant to your subject matter.

Last, be sure to express a sincere desire to work together and serve as the prospect's partner in success. These are the elements of the appreciation section of the close:

- ➤ Thank them for their valuable time and attention.
- ➤ Acknowledge those who invited you and who made the event possible.
- ➤ Express a sincere desire to work with them and support their success.

OUTLINE RECAP

Let's go back to Jim and see how he closed his winning presentation to the decision makers of the Columbus city government, as shown in Figure 4-3.

In this chapter, we've gone step-by-step through a proven presentation outline that persuades decision makers. Once you know your audience and have them at the forefront of your preparation process, you can develop a customized message that addresses what's most important to them. Begin with a captivating opening that establishes your credibility, grabs attention, and provides a road map. Next, develop three key compelling points with qualitative and quantitative supporting material, plus clear transition statements. Last, close the presentation with impact by summarizing your key points, issuing a call to action, and thanking the audience for their time and consideration. Then, if appropriate, you can segue into a question-and-answer session. The topic of handling Q&A with finesse and confidence will be addressed in Chapter 12.

Figure 4-3

Summary	Ladies and gentlemen, this brings me to the close. In summary, first you saw the results of the Benefits Realization Study and how it revealed several costly, time-consuming gaps in your current process (repeat this "bad news" slide):
	6,000
	$150,000
	20%
	Second, you saw how Acme's "RoadDirector" can not only solve these issues but also deliver these measurable results in the first year (show this "good news" slide):
	Yearly Labor Efficiency Gain of
	10,000
	$250,000
	50%
	A reduction of 10,000 labor hours yielding a $250,000 savings, plus a projected 50% increase in citizen satisfaction due to improved efficiencies in traffic management.
	And third, you learned that Acme is the leader in the industry and has a proven track record of saving other city governments $200 million in the first year
Call to Action and Next Steps	As a next step I'll leave you with a proposal to review. The proposal outlines the investment and timeline of implementing stage one of the software. Because our solution offers significant potential savings to the City of Columbus, I encourage this governing body to vote in favor of Acme as your vendor of choice.
Appreciation	Thank you very much for your time and consideration today. Madam Mayor and council members, thank you for the invitation. And many thanks to Sue Bell and her staff for helping us prepare the workflow study. The team at Acme welcomes the opportunity to work with you, and would consider it an honor and privilege to partner with the City of Columbus.
Segue to Q&A	I see we have about 40 minutes remaining. It would be a pleasure to answer any additional questions and hear your comments and ideas . . .

Presenters who follow this proven format enjoy more successful outcomes. It makes it easier for you to prepare, present, and persuade. It makes it easier for the audience to listen, remember, and respond. As Jim discovered after his outstanding success, you become accustomed to the approach through repeated use. You may even find it becomes automatic and enjoyable! With every additional presentation you make, you discover the power of Aristotle's ancient method: Tell them what you're going to tell them; tell them; then tell them what you told them.

CHAPTER 4: EXECUTIVE SUMMARY

Follow the "tell them" principle to develop a well-organized, persuasive presentation:

I. The opening (tell them what you are going to tell them)
    A) Introduction
    B) Attention-getter
    C) Executive preview

II. The body (tell them)
    A) Three key points
    B) Supporting material
    C) Transition statements

III. The close (tell them what you told them)
    A) Summary
    B) Call to action
    C) Appreciation

CHAPTER 5

Developing Content That Involves and Engages Your Audience

> Tell me and I'll forget; show me and I may remember; involve me and I'll understand.
>
> —CHINESE PROVERB

Once you have structured a compelling open, body, and close following the "tell them" principle, it's time to look over your outline and conduct what I call the "FAN" test: **F**requency of **A**udience i**N**volvement. One of the best ways to endear yourself to listeners and make them your "fans" is to frequently involve and engage them. Before looking at specific techniques to help you engage your audience, let's explore why audience involvement is critical to achieving results.

ADAPTING TO THE THREE AUDIENCE LEARNING STYLES

Audience members perceive and process information using three learning styles: visual, auditory, and kinesthetic. Visual learners process new information best when it is visually illustrated or demonstrated. As the presenter, you would appeal to this type of learner by using graphics, charts, illustrations, photos, props, and demonstrations. Auditory learners process information by hearing and listening. In other words, they learn best when spoken to. This would include listening to the presenter lecture or hearing other people speak. Kinesthetic learners gain knowledge by touching and doing. They process new information best when it can be physically felt or manipulated. This may include taking notes, examining an object, participating in an activity or exercise, or writing an assignment. To ensure that you connect with each of type of learner, it's essential that you develop and include balanced, blended content that appeals to each of the three learning styles.

Audience Involvement Optimizes Principles of Adult Learning

As adults, we are active, hands-on learners. Give your listeners an opportunity to participate and engage in the learning process. Create a presentation setting that is inviting, stimulating, and affirming. In the hundreds of surveys I've conducted with adult learners, I find they want presentations that focus on real-life problems and tasks rather than academic material. They desire a strong, how-to, focused approach versus theory. They become restless if their time is wasted. Learning is active: "Tell me, I forget. Show me, I remember. Involve me, I understand." By involving your listeners you help them make connections between the new knowledge and their existing knowledge, and construct meaning from their own experiences.

Adults see learning as a means to an end rather than an end in itself. They must know what there is to gain and they must see progress being made. Before devoting precious time and energy to the task of learning, they tune to radio station WIIFM and ask themselves, "What's in it for me?" Therefore, you must strive to constantly reinforce and emphasize the benefits they will gain as a result of doing what you are suggesting. State the payoffs in the beginning, throughout the middle, and at the conclusion of your presentation. Emphasize how the presentation or demo will apply to their everyday lives. Learning occurs in context. Without an appropriate setting, it's unlikely to succeed. Adults have a "here and now" viewpoint. They wish to focus on current issues that are immediately applicable today, rather than on futuristic concepts.

Let's not forget that adults bring considerable experience with them to the meeting room. Therefore, they usually want to speak, participate, and contribute to the proceedings. They usually dislike long lectures and one-way communication. It's important to plan time for Q&A, group discussion, and audience comments. Remember, adult learning is social. Learners benefit from working collaboratively in groups so that they can hear different perspectives and accomplish the learning tasks with the help of their peers and experts.

Regardless of which audience engagement techniques you use, it's critical you make the experience safe, rewarding, and affirming for the participants. Adults have something to lose. They have a strong need to maintain their self-esteem, especially in front of other adults who are likely to be their colleagues (and possibly their boss). Like most people, they want to appear credible and smart in front of the group, and minimize any risk of embarrassment. Therefore, set them up for success. Welcome their input; listen to them actively; and openly affirm their contribution. Invite diversity and encourage other viewpoints. If points of disagreement arise, respectfully challenge them, and agree to disagree. Remain upbeat, positive, and courteous.

Every few months I send surveys to individuals who have participated in one of my workshops the previous quarter. I ask, "What do you remember most about the presentation?" "What key takeaway(s) have you used and/or found most valuable?" "What have you applied in your day-to-day work?" Quarter after quarter, year after year, the results are the same. For the most part, the participants remember what they were involved in: preparing and rehearsing an impromptu speech; delivering a presentation; receiving feedback and coaching; participating in a group discussion; reporting on a case study; discussing and debating issues with their peers; pairing up with a partner for a listening exercise; winning a prize; telling a personal story; having the group listen to their challenges. Mostly, they recall what they said and did; they remember their moments of engagement; they learned most from their own participation. They seldom mention a point that I as the speaker pontificated upon; and they've never—not once—mentioned a single slide as a key takeaway. Every time I read these surveys it's a slice of humble pie! Yet, I'm grateful for the feedback. It reminds me constantly that it's all about them. I can tell them and they will forget. I can show them and they may remember. But if I take the time to involve them, if I develop content that engages them, if I create opportunities to interact with them, they will not only understand, they will consider the experience meaningful and memorable. Now let's explore ways to achieve that result.

TWENTY WAYS TO ENGAGE AND INVOLVE YOUR AUDIENCE

Though their styles may vary greatly, memorable speakers have one thing in common: they know how to create a connection with their listeners. Here are twenty proven techniques to help us do the same:

1. *Conduct a pre-session survey.* For starters, you can send attendees an online survey prior to meeting to engage them in thinking before they arrive. If appropriate, also send reading material to prep them for your topic. Attendees, especially decision-making senior managers, like to see their own data displayed. For example, I almost always send out questionnaires before a program including the question, "On a scale of 1–10 with 10 being the highest, please rate your level of proficiency in the following presentation categories . . ." Then, when the group is together, I show the rankings, which clearly display the perceived strengths and weaknesses of that particular group.

2. *Invite introductions.* This technique works well if there are fewer than twenty people in the group *and* they do not all know one another. I usually allot five minutes for this exercise. I introduce it by saying, "For the benefit of those who have not met everyone, let's take about ten to fifteen seconds each to briefly introduce ourselves. Please include your name, title, and anything you want this group to know about you." Inevitably, this open-ended invitation not only recognizes everyone and clarifies roles and responsibilities but also opens the door for them to share something personal. For example, at one session a chief operating officer introduced himself and added, "Plus, I spent thirty years in the U.S. Air Force and have served in two wars." Serendipitously, the date of the session happened to be Veteran's Day! The group immediately stood up and applauded his service. At lunchtime, someone arranged for a special cake in his honor. In a million years, I couldn't have written or planned anything that good in my outline. The best material comes from the audience, if you give them a chance to share it. Caution: If everyone in the group already knows one another, don't ask for introductions. Busy decision makers will consider it self-serving on your part, and a waste of their time.

3. *Record their wish list.* In the first few minutes of the presentation, be sure you clarify and verify what's most important to the audience. What's on their wish list to solve or accomplish? You may say something such as, "Your burning issues are the most important ones to address today. In addition to the ones listed here on the agenda slide, are there any others you would like for me to add to the list?" Write them down on a flip chart and be sure to either address them during the presentation or promise to follow up.

4. *Request a response or ask a question.* A very easy way to involve listeners right away is to request their input on your topic. Rather than spoon-

feeding them your information with one-way communication, invite them to think about a question you pose and share their thoughts aloud with you and the group. For example, Marc, the executive vice president of business strategy for a leading auto manufacturer, recently started a presentation by asking, "According to recent studies, what topics do you believe should appear on the experts' list of The Top Ten Business Risks for Multinational Firms?" Within five minutes, all fifteen decision makers in the room had chimed in. Marc listed their responses on a flip chart, and the session was off to a stimulating, engaging start. Marc took a red marker, circled one of the responses, and said, "Sarah, you win the prize—Regulation and Compliance is the number one risk according to the experts. Let's begin by discussing our industry's ever-changing regulatory environment."

5. *Show a photo.* A picture is worth a thousand words, maybe more. The president of an electronics equipment company reported to me that he believes a photo he used in a presentation helped save his company millions of dollars. Rather than the mundane charts, graphs, and spreadsheets he had been using to encourage his managers to cut costs, this time he showed two photos. First he displayed a photo of a ship and asked the audience to identify it. They quickly and correctly said in unison, "The *Titanic*." Then he said, "The *Titanic* was designed by experienced engineers, using some of the most advanced technologies and extensive safety features of the time. So what sank it?" Again, everyone replied correctly in unison, "An iceberg." He then showed a second photo of a whole iceberg: the tip was clearly visible above the water; the much larger portion was dimly visible below the surface of the water. He paused then said, "The same thing is about to happen to our company. Hidden costs—the dangers beneath the surface—are about to sink this company. I need your help." This visual metaphor spawned a creative, productive brainstorming session that led to every business unit manager diligently hunting for what they labeled the "icebergs." Use photos instead of text, when possible. Pictures engage the audience's imagination and make your message unique, memorable, and actionable. Also, consider including a photo of yourself on the title slide, or a picture of your team, or pictures of the listeners' facility and staff members.

6. *Play a video or audio clip.* Insert short clips so the audience can learn from clients, experts, or leaders. A well-produced video is an excellent addition to a presentation. It provides variation in the format and allows the audience to see remote facilities and hear from different speakers. The video

may include customer testimonials, a special message from the company president, or a promotional corporate message, to name just a few possibilities.

7. *Use creative props.* The CEO of a large insurance company who was an avid tennis player brilliantly used a tennis racquet to drive home the key points of his strategy at an employee meeting. Metaphorically he talked about "acing the competition"; "rallying" with partners; winning a "grand slam" through good customer service and quality products. Year after year, other speakers were compared to this leader's creative ability to rally the troops.

8. *Set up a demonstration and invite audience members to participate.* If you're selling a product that's small enough to transport, you should demonstrate the key features and benefits during the presentation and then invite the audience to give it a try. The executive vice president of sales for a major computer company wanted to convince a group of prospects to convert from their old laptops to his company's new tablet PC product. He overcame their skepticism and objections within thirty minutes: after demonstrating the product, he handed a tablet PC to each member of the audience and asked them to perform tasks as he narrated a guided simulation. They experienced for themselves the ease of use, the timesaving features, and the convenience. He closed the order that day, became the vendor of choice for his new client, and sold more than 2,000 units to the company's sales force.

9. *Conduct a quiz or host a game show.* Leslie, the vice president of public relations for a major beverage company, had a vision to produce a one-of-a-kind marketing campaign that would teach the public about her company's impressive, long-standing history and build brand loyalty. Focus group studies indicated customers were confused about the brand and lacked top-of-mind awareness. When she delivered her presentation to skeptical and frugal decision makers to gain the necessary funding, they doubted the need for the campaign. In a whimsical, nonthreatening way, she conducted the same quiz with them that she had conducted with focus groups. They failed the test! She proved her point about lack of brand awareness and convinced them they needed to invest dollars to fund her campaign. A simple quiz helped her walk away with the order! You may also consider using one of the many game show software products available. These tools enable you to turn routine reviews and dry presentations into funny, TV-style quiz shows that boost attention, participation, and retention.

10. *Give away prizes.* Everybody likes to be a winner, regardless of one's hierarchy on the corporate ladder. In my presentations, which often range from six to eight hours a day, participants have a chance to win a prize once an hour. It's built into the slide deck. At every major transition between key points, a large colorful photo appears featuring a brightly covered gift bursting open with neon ribbons. I simply ask, "Okay, who's ready to win a prize?" Attendee names are in a grab bag and someone from the audience chooses and announces the winner's name. Popular prizes range from gift cards for coffee, books, and music to leather portfolios, coffee mugs, T-shirts, and corporate-branded paraphernalia. Caution: Be sure to check with company officials to ensure that gifts are allowed and, if so, what the limit is on the gift amount.

11. *Ask the audience questions during the presentation.* My rule of thumb is to stop and ask the audience a question after every major point (usually once every couple of slides). Constantly check in to ensure your audience is on track, understands your message, and has the opportunity to ask their questions as they arise. This list may include questions such as, "What do you think of the content you've seen so far?" "How do you see this solution fitting into your current environment?" "Has this situation ever happened in your organization?" Relevant reflective questions generate discussion and keep your audience engaged. Remember, the decision maker will likely recall the content that most engages him or her, the moments that are learner-centered versus speaker-centered. This means that as the presenter you must wrestle with the paradox of establishing control by risking giving it up! By giving up the need to feel that you are expertly delivering every point and controlling the agenda, you gain the kind of facilitative control that is most effective for adult listeners.

12. *Use activities, games, or exercises.* Terry, the chief executive officer of a major home appliance company, wanted to communicate to his resellers that it takes hard work, persistence, and the willingness to go the distance to yield the greatest results in business. He could have placed this platitude on a slide as a bullet point and talked about it. Instead, he opted to try an activity. Midway through his presentation he said, "Okay, I want to give away some money now." Audience members began to sit up a bit straighter and lean forward. Reaching for his wallet, he pulled out a five-dollar bill. "Who would like five dollars?" A few hands shot up. He walked over and handed the bill to the person whose hand first went up. "There, that was easy, wasn't

it?" The recipient nodded. Then he pulled out a twenty-dollar bill. "If you want this twenty, please step forward to the stage." A few people hurried forward. He handed the twenty to the first person who arrived. "Now, I'm going to give away this hundred-dollar bill. Who would like it?" Every hand in the room went up. Then he said, "Okay, you're going to have to work for this one. Please look inside your wallet. If you have three bills of any face value that are dated on or before the year 2006, you may have this hundred-dollar bill." Some participants looked confused; others did not want to go to the trouble of pulling out their purse or wallet; a few reached into their wallets, grabbed a handful of bills, and quickly thumbed through them. A hand shot up in the air. Terry said, "There's our winner!" The man came forward; Terry checked the dates and gave him a crisp $100 bill. Terry then pointed out that there are three levels of success for resellers. For those who sit back and wait for success to come to them, there is minimal return. Others put forth a comfortable amount of effort and receive a moderate return. But those who go the extra mile and make the extra effort will receive the greatest return.

13. *Ask for volunteers.* Audience members are usually happy to write on a flip chart, track the time, record action items, assist with an activity, or draw a name out of a hat. They're just waiting for an invitation.

14. *Play fill-in-the-blank.* Ask listeners to guess certain facts or data, or leave blanks on your slides and ask them to fill in the missing words. This level of audience participation keeps people engaged and active in your presentation.

15. *Facilitate a discussion.* Encourage dialogue. Ask listeners to discuss concerns or topics with one another in pairs or at tables. Then discuss small-group ideas in the large group. I'm constantly reminded how important this is. Audience members are likely to recall what *they* say and do (not necessarily what you, the speaker, say and do). By getting your decision makers involved in the discussion and letting them talk, you significantly increase the impact of your message.

16. *Focus on benefits to the audience.* Ask them to confirm the benefits that are important to them. Throughout the presentation, notice when listeners affirmatively nod their heads, take notes, or smile in agreement. Use this opportunity to check in and say, "Sue, I can see you like the idea of reducing downtime by 15 percent. How would this benefit affect your particular department in terms of dollar savings?"

17. *Provide practice or application opportunities.* Rosanne, the chief officer of diversity at a major bank, presented to her senior executives on the importance of appreciating the various cultures and native languages represented in their employee base. She taught them basic greetings and phrases in seven different languages. She then invited them to practice their new language skills by moving around the meeting room and saying them to their colleagues. It was the job of the listener to identify which language his or her partner was speaking.

18. *Use learning aids.* Tactile-kinesthetic listeners especially enjoy having an item on the table to hold, squeeze, or manipulate. The physical involvement keeps them engaged and alert. For ideas, enter "office toys" in your search engine. The choices are almost endless including stress relief balls, bendable toys, Slinky toys, cube puzzles, finger puppets, and Koosh Balls. These grown-up toys can help illustrate points, entertain, increase learning, entice participation, promote your company, build your brand, and inject fun into your presentation.

19. *Use humor.* Everyone likes to laugh. A tasteful cartoon, clever quote, humorous story, or funny comment by an audience member works wonders for audience connection. Please see the following section for specific techniques on how to incorporate more humor into your presentations and conversations.

20. *Tell a story to illustrate your points.* Of all the tools in your kit, telling a well-crafted story is among the most powerful. In fact, storytelling is so important that there's an entire section dedicated to it later in this chapter. As you begin to think about your story, consider these questions: What were your pain points? How did you overcome them? What's unusual about your particular journey? What are your lessons learned?

TECHNIQUES FOR INCORPORATING HUMOR

There's a Norwegian proverb: "He who laughs, lasts." Humor is a powerful communication tool. It helps you gain attention, create rapport with your audience, and make your presentation more memorable. When applied appropriately, it can also relieve tension and reinforce key points. Are you concerned you're not naturally funny? Don't worry—most of us aren't. There are still plenty of ways to tickle your listeners' funny bones without being a comedian.

Personal Stories and Anecdotes

These are brief stories based on a real-life experience, either yours or someone else's. They are easy to tell because you have lived them and they spring from your own personal experience. They may include stories from childhood, friends, relatives, work, home, vacations, or embarrassing moments.

Cartoons and Quotes

Collect your favorite cartoons and keep them in a file. You can use them to add wit and make important points in a presentation. To research cartoons, type the words "business cartoon" into your favorite web browser; you'll find hundreds from which to choose.

Quotations can also serve as an indispensable aid in your presentations. They not only support your point and add humor, they also inspire and enlighten. For example, I always use this classic advice to add levity when there's conflict or disagreement among parties: "When two people agree on everything, one of them is unnecessary."

Sayings on Signs, Billboards, Bumper Stickers, and T-Shirts

When you see sayings that make you laugh, chances are your audience will, too. Jot them down and find ways to tie them into your presentation (making sure the message is clean, relevant, and non-offensive). I once saw this bumper sticker that read: "Been dieting a month. So far I've only lost 31 days." I now use this saying to kick off a discussion on goal setting.

Twist in a List

Try including a list of some kind in your presentation and add a surprise ending. For example, a vice president of sales and marketing used this technique to coach his entry-level managers: He opened up the presentation by saying, "Let's discuss the Five Ts of Becoming an Effective Manager: Taking Charge, Time Management, Training, Teamwork . . . and Tylenol!" It got a big laugh, showed his sense of humor, and opened the door for a helpful discussion on stress management when he covered the "Tylenol" section.

Photos and Images

A picture can communicate a message instantly, and get a laugh. The chief information officer of one of the world's largest consumer electronics companies needed to convince investors that his organization was responsive to economic change thanks to its well-balanced portfolio. He opened his talk with a photo featuring an elephant balancing on a bright beach ball. In a friendly tone he opened by saying, "It *is* possible to be big and agile." This photo was the theme of his presentation, handouts, and follow-up e-mails. Ultimately, the idea was used to brand an entire advertising campaign.

Headlines

Easy to find and fun to use, headlines can make your topic relevant. Because the funny headlines usually reflect errors in language or grammar, you can use them to emphasize a need for clarity in communication or discuss the possibility of multiple meanings in business. Type "Funny Headlines" in your favorite search engine to explore some that may work for you. Here are some of my favorites:

- ➤ Cold Wave Linked to Temperatures
- ➤ If Strike Isn't Settled Quickly It May Last a While
- ➤ Milk Drinkers Are Turning to Powder
- ➤ Hospitals Are Sued by Seven Foot Doctors
- ➤ Safety Experts Say School Bus Passengers Should Be Belted

Interesting Definitions

Select a key word or phrase from your presentation and define it in an amusing way. Again, using your favorite search engine, type in "Funny Definitions" and discover all the options. Here are a few that I've used:

- ➤ Committee: The confusion of one person multiplied by the number present.
- ➤ Dictionary: The only place where success comes before work.
- ➤ Smile: A curve that can set a lot of things straight.

Audience Interaction

One of the best sources of humor is your audience. Ask them how they would define a particular term; allow them to generate a list; invite their responses to a question; instruct them to share their ideas with a partner or in small groups and report their observations to the entire audience; have them draw, write, speak, demonstrate, and participate in your presentation. They will inevitably interject their unique sense of humor, wit, and funny experiences into the mix. Listen, laugh, and allow them to entertain one another.

THE ART OF EXECUTIVE STORYTELLING

A big part of your job as a leader and presenter is to motivate people to reach certain goals; to influence their thinking; to adopt your point of view. To do that exceptionally well, you will need to engage their emotions. A good story is key.

As children, we were naturally good at telling stories. It was in fact our main mode of communicating with the world. It's also how we learned from others about the world around us. But as we grew up, things changed. We learned that serious people—everyone from schoolteachers in the smallest towns to bosses in the biggest cities—relied mostly on presenting facts and figures.

We witness it every day. The average presenter builds a case with slides, statistics, and bullet points. However, as Aristotle teaches us (and as we discussed in Chapter 2), people are not inspired to act based on reason or Logos alone. It also requires Pathos, or engaging the emotions. There's a reason why movies compose a big portion of the multibillion-dollar entertainment industry: people enjoy good storytelling. The key for us, then, is to fuse our idea or recommendation with the listener's emotion. This is best done through a well-crafted story.

Consider Laura, the president of customer operations for one of the world's largest healthcare technology firms. Her company's electronic document imaging product converts a hospital's volumes of paper records into electronic images on a computer. As you might imagine, this frees up tons of physical space in the hospital because there's no need for storage rooms and filing cabinets. She knew her prospect needed more space in the emergency department to accommodate the growing number of patients, so Laura opted to turn off the PowerPoint presentation and tell the following story instead:

> Two weeks ago I was visiting one of my customers in California—a large 800+ bed hospital similar to your size here at Memorial General. Cindy Smith, director of patient services, told me about a little boy named Roy who had fallen off his bike and skinned his knee badly. That's no big deal for kids—you know how resilient they can be, right? However, Roy's

mother saw the scene out the kitchen window, shrieked, and raced him to the hospital. Why the panic? Roy is a hemophiliac. Last year, after a similar incident, he almost died due to blood loss because of the extreme wait in the emergency department. They didn't have enough beds to serve the patient population. Roy's mom knew this. As she frantically drove, she prayed, "Please, let them be able to see him right away." This time, when the son and mother arrived, it was a different story. Roy was in a bed with the bleeding stopped in less than five minutes. You see, since last year, this hospital was able to add five new treatment rooms, without a single capital expenditure. By using the XYZ document imaging solution, they freed up 5,000 square feet of space—formerly used for medical records—and converted it to patient rooms. As a result, the hospital's patient satisfaction ratings are sky-high. The physicians and clinicians are happier. Plus they're treating 20 percent more patients and realizing increased revenues at a lower cost structure. Through a simple choice called electronic document imaging, they've devoted newfound space where it was needed most: the emergency department . . . and Roy's knee. And how about your team here at Memorial General? Does this story sound familiar? How many more "Roys" could you serve with a few extra emergency department rooms? And what would that extra capacity mean for patient and employee satisfaction, not to mention increased revenue? The purpose of today's presentation is to explore how the XYZ document imaging solution can benefit Memorial General."

Good storytelling, like other parts of your message, requires preparation and organization. Most good stories have at least eight elements: characters, setting, foreshadowing, a protagonist, an antagonist, conflict, climax, and point of view. For business audiences, may I add a ninth? Brevity. No decision maker has the time to listen to a long-winded tale that rambles along and delays getting to the point, regardless of how well a speaker tells it. On the contrary, when you craft a story that gets to the point quickly (ideally in less than two minutes), you reveal a clear beneficial message, evoke emotions within the listener, and make the point more memorable. It's one of the most persuasive tools in your repertoire.

Let's revisit Laura and examine how she crafted her experience to tell a compelling story to her group of prospective customers. She used what I call the "five-part STORY method" to craft the tale into a concise and meaningful engagement opportunity.

1. **S:** Set the scene with time, place, and characters. Present briefly the necessary facts and create the context within which the story takes place. Also add your point of view—where you fit in story.

> Example: Two weeks ago I was visiting one of my customers in California—a large 800+ bed hospital similar to your size here at Memorial General. Cindy Smith, director of patient services, told me about a little boy named Roy who had fallen off his bike and skinned his knee badly. That's no big deal for kids—you know how resilient they can be, right?

2. **T:** Tell the trouble. What's the obstacle, conflict, problem, or scary part of the story? Who or what is the enemy? Can you include foreshadowing to imply what may happen in the future?

> Example: However, Roy's mother saw the scene out the kitchen window, shrieked, and raced him to the hospital. Why the panic? Roy is a hemophiliac. Last year, after a similar incident, he almost died due to blood loss because of the extreme wait in the emergency department. They didn't have enough beds to serve the patient population. Roy's mom knew this. As she frantically drove, she prayed, "Please, let them be able to see him right away."

3. **O:** Overcome the obstacle. This is where the teaching, hope, good news, and inspiration occur in your story. What is the climax of the story? How did you or the characters overcome the obstacle? What happened? Who helped?

> Example: This time, when the son and mother arrived, it was a different story. The nurses had Roy in a bed with the bleeding stopped in less than five minutes. You see, since last year, this hospital was able to add five new treatment rooms, without a single capital expenditure. By using the XYZ document imaging solution, they freed up 5,000 square feet of space— formerly used for medical records—and converted it to patient rooms.

4. **R:** Reveal the reward. What was the happy (or unhappy) ending? What lesson was learned? What benefits were gained from the experience?

What's the point of the story? This is where you reveal the moral—the main message or result—of the story.

> Example: As a result, the hospital's patient satisfaction ratings are sky-high. The physicians and clinicians are happier. Plus they're treating 20 percent more patients and realizing increased revenues at a lower cost structure. Through a simple choice called electronic document imaging, they've devoted newfound space where it was needed most: the emergency department . . . and Roy's knee.

5. **Y**: You-focus. This section speaks to relevance. Ask a question or make a point that transfers the story to the audience and their action. Employ a *you* question. "How about you?" "Imagine if you . . ." "Have you ever . . .?"

> Example: And how about your team here at Memorial General? Does this story sound familiar? How many more "Roys" could you serve with a few extra emergency department rooms? And what would that extra capacity mean for patient and employee satisfaction, not to mention increased revenue? The purpose of today's presentation is to explore how XYZ document imaging solution can benefit Memorial General."

Before delivering your presentation be sure to review your opening, body, and close, paying close attention to how many times you're reaching out to involve and interact with your audience. A key concept in adult learning is to keep the audience engaged. Whatever techniques you choose to use, remember to involve your listeners as often and soon as possible.

CHAPTER 5: EXECUTIVE SUMMARY

- ➤ Be sure to create content that helps your presentation pass the "FAN" test: **F**requency of **A**udience i**N**volvement.
- ➤ Strive to develop content that appeals to all three learning styles: visual, auditory, and kinesthetic.
- ➤ Develop content that honors adult learning principles: Active, hands-on, applicable, beneficial, two-way, social, safe, meaningful, and memorable.

➤ Apply one or more of the top twenty ways to engage and involve your audience:

1. Conduct a pre-session survey.
2. Invite introductions.
3. Record their wish list.
4. Request a response or ask a question.
5. Show a photo.
6. Play a video or audio clip.
7. Use creative props.
8. Set up a demonstration and invite audience members to participate.
9. Conduct a quiz or host a game show.
10. Give away prizes.
11. Ask the audience questions during the presentation.
12. Use activities, games, or exercises.
13. Ask for volunteers.
14. Play fill-in-the-blank.
15. Facilitate a discussion.
16. Focus on benefits to the audience.
17. Provide practice or application opportunities.
18. Use learning aids.
19. Use humor.
20. Tell a story to illustrate your points.

CHAPTER 6

Designing and Presenting Effective PowerPoint Slides

> It has become appallingly obvious that our technology has exceeded our humanity.
>
> —ALBERT EINSTEIN

Try to imagine Martin Luther King Jr. delivering his "I have a dream" speech using computerized graphics. There he is on the steps of the Lincoln Memorial in Washington, D.C., on August 28, 1963, delivering his stirring speech for racial equality to a crowd of thousands. He turns away from his audience, faces the screen, clutches a remote mouse, and advances his laptop to display dozens of snazzy slides illustrating his strongest points. The visuals are complete with richly colored bar charts and graphs, bullet points, creative animation, and even sound effects.

Thank goodness the technology did not exist back then. The world would likely have been robbed of one of the most inspirational speeches in history.

YOU ARE YOUR BEST VISUAL AID

Great speakers are successful with or without PowerPoint. They know how to connect with an audience with or without slides. As a persuasive presenter, you are your best visual aid. You are the message; the technology is not.

What is more, you are your most reliable and dependable visual aid. Projectors, laptops, software applications, and Internet connections often fail. I've had the electricity go off in the middle of a presentation more than once. Murphy's Law may prevail with every visual aid except the most important one—you.

SURVIVING AND THRIVING WITH OR WITHOUT POWERPOINT

Steven, the chief executive officer of a large furniture manufacturer, demonstrated this point at a conference of more than 2,000 customers and resellers. He and I had prepared and rehearsed for his 45-minute keynote address complete with twenty slides. When the emcee introduced him, he walked on stage to enthusiastic applause. He opened with a warm word of thanks and then clicked to his first slide. Nothing happened. He clicked again. Nothing. Without missing a beat, he smiled, stepped forward, looked into the eyes of his listeners, and said, "In lieu of showing you a bunch of slides with text and data, I'd just like to have a conversation with you this morning about how this company is going to help increase your sales this year. Would that be all right?" The audience instantaneously applauded.

Despite the frozen computer back stage, Steven was prepared and familiar enough with his outline that he was able to cover almost every point, as though it were a friendly discussion over dinner. First, he shared his perspective on the macroeconomic and industry conditions plus showed understanding and empathy for the audience's main business challenges. Next, with a clear transition, he moved effortlessly into his second section. He discussed his plan to drive customer value through innovation and described the company's new products, marketing campaigns, and educational programs. Third, he spoke about partnership and accountability; he laid out a mutual to-do list for both his company and the customers. And he closed with a personal story about his first job, working in his father's furniture store in a small town in North Carolina during the Great Depression. It was there that he learned the importance of enduring hard times, producing quality products, and taking care of the customer. After a long pause, he said, "Every good conversation is two-way. I've been talking about twenty minutes—now I'm going to be quiet and start listening. I'd love to hear your thoughts, and will be happy to answer any questions you may have." Steven filled the next twenty-five minutes with a lively interactive Q&A session.

Twelve other speakers presented on the same stage that week including industry experts, company executives, and best-selling authors. They did not experience any technical glitches and had the advantage of copious slides to help tell their story. Yet, in the end, the audience evaluation forms clearly ranked Steven's "conversation" the highest.

Why? It could be because he's a celebrity in his industry and greatly admired. Maybe it's because he's the CEO and some people rate a title the highest out of respect. Or, to paraphrase Albert Einstein, it may have been because Steven didn't allow technology to exceed the importance of humanity. He first and foremost made an emotional connection. He communicated to his audience he was there to support their success and just wanted "to have a conversation" with them. With or without his slides, he was confident and in command. What's more, he communicated the idea that connection is more important than content.

USING POWERPOINT PRESENTATIONS EFFECTIVELY

Steven's story does not mean that we as presenters should not use slides. Despite the ample criticism that surrounds PowerPoint, I like the tool and recommend using it when the message calls for it. When used effectively, it can complement and enhance your presentation.

The key to remember is this: You are the message. Slides do not persuade, inspire, or connect with an audience—only people do. Therefore use slides to support you, not replace you, upstage you, or distract from you. By all means, please don't use them as your note cards or crutch. Do use them to reinforce your most significant points and graphically illustrate abstract ideas. Use them to grab attention, inject humor, create interest, and stimulate thought. Use them to show important relationships or comparisons through simple charts and graphs. Slides help your listeners visualize, understand, and remember your key points, so do use them when appropriate. Just remember that as with building a house, a car, or a garden, there are guidelines and best practices to ensure a quality design and delivery.

POWERPOINT BEST PRACTICES

I remember the day when Microsoft PowerPoint was officially launched: May 22, 1990. I was sitting in a conference hall at a high-tech trade show, watching presenter after presenter display hundreds of foils, also known as transparencies, using an overhead projector. Oh my, how things have changed. Today, it's rare to see a presentation delivered without the use of slides. In the last two decades, I've observed and evaluated thousands of PowerPoint presentations and also gleaned many helpful shortcuts and techniques from my clients. Here's a condensed checklist of my PowerPoint Best Practices in the areas of design, rehearsal, and delivery of slides. I recommend keeping this list on hand and referring to it as you prepare and practice your slide presentation.

Design

First, let's look at the top best practices for effective slide design to help ensure we visually present our message with impact.

- ► Ensure legibility. Be sure every word and number on every slide is readable from the back of the room. This usually requires using a 28–30 point font. Stick with a simple, sans serif font.

- ► Apply the 6x6 Rule—limit text to six lines of copy per slide/no more than six words per line (thirty-six words total).

- ► Use clear, concise phrases, not full sentences. Sentences use too much real estate, break the 6x6 rule, and clutter the message.

- ► Use compelling, relevant photos instead of text as often as possible.

- ► Contrast the background color with text color; for example, a white background with navy or black text. This ensures that the text is clear and readable.

- ► Minimize animation of text. That is, avoid applying effects such as Blinds, Box, Checkerboard, Diamond, and so on. Simply opt for the text to appear with no special effects. Also omit unnecessary sound effects.

- ► Limit each slide to one point.

- ► Use a simple sans serif font. For example, Arial is easier to read than French Script.

- ► Use initial caps and lowercase. Avoid all caps.

- ► Apply what is commonly known as the 10–20–30 Rule when possible. Use no more than 10 slides, speak no more than 20 minutes, and use a 30-point font. This guideline especially holds true when you are presenting to results-driven decision makers who are usually short on time, have limited attention spans, and want the crux of the message right away.

- ➤ Ensure proper spelling and grammar.

- ➤ Use parallel structure: Ensure that all bullet points start with the same type of word—usually an action verb: *Improve* efficiencies; *Enhance* customer service; *Boost* the bottom line.

- ➤ Limit numbers to three per visual with a maximum of five digits per number. For example, if you're showing a spreadsheet or a graph on the slide that may include many numbers, highlight and enlarge the three numbers that are most important and talk about those.

- ➤ Be consistent. Use the same font and color palette throughout the presentation. Unify your visuals by using the same color for your slide title and the bullets.

- ➤ Design a title slide. Include a compelling benefit-oriented title for the presentation, your name and title, your company's logo, your customer or prospect's logo if permitted (be sure to check), and the date. Ideally incorporate a relevant photo(s) on the title slide.

- ➤ When presenting a list, reveal the lines one at a time. If you show the entire list at once, the audience will most likely read ahead. This means they're on the last point, while you're still speaking about the first one.

- ➤ Connect each slide title to its corresponding parent point on the agenda. For example, if your three key points are People, Products, and Process, make sure that each slide in the People group has the word "People" in the title; the subtitle serves as the specific descriptor of that slide. For example:

Slide 1 Title: People Are Our Greatest Asset   Subtitle: We're 26,000 Strong and Growing

Slide 2 Title: Our People Are Industry Experts   Subtitle: Ways You Benefit from Their Experience

- ➤ Create an agenda slide showing three to five key points. This clearly announces the key points you intend to cover and provides a road map.

- ➤ Repurpose the agenda slide between key points. Use the agenda as a transition slide to provide clear, smooth shifts from one topic to the next. For example, when you're transitioning from your first key point to the second, show the agenda slide again and pause. Say, "Are there any questions or comments about point number one, 'People,' before we move on to our second point, 'Products'?"

➤ Practice data chunking: Check to ensure that all information related to one topic is together. For example, all the people-related slides go under the "People" section, product-related slides go under the "Products" section, and so on.

➤ Customize slides for every audience. Avoid giving a "canned" presentation. Design some of your slides to show the audience you've done your homework. For example, create slides that display relevant specifications of their facility; specific metrics, numbers, and stats that apply to them; photos of their people or facility; quotes from their leaders or staff members.

➤ In closing your presentation, be sure to provide a summary slide that includes the key messages and takeaways you want the audience to remember. Also include a slide that clearly outlines action items and next steps.

➤ Number your slides. When audience members have questions about a particular point during your presentation, and don't want to interrupt your flow, they're able to note the slide number and ask you later to return to it.

➤ Follow the two-minute-average guideline. I've videotaped and timed hundreds of presentations across many industries, delivered by presenters who all speak at different paces. In most cases, the average time a presenter spends discussing a slide is two minutes. Of course, some slides may require more or less time, depending on the topic and level of audience interest. I've seen presenters spend anywhere from thirty seconds to ten minutes or more on a single slide. But when all is said and done, the average is around two minutes.

This best practice is especially helpful when planning the number of slides, given your time allotment. Base the number of slides you use on the allotted time available. For example, using the two-minute-average guideline, let's say you've been given one hour to present. You want half the time to be used for Q&A and discussion, so that leaves thirty minutes for your presentation. Thirty minutes divided by two minutes per slide equals fifteen slides. If you limit the number of slides to fifteen, you will likely cover all your points in a deliberate, unrushed fashion with plenty of time left for audience Q&A.

Rehearsal

Second, after you design effective slides, it's important to rehearse with them to make sure you have a smooth, confident delivery. Following are a few practice tips for presenting with slides.

Time your presentation

Talk through your presentation aloud to see how much time you use for each slide. For rehearsal, set the automatic slide transition to the amount of time you want to spend discussing each slide. Decide if you want to remove the automatic slide transition feature before giving the presentation.

Rehearse using the three-tiered pyramid approach

Must say; need to say; want to say. Imagine that the notes section of every slide is shaped like a pyramid. The pinnacle of the pyramid represents the main idea of the slide—the key takeaway. This critical content is what you "must say" about the slide. Be able to state this point in ten to fifteen seconds—clearly and concisely. The middle of the pyramid represents the next layer of detail, which expounds a bit further on the pinnacle point. This is what you "need to say" to the audience to provide key evidence and support. Be able to articulate this second tier of important content in sixty seconds or less.

Last, at the bottom of the pyramid, lies the widest section. This represents what you "want to say" if time permits. It's the nice-to-know information that typically holds too much detail for the decision maker. This section can take anywhere from two minutes to two hours. Sadly, many presenters begin talking about the slide at this broad level, feeling the need to build their case step by step, finally culminating at the pinnacle point. This critical mistake often loses decision makers, causes them to disengage (or interrupt), and risks burying the key message of the slide in too much detail.

Use this three-tiered pyramid approach when you rehearse. Click through all the slides, spending about ten to fifteen seconds on each, articulating the "must say" messages. If time permits, click through them again. This time, when you finish the "must say" part, add the "need to say" content. If you go into a presentation being able to clearly articulate the "must say" and "need to say" on every slide, your message will likely be perceived by the decision-making audience as clear, concise, and confident.

Practice with the equipment

I encourage you to invest in a presentation remote with the blackout feature. Blacking out the screen at the appropriate times and getting familiar with the device requires some practice. If you're navigating a mouse, using the keyboard, facilitating a demo, or using an Internet connection, be sure to practice ahead of time to ensure a smooth choreography with all the moving parts.

Make inherited slides your own

Sometimes you may "inherit" a set of slides (for which you feel no ownership) and be instructed to go give the presentation. Marketing departments develop presentations and distribute them for delivery; the boss may send slides to you and say, "You're giving this presentation Monday morning at 9." Whatever the reason, you're stuck with slides you don't necessarily know, like, or even understand. And there's usually a script (written by someone else) thrown in for you to learn.

When this happens, a number of problems can ensue: you, the presenter, may feel detached from the message and insecure about delivering these foreign slides; you may diligently try to cover every single point listed on the slide out of obligation or respect for the author; you may even read the slides (due to unfamiliarity) and talk to the screen instead of focusing on the audience. If you get bogged down in the content, your audience will likely feel anxious and bored. Instead, take a deep breath, think about the audience, and tell the story in your own words. Certainly prepare by reading the script, studying the bullet points, and practicing the flow. But ultimately, if you want to have impact, you must make the message your own. Don't feel you have to cover every point on the slide. In fact, it's often better if you don't. Audiences can read. It's often even more effective (and concise) when you say, "As you can see, there are six important points here, but the most critical is number three—reducing your total cost of ownership. In respect of time, let's focus on this one." Then talk one or two minutes on point three and move on.

The key is to take every pre-scripted "canned" slide and figure out how to make it your own. What point is the slide trying to make? Identify the key message and say it in your own words. Blend in your content—add a story, use a quote, inject humor, share a customer example, ask the audience a question. Remember, the first goal is to connect with your audience.

Presenting

After you've designed the slides and completed a few rehearsals using them, it's time to raise the curtain and deliver them to the intended audience. Here are some of my favorite tricks and techniques for presenting slides effectively.

Toggle the screen to black periodically

Sometimes it's effective to make the image on the screen disappear so that the audience is focused solely on you, the presenter. It also avoids casting a shadow on the screen by stepping into the projector's light beam. For example, let's say you want to kick off the presentation with a strong two-minute opening, standing in the center of the room, where all eyes are on you, not the screen (and certainly not your shadow on the screen). Then, later in the presentation, you want to tell a story, have a conversation, elaborate on a point, or move into the audience where no slide is visible. Or, to ensure you connect equally with listeners on both sides of the room, maybe you want to casually cross over from one side to the other without casting a shadow on the screen. All of this is possible by simply blanking (or blacking out) the screen.

There are two ways to create a blank screen. First, as mentioned in the previous section, you can use a presentation remote that has the blackout feature. This allows you to control the slides from anywhere in the room. Second, you can press the "B" key on the computer keyboard (for "blackout" or "blank"). To restore the image on the screen, press any button on the presentation remote or any button on the keyboard.

Seamlessly navigate to any slide

Let's say you're in the middle of your presentation, speaking to slide number 10, but the decision maker in the audience is thinking ahead. He asks a burning question that you hadn't planned to answer until slide 20. Many presenters would frantically click forward ten slides, or they would escape out of the presentation, go to slide sorter, search, then double-click on the desired slide to re-enter slide mode. But PowerPoint provides a more professional, smoother approach by way of a feature that allows you to move quickly and seamlessly to any slide in your presentation. Once you know how to use it, you can simply type the slide number on the keyboard, click "Enter," and the desired slide will appear.

To properly use this great feature, you need a printout that shows you all the slide numbers. Here's how to do it: After your presentation is finalized, click "Print." Next, under "Print what," select "Handouts." Opt for nine slides per page with a horizontal orientation. Next, click "Frame slides." If you've hidden any slides in your deck, be sure to check "Print hidden slides." Then click "OK" to print. On the printout, underneath each slide, manually number the slides horizontally left to right.

With this preparation done, you would listen to the decision maker's question and say, "Yes, I'll be glad to address that concern. Let me navigate to that slide in my presentation." Glance at the printout, see that the slide you need is number 20, enter "20" on the keyboard, and press "Enter." Voila! It's a presentation on demand. When you are finished discussing slide 20, return to slide 10 by right-clicking on the screen and selecting "Last Viewed." You're right back where you started. To jump to any slide, just enter the slide number on the keyboard and press the "Enter" key. This technique is useful for moving to a prepared summary or Q&A slide, or for skipping parts of your presentation if you run short on time.

Given your audience of senior leaders and decision makers, you may be required to jump around within your slide deck to accommodate their requests. Therefore, be sure to frontload your presentation with the top ten "must say" slides. After these ten, insert a blank slide labeled "Extra Slides." You can have as many slides as you want in this section, as long as you prioritize and place the ten most important at the beginning. These extra slides come in handy during Q&A sessions. And now that you have a printout with all of your slides manually numbered, you can easily and seamlessly jump to any slide in the deck.

Draw on your slides

Sometimes it can be valuable to add a drawing to your slides to illustrate a particular point or item as you're presenting. It also creates audience interest and shows spontaneity. Perhaps you want to highlight a word, add a number, circle an item for emphasis, or draw an object. This can be done in the following way. In slide mode, press the Ctrl+P key combination, which transforms your cursor into a small black dot on the screen. Then, using the right mouse button, click "Pointer Options" to select a pen style (highlighter, felt tip, or ballpoint) and the ink color. Using the left mouse button, draw on the slide as you wish. To erase your drawings and doodles, press the E key.

Face the audience—don't read your slides

It's fine to glance at the screen occasionally. Just make sure your shoulders remain open and squared to the audience (not in profile facing the screen) and that you maintain good eye contact with your listeners.

Refer to your laptop more than the screen

If possible, position the presentation computer directly in front of you so that you can glance at the laptop display more than the large screen behind you. It serves as a cue card, keeps you facing forward, and prevents the need to turn back and look at the screen too frequently.

Use a laser pointer

I've seen many presenters step in front of the projector light beam and use their arm to point or gesture to the screen. This casts a distracting shadow and looks unprofessional. Avoid using your arm to point to the screen—use a laser pointer instead to highlight the item on the screen.

Stand up when presenting slides

In most cases, I recommend that you stand when you deliver a presentation. There's often a temptation to remain comfortably seated at the table and deliver your presentation from this position. However, if slides are being projected onto the screen, the presenter ideally stands beside them. This keeps you in close proximity to your visual aids and makes it easier for the audience to look both at you and the screen. Standing also connotes confidence and credibility, and ensures that you won't be upstaged by a huge screen that's larger than you appear to be if you're seated. If you are going to present slides to one or two people and wish to remain seated due to the casual nature of the meeting, consider using your laptop or bringing a table monitor.

Stand to the audience's left

Presenters have a tendency to migrate and stay on one side of the screen or the other. If you can choose which side to stand on to present your slides, stand to your right of the screen (your audience's left). Because most people in the Western world read from left to right, the audience members' eyes rest on you to the left, then read the slide on the right, then return to you on the left. Subliminally, this pattern is more comfortable than right to left.

Distribute handouts after the presentation

I've seen it a hundred times—a presenter distributes the handouts before the presentation and the decision makers in the room immediately turn to the back page to read the summary and key takeaways. To help ensure your audience is in sync with you, distribute handouts afterward. Announce to the audience that you will distribute copies of the slides following the presentation.

Create two slide presentations: the "show" version and the "handout" version

The show version is the deck you use to present—the one the audience sees. These slides are clean and uncluttered, with minimal text. They display all the effective design principles discussed in this chapter. As the presenter, you provide the detail and subpoints—the slide does not. Conversely, the handout version can be much more detailed (and can break the rules) because it is a take-home reference tool intended for reading and study.

CHAPTER 6: EXECUTIVE SUMMARY

- ➤ You are the message.
- ➤ Slides support your message; they do not replace you.
- ➤ When used effectively, slides enhance your presentation.
- ➤ When preparing and rehearsing, keep the PowerPoint best practices handy and refer to them frequently:
    - ➤ Face the audience, not the screen.
    - ➤ Ensure readability by using a 28–30 point font.
    - ➤ Follow the 6x6 Rule.
    - ➤ Use compelling relevant photos.
    - ➤ Manage time and number of slides with the two-minute average.
    - ➤ Rehearse with slides using the pyramid approach.
    - ➤ During your presentation, black out the screen periodically.
    - ➤ Seamlessly navigate to any slide by using a printout of numbered slides.

Mastering a Confident, Dynamic Delivery Style

CHAPTER 7

Preparing for a Powerful Performance

> Start by doing what's necessary, then do what's possible; and suddenly you are doing the impossible.
>
> —ST. FRANCIS OF ASSISI

If we were attending the Nervous Nellies Convention, we would see an assortment of interesting mannerisms: Hands in the pocket jingling coins and keys, eyes staring at the floor, arms locked behind the back. There would be some hand wringers, pen clickers, and pacers; possibly a few ring twisters, scowlers, and fast talkers as well. All of these behaviors are unconscious expressions of uncontrolled nervousness that presenters often exhibit.

Tom was an outgoing senior-level executive and sales leader. Before I began coaching him, Tom attended a national sales meeting at a consumer electronics convention. While standing in front of the entire sales staff, he forgot what he was supposed to say. He just froze. Luckily, one of the other presenters jumped in and took over. After working with Tom for a while, I realized his anxiety about public speaking was so deep that I advised him to seek psychological counseling. The following year, after some sessions with a therapist and some coaching from me, Tom gave one of the highest-valuated presentations at the conference.

I found myself in a similar situation when I was in tenth grade. I was assigned by Ms. Weaver to deliver an oral book report on *Great Expectations* by Charles Dickens. It was my first time to present in front of an audience and I was very nervous. I had a thick Southern accent and I had trouble pronouncing the "S" and "R" sounds. I thought everyone was going to laugh at me as soon as I opened my mouth.

When my turn came, I walked slowly to the front of the class, like a prisoner walking to the gallows. I organized my three-by-five cards, looked down, and studied them for a moment. I felt my hands shaking, heart racing, knees knocking, and palms sweating. Then I looked up at the audience of students. As soon as I made eye contact with them, everything changed—all the nervous mannerisms went away. I didn't have to worry about my presentation skills or whether they would laugh at me. Instead, I fainted.

When I awoke in the guidance counselor's office, Ms. Weaver was standing over me. She looked me in the eye and said, "You *can* do this, and you *will* do this—*next* Tuesday morning at eleven." Ms. Weaver made me work with her after school every day for a week to rehearse my speech. All of that practice really helped when Tuesday came around. This time, I didn't faint, and although it was not an Academy Award–winning performance, I wasn't terrible, no one laughed, and I remained vertical.

Ms. Weaver convinced me to join the Drama Club, the Debate Team, and eventually the Student Council. I remember a humorous adage she shared with me as we were practicing after school. She said, "You can't get rid of the butterflies, but you can teach them to fly in formation."

CONTROLLING NERVOUSNESS AND ANXIETY: FROM STAGE FRIGHT TO STAGE MIGHT

Truth be told, you don't want to get rid of the butterflies because they're carriers of energy and enthusiasm. Adrenaline is your friend. Years ago, one of the best speech coaches I ever trained with said to me, "Welcome the nerves, Darlene. They're a sign that you care and want to do a good job," to which I replied, "Boy, I sure care a lot!" The key is to control, harness, and focus that surge of adrenaline so that it works for you.

If you find yourself fighting nervousness when you present, and are afraid you'll end up frozen stiff like Tom (or passed out like me) at the front of the room, try the following tips to help you train those butterflies. I've created an acronym called STAGE MIGHT featuring my top ten favorite techniques for managing anxiety.

Smile at yourself in the mirror before you speak, when you're introduced, and during your speech as appropriate. The physiological effect of smiling emits brain chemicals that calm the nerves and promote relaxation.

Always remember that a smile is the shortest distance between two people. It shows your audience that you're happy to see them and enthusiastic about the message.

Talk positively to yourself and visualize your success. Even though you might not feel 100 percent confident at first, tell yourself you can do it! Experts in sports psychology have proven that an athlete's self-talk and visualizations create self-fulfilling prophecies—good or bad. Thoughts create action, and actions create outcomes. Therefore, why not make your thoughts positive and reap the rewards? See in your mind your confident stride, warm smile, and adoring audience. Say to yourself, "I am a dynamic speaker." "I am enthusiastic and engaging." "I am liked by my audience." "I am prepared and confident." "I am on fire!" It really works.

Acknowledge the three audience truths: (1) They believe you're the expert. The audience perceives you as the recognized authority simply because you're the one speaking. Plus, you know more than they do about the topic. (2) They want you to succeed. The audience really wants you to be good and add value—otherwise it's a waste of their time. (3) They don't know what you're going to say. In the unlikely event you forget something or reorder your points, don't announce the error or apologize. They won't know.

Greet the audience before you speak. Shake hands with and meet as many people as possible ahead of time. This shows the audience you're approachable and personable. It relaxes you and turns "public" speaking into "personal" speaking, which makes the presentation feel like a continued conversation.

Exercise lightly backstage or privately before you speak. This will rid your body of excess adrenaline. It's critical to prepare the body for the physical activity of public speaking. Do some light stretching, a few knee-bends, or take a brisk walk around the building. Take a few deep breaths: inhale through the nose on a slow count of three, and then exhale through the mouth on a slow count of three.

Memorize the first and last minutes of your presentation. Knowing the first words that will come out of your mouth gives you confidence and calms your nerves. It also enables you to look directly into the eyes of your audience and optimize the first impression when you begin. Likewise, if you nail the closing, they'll remember you as confident and self-assured. Know your material.

Interact with your audience in the opening. Within the first five minutes, involve the audience. Ask a thought-provoking question; conduct a survey by show of hands; ask audience members to introduce themselves, if appropriate; generate responses and make a list; do a learning activity; hold up a prop or give them a learning aid; tell a funny or compelling story. By immediately engaging your listeners, you focus the attention and interest where it belongs—on the audience, and off of you, which relieves some pressure. You're also doing something very natural and comfortable—interacting with human beings, rather than engaging in the dreaded "public speaking."

Give, give, give. Focus on giving to the audience. Often I'll ask people in my presentation workshops if they get overwhelmingly nervous when giving a birthday gift to a loved one. The answer is almost always no. Instead they feel anticipation, excitement, and joy. They look forward to giving the gift, and they eagerly await its unwrapping. As a speaker, think about your presentation as a gift to the audience—one they will actually enjoy, that is full of valuable information, helpful ideas, and meaningful content. The mental attitude of giving empowers you and frees you to focus on the purpose of the presentation—to inform and enrich the audience.

Hold a dress rehearsal. Comfort breeds confidence. The more you do it, the better you get. There's no better way to ensure a winning presentation or speech than to walk through it, say it aloud, practice your body movement, go through the slides, warm up your voice, and familiarize yourself with the content and flow. Ideally, you should videotape or audiotape the rehearsal and review your performance. Also, time the rehearsal to ensure you stay on schedule.

Trust yourself. There was a time when I was paralyzed by the fear that I would not have all the information I needed when making a presentation. One of my cherished coaches said to me, "Darlene, when you're making vegetable soup and you chop up ten carrots and place the pieces in the pot to simmer, do you worry the carrots will be missing when you return an hour later to serve it?" I answered, "Of course not." He said, "If you just relax and trust yourself, your content will be like the carrots. If you've prepared it, it'll be there for you when you lift the lid to serve—just believe in yourself." Trust yourself to be outstanding and you'll likely live up to your expectations.

Those are my tried and true tactics for turning stage fright into STAGE MIGHT. Putting them into practice will help tame your butterflies and teach them to fly in formation.

REHEARSAL TECHNIQUES TO OPTIMIZE DELIVERY

Most of the time, what presenters give the audience is their rehearsal presentation. Think about it this way: If you have not practiced the entire presentation beforehand, you are giving a dress rehearsal—and it shows.

If you went to New York City and bought a ticket to a Broadway play, that ticket might cost you $200 or more. How would you feel if the curtain opened and the actors were in street clothes, holding their scripts, and the director was constantly feeding lines ("Pick it up from 'To be or not to be.'")? On Broadway, the actors rehearse for weeks before the show opens. Because of this, the show we see is usually spectacular.

One sales manager I know makes all of his sales representatives give him a dynamic presentation before he lets them out into the field to sell copiers. This leader must personally approve each and every sales representative in the country. If the presenter does not meet his criteria, he cancels the demo with the customer. His motto is, "No impression is better than a bad impression." Like the director of a play, he makes sure they are rehearsed and ready for a Broadway-quality performance with their first presentation. It's no wonder his division sells more copiers and closes more deals than any other team in the company, worldwide.

Here are several techniques you can employ to make sure your presentations are not dress rehearsals, but award-winning performances:

- ➤ Visualize your success. The body helps manifest what the mind's eye sees.
- ➤ Keep a microcassette tape recorder handy. Record the main parts of your presentation and listen to them repeatedly while driving, walking, etc., to familiarize yourself with the content.
- ➤ Stand up and deliver your presentation aloud. Imagine the audience is sitting in front of you.
- ➤ Deliver it to a dress-rehearsal audience in the actual setting if possible.
- ➤ Videotape at least one rehearsal, followed by playback and evaluation.
- ➤ Time the presentation.
- ➤ Rehearse often enough to be comfortable, but avoid over-rehearsing.
- ➤ Memorize the first minute and last minute of your presentation. This allows you to master the opening and close plus maintain confident eye contact with your audience to create a positive first and last impression.

> ➤ Repeatedly recite the top three to five benefit statements and the main ideas of your presentation. Practice telling them to a friend in the form of a story or conversation. These important statements should be delivered smoothly and confidently, eye-to-eye with your audience.

> ➤ Create a color-coded outline and/or storyboard. For example, blue for lecture, yellow for audience interaction, pink for a personal story. Draw pictures to link main ideas. Form acronyms to help remember key points. These visual cues aid memory and the flow of thought.

> ➤ Anticipate tough questions that the audience may ask. Prepare and rehearse your answers aloud.

> ➤ On the day of the event, arrive early and do a technical run-through to ensure smooth, proper use of visuals, equipment, microphones, connections, and lighting.

TOP TEN WAYS TO CREATE A GREAT FIRST IMPRESSION

As the old saying goes, "You never get a second chance to make a good first impression." With that in mind, here are my top ten tips for making a great first impression every time you present.

1. *Dress for success.* Decision makers perceive your work clothes as a symbol of your competence. Therefore, look professional and capable. As the eighteenth-century novelist and clergyman Laurence Sterne once said, "A man cannot dress, but his ideas get clothed at the same time."

2. *Be well groomed.* Know that people will look at your face and neck first. Look neat from head to toe with a current hair cut and style, high-quality (but simple) jewelry, smooth hands, manicured nails, and polished shoes.

3. *Walk with purpose.* Hold your shoulders back, keep your chin up, and have a mission in mind. Let your entrance announce that you're a person with a purpose. Confident people have a rhythm to their movements and energy in their stride.

4. *Smile.* A genuine smile starts in the heart, shows on the lips, and finds its way to the eyes.

5. *Use good direct eye contact.* It conveys believability, sincerity, and confidence.

6. *Shake hands.* A good, confident handshake consists of a full and firm handclasp. Shake up and down once or twice, while smiling and maintaining eye contact. And remember: when shaking hands, treat men and women with equal respect. Gender makes no difference, and either may initiate the handshake.

7. *Show sincere interest* in the person you are greeting. Initiate conversation. Upon meeting, immediately ask a thoughtful question or bring up a subject of importance to that person.

8. *Remember names.* People's names are the most important words they hear. Using a personal name instantly captures attention and shows you care enough about the person to remember. When you first learn someone's name, use it immediately in conversation, and repeat it silently to yourself while the person is talking. Use visual association by connecting each name or face to something familiar.

9. *Use an enthusiastic tone of voice.* Speak with energy and volume, allowing your voice to convey sincerity, cheerfulness, and confidence.

10. *Give sincere compliments* or offer congratulations if appropriate.

CHAPTER 7: EXECUTIVE SUMMARY

➤ Control your nervousness and anxiety by practicing STAGE MIGHT:
  ➤ Smile.
  ➤ Talk positively to yourself.
  ➤ Acknowledge the three audience truths.
  ➤ Greet and meet the audience before you speak.
  ➤ Exercise lightly beforehand.
  ➤ Memorize the first and last minute of your presentation.
  ➤ Interact with your audience immediately.
  ➤ Give yourself to the audience.
  ➤ Hold a dress rehearsal.
  ➤ Trust yourself.

➤ Rehearse your presentation aloud ahead of time, time it, and visualize your success.

➤ Practice the top ten techniques for creating a great first impression, including a confident handshake, professional presence, and remembering names.

CHAPTER 8

Using Effective Body Language to Show Confidence

> **What you do speaks so loudly that I cannot hear what you say.**
>
> —RALPH WALDO EMERSON

When you present, you send two kinds of messages to your listeners: verbal and nonverbal. While you may be communicating verbally through the words you speak, a more memorable message is conveyed nonverbally by your body language and voice tone. Almost always, you will influence your audience more by how you say something (body language and voice tone) than by what you say (words alone). In this chapter we are going to explore how to use your entire body as a powerful instrument of speech and to make your body speak as eloquently as your words. We'll address issues related to effective voice tone in Chapter 10, and persuasive language in Chapter 11.

In the realm of body language, you are equipped with at least five powerful tools to communicate your message:

1. Eye communication
2. Facial expressions
3. Gestures
4. Posture
5. Body movement

You cannot avoid sending nonverbal messages to an audience, but you can train yourself to send the right ones. Let's begin by exploring the importance of good eye contact.

EFFECTIVE EYE COMMUNICATION

Ralph Waldo Emerson put it succinctly when he said, "When the eyes say one thing, and the tongue another, a practiced man relies on the language of the first." Knowing your material and having control over your verbal message is essential for establishing effective eye contact with your listeners. Strive to know your presentation so well that you do not have to devote undue mental energy toward remembering your next point.

Eye contact is the most important nonverbal tool you have; it is the cement that bonds a speaker with her audience. As the Yiddish proverb asserts, "Eyes are the mirror of the soul." When you speak, it is the caliber of your eye contact—more appropriately termed *eye communication*—that tells listeners how you feel about them, your message, and yourself. Listeners look to your eyes first to see if you're sincere, enthusiastic, and confident. Eyes, more than any other nonverbal cue, can make your presentation seem personable, authentic, friendly, conversational, and connected. Conversely, there is no surer way to break that bond than by failing to look into the eyes of your audience members. A lack of eye contact implies a list of offenses: disinterest, detachment, insecurity, insincerity, shiftiness, or arrogance.

Regardless of the size of an audience, each listener wants to feel important. Each listener wants to feel that you are communicating directly with him or her. Eye communication is a symbol of sincerity. It tells your listeners, one by one, that you are interested in them, and that you care whether or not they accept your message.

While presenting, your eyes can also function as a control device. Simply by looking into the eyes of your listeners, you have an influence on their attentiveness and concentration. On the other hand, if you do not look at them, they will tend not to look at you, and the impact of your message will suffer. Make a diligent effort to look at each and every individual in a way that they will notice. Whether your audience is seated in front of, behind, or beside you, create rapport by enveloping everyone with your eyes. It is the best way of knowing whether or not you are connecting with them.

Eye contact can also guide your audience's responses. If you want to say something that's funny, put a smile in your eyes during the delivery to let your listeners know it is okay for them to laugh or smile. If you want to emphasize a serious or profound point, have a serious look in your eyes. Your audience will take their cue from your eyes and face.

Another benefit generated by your effective eye contact is your own personal comfort. Eye contact to and from your audience is a tremendous source of strength and encouragement; it helps dissipate any nervousness or tension you may feel. When you see how interested your listeners are in what you have to say, you get an encouraging boost of confidence and enthusiasm.

A CEO once told me, "I don't care what kind of fancy materials they send, I'm not making a decision until I can see the whites of their eyes—that'll tell me what I need to know."

Certainly, feel free to use notes during your presentation. It's fine to glance down at them occasionally, but do not allow notes, slides, or visual aids to stand between you and your audience. You are the best visual aid, and your audience is there to see and hear *you*. Remember to keep your eyes on your listeners. A skillful presenter's attention is always on the audience.

It's important to establish a personal visual bond with each listener. You have probably heard the phrase "ties that bind." In the realm of effective presenting, it is the *eyes* that bind. When you present, you are communicating with a group of individual people—human beings who think, feel, see, listen, and respond similar to the way you do. Making effective eye contact means more than just passing your gaze across the room; it means focusing on individual listeners and creating person-to-person relationships with them.

Sometimes it is tempting to think of an audience as a single unit, a common collective mass of people: the "public" in "public speaking." Avoid this viewpoint at all costs! In fact, coin a new term for yourself: "personal speaking." Indeed, you may be speaking to a group of fifty people, but that's not the way they see it. In *their* minds, you are actually speaking to each one individually. There just happen to be forty-nine others in the room.

Creating an visual bond with as many people as possible in the audience is the key to being perceived as sincere. You cannot appear sincere and distant at the same time. Make the experience more meaningful to your audience by connecting with them one at time, eye-to-eye.

So, how do you do this? Begin by selecting one person, perhaps a friendly audience member you met prior to the presentation. Look directly into that person's eyes and just talk to him as you would in any other conversation. Hold his gaze long enough to establish a visual link—about two to three seconds, or the length of time it takes you to complete a thought. Then, move your eyes to another person and do the same thing. Soon, you will see everyone in the room and they will feel connected to you.

Evaluate Your Audience's Body Language

Effective eye communication affords you the opportunity to watch your listeners. By keeping your eyes on them, you can monitor and respond to their nonverbal messages.

For example, do your listeners look confused or puzzled? If so, you may want to stop and ask, "Are there any questions at this point before we move on?" Or, you can simply respond to their perplexed look by offering a bit more information. Then, when you see clarity and understanding register on their faces, continue to the next point.

If your audience members aren't looking at you, chances are they aren't listening either. Perhaps they cannot hear you. If you are using a microphone, speak louder and see if that gets a positive reaction. Better yet, ask them, "Can everyone hear me clearly?"

If they are bored, their bodies will tell you—chins resting in palms, eyes gazing off into the distance, fingers tapping on the table, hands doodling with a pen, eyelids getting heavy, and loss of eye contact with you. When interpreting nonverbal language, be sure to look for a *combination* of cues. A single mannerism does not necessarily indicate a specific emotion or attitude. For example, doodlers may be kinesthetic learners—people who grasp and retain information more effectively when a physical part of them is in motion. On the other hand, if audience members are doodling, nodding off, *and* tapping their pens, it's probably time to vary the pace.

Realize Eye Contact Is a Two-Way Communication Process

Your listeners watch your eyes for confidence and conviction; you, the presenter, watch theirs to confirm your connection with them. For this reason, make sure there is enough light in the room, both on you and your listeners, to see one another. They must see your face, and equally important, you must see theirs.

If at all possible, avoid wearing eyeglasses during your presentation, especially those with dark or heavy rims. Although eyeglasses are a necessity for many of us, they typically prevent your audience members from clearly seeing your eyes—your most expressive tool. Glasses usually cast a shadow on your cheeks and eyes; they may also reflect glare, which is distracting. If possible, wear contact lenses instead. If you must wear your glasses, at least remove them from time to time for emphasis, or invest in a pair of rimless glasses.

Avoid These Eye Contact Patterns

Most speakers know they need to establish eye contact. Some try to create a set pattern for making it happen. The trouble is, it becomes distracting, or worse, discrediting. Here are several commonly rehearsed patterns of eye contact and head movement you should avoid:

► *Tricks.* Avoid ineffective tricks such as staring over the tops of audience members' heads, looking at their foreheads, or gazing at their cheeks instead of their eyes. You cannot fake sincerity. Besides, you have nothing to hide or be afraid of—and everything to gain—by looking at your listeners squarely and sincerely in the eyes.

► *Oscillating Fan.* This is where the speaker slowly scans his or her audience back and forth, left to right, from side to side. Although this scanning pattern does keep a speaker's face up and exposed to the audience (which is a good thing) no one person receives any direct eye contact or attention.

► *Ducking.* You may have seen this one. A speaker stands behind the lectern and looks down at his notes, then up at the audience, then down at his notes, then up at the audience in an almost timed, repeated fashion. Again, not very meaningful for either the speaker or the listener.

► *Eye Dart.* Have you ever seen presenters who glance quickly from person to person without actually pausing long enough to connect? Technically, you could call this "eye-dart eye contact," but it's not communication.

► *Looking Down.* Looking down while speaking to an audience suggests timidity and insecurity; it weakens you in the eyes of others. Oftentimes when our brains are intensely focused on a task or heavily processing information (such as what we're supposed to say next), the eyes tend to disengage from the distractions of the outer world and look down to aid concentration. When there's an audience in the room, this becomes a problem. This is why rehearsal and preparation are so important. By practicing and knowing your content, you have more awareness and energy available to focus your eyes on your audience.

Your eyes should not follow any set pattern. Allow your natural flow, rhythm, and spontaneity to carry your eyes from one listener to the next, pausing on each person long enough to make a meaningful connection.

I'm often asked the question, "When you're presenting, should you look at everyone in the room equally, or give some audience members more eye contact than others?" As a general rule, look at everyone equally and engage the entire audience with your eyes. If someone has been invited to the presentation, that means his or her opinion counts. Therefore, establish a visual bond with everyone. However, there are at least two instances where you want to look at a particular audience member longer than others. The first is when you're making a specific point that relates to a particular audience member. For example, if you know the financial officer's primary concern is cost, then focus a bit more on her when you're describing your solution's return on investment. If you're emphasizing the speed and ease of your solution's software implementation, look directly at the technical experts in the room to deliver that point. The second instance is in the closing. When you deliver your call to action, look directly at the individuals responsible for approving your proposal and committing to your recommended next steps.

Optimize Eye Communication with Large Audiences

Effective eye communication is relatively easy to establish with an audience the size of a typical business presentation—about ten to twenty people. That's because everyone is fairly close. But, in larger rooms with larger groups—such as a product user conference or trade show—it's almost impossible to look at each person in the eyes.

However, it will not seem that way to the audience if you do the following: Pick out two or three people in each section of the room and establish an eye bond with them; hold your gaze on them, or at least in their direction, for three to five seconds. This approach works very well in larger rooms with bigger groups because when you steady your attention and look at one person, dozens of people around her think you are looking and talking just to them.

EFFECTIVE FACIAL EXPRESSIONS

A man without a smiling face should not open a shop.

—CHINESE PROVERB

When you speak, your face serves as a billboard communicating to others your attitudes, feelings, and emotions. People recognize almost every emotion simply by observing a person's facial expressions; feelings as distinct as surprise, fear, happiness, confusion, excitement, anger, interest, disbelief, nervousness, confidence, confusion, pleasure, sadness, and apathy.

Smile

People are drawn to people who have a genuine smile. While frowns, scowls, and deadpan expressions all push people away, the smile draws them in, making a speaker attractive to his or her audience. A genuine smile conveys interpersonal warmth, empathy, and friendliness. It shows you're interested in the audience and topic; it expresses a glad-to-be-here attitude. Moreover, smiling is contagious. If you smile easily, your audience is likely to as well. Smiling also has a side benefit. It's a natural drug that sends endorphins and other positive chemicals through your body. It relaxes you and has a calming effect on the audience. Try this technique: When you begin your presentation, lock eyes with one person, smile, and say your first sentence to him or her, e.g., "Good morning and thank you for joining us for today's presentation." Then move to another person. Look him in the eye and smile. Then, complete another sentence while smiling.

Feature Your Aliveness

Allow your face to billboard your attitude and message. Be as animated and lively as your subject will allow; your listeners appreciate it. For example, raise your eyebrows and widen your eyes to emphasize a particular point or show wonder. If you are describing a past event, try closing your eyes and tilting your head back slightly, as though visually reaching for the information. Do you want to imply doubt or suspicion (perhaps when talking about the competition)? Just raise one eyebrow and smirk. If a picture is worth a thousand words, a picture painted on your face is worth ten thousand!

Be Aware Your Listeners Reflect Your Facial Expressions

The next time you are in a movie theater, notice the people sitting around you (after the lights go down). Once they are involved in the movie, watch their faces and you will notice they unconsciously mirror the expressions of the characters on the screen.

As a speaker, your audience reflects what you do. When you act natural, relaxed, and pleasant, most of your audience will too. Conversely, if you notice they look unusually pensive or tense, check *your* facial expressions. Maybe you are unconsciously frowning, furrowing your brow, or appearing too serious. When you show you are involved and glad to be presenting, your audience will show that they too are involved and glad to be listening. Your face sends a powerful message—make sure it is your *intended* message.

Avoid a Deadpan Expression

Some speakers believe they are perceived as more authoritative and in charge if they look serious and somber. Others try to hide their anxiety with a deadpan expression. Either case carries the risk of sending your listeners a negative message. A neutral expression is fine, but avoid appearing too pensive or lifeless.

Remember, you have the power to create the emotions you want your audience to feel, and your face helps you do it. "Just put on a happy face" and watch your listeners' expressions change! Remember, you are confident and in control; you're their leader for the duration of the presentation. And, when you indicate pleasure, interest, and close attention, your listeners will reciprocate.

NATURAL GESTURES: VISUAL PUNCTUATION

A gesture is any physical movement that helps express an idea, opinion, or emotion. Gestures are bodily indicators of your own personality. They are highly individual. Regardless of your natural style—conservative and reserved, or casual and animated—the goal is to have your motions match your message.

Gestures are the punctuation marks of body language. Imagine how jumbled and confusing our written language would be if all the words on a page ran together without the use of periods, commas, exclamation points, hyphens, parentheses, and colons. Instead, these useful marks of emphasis give meaning and interpretation to the words around them.

The same is true of gestures surrounding your spoken words. They support your message and help the audience interpret your meaning. They are marvelous tools of communication. When used effectively, gestures increase a listener's understanding, attentiveness, and retention. And since much of the impact of your message stems from your body language alone, confident gestures contribute significantly to your effectiveness as a presenter. In fact, no other kind of physical action can reinforce your message in as many different ways as gesturing.

Reinforce Your Verbal Message

Gestures strengthen the audience's understanding of what you are saying. For instance, gesturing with an open palm held upward and outward toward the audience subliminally suggests that you have nothing to hide; it implies you are open, giving, and approachable. Conversely, if you turn the hand over and gesture with the palm facing the floor, this will likely signal suppression, secrecy, or a condescending attitude. A hand held outward with the palm facing the audience suggests denial or resistance.

If you want to indicate a change in measurement of any kind—such as length, width, height, growth, or reduction—use your hands to show how big or small, long or short, high or low. You can use gestures to help your listeners visualize the quantity, size, shape, movement, location, or function of what you are talking about. For example, if you are introducing three benefits, use your fingers to count them off as you say them.

Gestures can also suggest a certain mood or emotion. A shrug of the shoulders indicates perplexity, resignation, or lack of knowledge. A clenched fist suggests determination. Placing your hand over your heart shows earnestness and conviction.

Stimulate Audience Participation

Gestures help initiate the response you want from your audience. If you want your listeners to raise their hands, raise yours first and say, "By a show of hands, how many of you are familiar with this product?" If you want them to applaud, begin the applause. Remember, your listeners mirror you. Whatever you want your audience to do, lead the way and do it first.

Alleviate Anxiety

When you allow your gestures to flow naturally and purposefully, that physical action helps relieve nervous energy that is inherent in any public speaking situation. Gestures serve as a positive, effective outlet for extra adrenaline; conversely, small, stiff motions and lack of movement keep the surplus energy fastened inside. Loosen up and let your body move naturally.

Follow These Guidelines for Using Purposeful Gestures

First, realize that gestures are subconscious. They flow from your core and reflect how you feel about your environment and what you are presenting. Your listeners intuitively know this. From their perspective, your gestures help reveal the level of your mental and emotional involvement in your message. That's one reason why audience members will trust what they *see* over what they *hear*. When they see that your gestures are natural, lively, purposeful, and spontaneous, it's evident that you enjoy what you are doing, and that makes you believable because your actions match your words. Remember, good presenting is from the inside out.

Second, gestures reflect your own personality. They're highly individual. For this reason, there are no "carved in stone" rules of gesturing. Simply consider the following guidelines for refining *your own* natural style.

Be Genuinely and Spontaneously Yourself

Allow your body instinctively to punctuate what you are saying. It is totally natural for a person to gesture—at least to some degree—when he is speaking. And it looks unnatural not to. Regardless of your personality or cultural background, you most likely have a natural impulse to emphasize your message with movement. It's critical that you trust yourself enough to respond positively to that instinct and allow your body to naturally support what you say.

Try not to inhibit your own nature by hiding behind a stoic mask. In fact, if you constrain your natural impulse to gesture, you will probably become tense and risk appearing rigid and stiff. On the other hand, avoid mimicking the gestures of another speaker. If you impose artificial gestures onto your natural style, your audience will probably sense that something seems unnatural and you may be perceived as nervous, mechanical, or insincere.

The best advice is to be your own genuine and spontaneous self; respond naturally to what you think, feel, and say. For instance, if you use your arms and hands freely when you converse informally, use them freely when you present to a group. If you are by nature a reserved, low-key person, don't feel as though you have to change your personality just to suit your presentation. Some people are naturally animated, while others are naturally reserved. Focus on your purpose, respond instinctively to your audience and message, and your body will do a beautiful job of supporting you.

Gesture Wide and Large

Effective hand gestures start from the shoulder—not the elbow. Avoid looking like your upper arms are permanently attached to your body. Involve the whole arm by freely extending it outward, creating space between your upper arm and body—think of it as putting air under your wings.

The style of gesture perceived as most confident is low (around the waist and hip area), smooth, and expansive. By using broad gestures that start and end in the central region of your body, you convey several positive messages to your audience: you reveal more of your body and therefore show you are secure and comfortable with it; you freely use the space around you, which indicates you belong; you appear calm and poised; and your audience members are better able to see these gestures simply because they are wider and larger.

For bolder gestures, you may want to raise your hands above your elbow or head. Gestures at the head level and above generally indicate a sense of vision or profound thought.

Use Open-Palmed Gestures

One of the most effective gestures for a presenter is an outstretched arm toward the audience with palm up and open, as though you are lending a hand. This will be perceived as friendly and giving. Whether your arms are in motion or in a resting position at your waist, make a conscious effort to keep the palms up and open. It will appear inviting and imply that you have nothing to hide. Also, strive to keep your fingers and wrists supple and natural—never clenched or stiff.

And speaking of fingers, some presenters have a tendency to use their index finger to gesture—pointing or shaking it at their audience to emphasize a point. This frequently comes across as bossy or scolding. A more effective gesture is simply to use two fingers or the entire hand with the palm facing up. Your point is still accentuated by movement, but the gesture carries no hidden or negative meaning.

Occasionally, try placing your hands in front of you in the waist or hip area with all fingertips lightly touching in a modified praying-hands position, aka "the steeple position." This is a good rest stop for your hands. From the steeple position, they will move naturally without your thinking about them.

Use the Home Base Position

When you are not gesturing, let your arms hang naturally by your sides. Some presenters comment that this position feels rather unnatural; however, to the audience member it looks relaxed and at ease. Try it for yourself: Stand tall and straight in front of a mirror with your arms hanging naturally by your sides where they belong. There is no movement, no fidgeting, no jerkiness—just poise and confidence.

Avoid Distracting Mannerisms

Since most nervous behaviors are unconscious, you may need to enlist the help of a friend or coworker to inform you of any distracting movements. Common pitfalls include a furrowed frowning brow, twitching nose, shifting eyes, clenched fists, and excessively crossed arms. You also need to avoid licking or pursing your lips, twirling your hair, wringing your hands, tapping your fingers, fidgeting with an item in your hand such as a pointer or pen, twisting a watch or ring, slouching or slumping, swaying, pacing, and tapping your feet.

What about placing your hand in your pocket? Some presenters intentionally do this to show a casual attitude. That's fine; just do not keep it there for too long, and make sure it does not move or jingle coins. As a general rule, keep your hands visible rather than hidden.

You may want to consider joining a speaker's club such as Toastmasters International. Each time you speak before the group, you will receive verbal and written evaluations including valuable suggestions for improvement.

Immerse Yourself in Your Topic and Audience

Here is the best advice of all: When you are excited about and totally involved in communicating your message to your listeners, your enthusiasm and passion show. It simply does not occur to you to think about what your arms and hands should or should not be doing—they are taking care of themselves. Immerse yourself in your mission. You'll find that your body naturally, spontaneously, and appropriately supports your message and responds to your listeners. Stay focused on your purpose, and your gestures will be purposeful.

POWER POSTURE TO EXUDE LEADERSHIP AND AUTHORITY

Good speaking posture involves your whole body from head to toe. It's a revealing indicator of self-assurance, attitude, and energy level. It demonstrates your command of the situation and shows you are balanced, stable, and in control. Not only does good posture make a positive visual impression on your audience, but it also helps you sound your best. Good posture aligns your body to optimize breathing. This allows you to project your voice more effectively.

Follow These Guidelines for Confident Body Posture

To evaluate your posture, stand with your back against a wall. Align your spine with the wall, making sure both shoulder blades touch the wall. Then, step away. Relax your shoulders while holding them back—nice and straight. If this feels uncomfortable, chances are your posture is not as good as it could be. If this wall test indicates you have droopy shoulders, try the following:

➤ *Pull in your stomach.* This automatically helps align your spine. Wear a lightweight back brace or elastic support garment underneath your clothing to help adjust your posture. When you sit in a chair, train yourself to hold your shoulder blades against the back of the chair with your upper body tall and straight. Also, ask a family member or coworker to give you a friendly reminder each time she sees you slumping or slouching. With daily effort, those droopy shoulders will transform into good posture in no time.

➤ *Balance your weight evenly.* As a persuasive presenter, you want to impart the message of strength and stability. Since your body is your most influential visual aid, it is imperative that you use it wisely and effectively. When standing, balance your weight evenly on both feet, placing them about eight to twelve inches apart. Imagine a twelve-inch ruler on the floor between your feet. Keep your knees straight but not locked. This picture gives your audience a vision of symmetry and steadiness. In addition, lean ever so slightly forward and situate most of your weight forward on the balls of your feet as if you are going to bounce up and down. This is known as the "ready position." It conveys energy and involvement. Refrain from swaying back and forth, leaning backward on your heels, or situating your weight asymmetrically on one hip. Think balance.

➤ *Keep your head and chin up.* To persuade listeners in the most effective way, your face and eyes must be visible. A technique to keep your face fully exposed to your audience is to keep your chin level with the floor. This simple rule of thumb allows your listeners to experience your most expressive persuasive asset—your face. Behaviors to avoid include tilting your head down, staring at the floor, burying your face in your notes, looking at your audience over the rim of your glasses, or keeping your head turned toward the screen. Avoid turning your head away from your listeners unless it is to briefly refer to a visual. Caution: Do not lift your head so high that you look over the heads of your listeners. Remember the importance of maintaining eye-to-eye communication.

Avoid These Postures

Refrain from standing "at attention" with your hands behind your back. This stance tends to look militaristic and a bit unnatural. For the most part, your hands should stay exposed for your audience to see. Another posture to avoid is the proverbial fig leaf position where you hold, fold, or clasp both hands for a length of time directly in front of the groin.

Remember the home base position. The easiest way to avoid a posture that undermines your credibility is to return to home base—stand tall and straight, head up, weight evenly balanced, and arms hanging naturally by your sides. Practice standing and speaking in this position; you'll find that it cures a multitude of nonverbal mishaps.

Does home base position feel comfortable for you? If not, try repositioning your feet slightly until your body feels balanced and natural. Certainly, move from one spot to another, step into your audience, gesture with your arms and hands, vary your stance, and work with visual aids—but return to home base once a purposeful gesture or movement is completed.

BODY MOVEMENT TO ENGAGE YOUR AUDIENCE

The Roman satirist Petronius wrote, "From a man's face I can read his character; if I can see him walk I know his thoughts." Meaningful body movement is a tremendous asset to your delivery style. It helps maintain audience attention, shows that you are natural and relaxed, and adds impact to your message. Whether you are gesturing, changing position, or walking from one location to another, make sure your movement supports what you are saying. Here are a few guidelines on how to move with meaning:

➤ Step away from the lectern. The more of your body the audience sees, the more of your message they believe. Therefore, place your body—head to toe—in full view of the audience as often as possible. If you must use a lectern, do not hide behind it or clench its sides. Plan and rehearse strategic opportunities within your presentation to step away from it and stand in full view of your listeners—perhaps when you want to emphasize a particular point or issue a call to action.

➤ Some lecterns have stationary microphones that tie you to one spot. Avoid this if possible. If you need a microphone, arrange ahead of time to have a mobile one available so you are free to move.

➤ Use your body to transition between points. As you change topics, change your body position to support the transition. For example, while delivering your transition statement between the first and second key points, pause for three seconds, take at least two steps to the left or right, and begin your new thought. The physical change supports the mental change and helps keep your audience on track.

➤ Step forward for emphasis. When stressing a particular point or benefit, use a body movement to reinforce the idea. For example, as you say "With Product A, you get 30 percent more system uptime," take two steps toward the audience. This forward movement adds impact to the benefit.

➤ Move into the audience. The most persuasive presenters are connected and involved with their audiences. To better interact with your listeners, move into the audience. If you want to initiate a discussion, recruit volunteers, elicit feedback, or conduct an activity, move closer to your audience members. This promotes a friendly relationship. It tells your audience that you want to get to know them.

➤ Avoid perpetual movement. Pacing and swaying are examples of *non-meaningful* movement. When your body is in constant motion, you dilute the meaning of any single movement or gesture you wish to make for emphasis. Plus, since the human eye naturally follows movement, your incessant action can distract, tire, and even annoy the audience. A stationary position is just as powerful as movement. The key is to use a combination of both meaningful movement and serene stillness.

➤ Watch a great presenter at work; it's like a well-choreographed dance. You will see her walk to center stage and present the first two minutes without a slide. Then, she walks to the side and the first slide appears. At a logical transition, she turns the slide off again and walks to the center to interact with the audience. Then she crosses to the other side of the room to deliver a few more slides. She uses these breaks and movement to make a personal connection with the audience.

➤ Move to both sides of the room. Refrain from favoring one side of the room over another; be equally attentive to both. Working both sides and the center of the room makes you, the presenter, equally approachable and accessible to everyone in your audience. Listeners want to *see* their speaker up close and personally. Likewise, you want to *see* each of your listeners. This technique also helps develop and maintain effective eye communication and build rapport with participants.

To remind yourself to follow these guidelines, plan and rehearse appropriate moves within your presentation. It may help to highlight or mark particular phrases or points in your notes to prompt a shift in movement. Professional trainers and speakers will often mentally mark the room and rehearse speaking from four points:

- ➤ Front and center (at the front row of chairs or as far forward as possible while still being able to see everyone in the audience)
- ➤ Back and center (usually near the screen, lectern, laptop, or presentation aids)
- ➤ Left side
- ➤ Right side

When beginning your presentation, establish yourself on the front and center mark where everyone can see you and you can see everyone. This is a powerful position and an excellent location from which to welcome your listeners and display confidence and openness. It also serves as the best spot to deliver your concluding comments and call to action.

When you deliver the body of your presentation, you may spend most of your time at the back and center spot, or to the left or right of the screen. You may, after all, need to access your computer equipment, look at your notes, and refer to the screen. Beware, however, of the common temptation to stay locked in a single position. The screen, lectern, and presentation equipment are stationary throughout the presentation, but you are not! Remember to maximize your effectiveness by moving.

For example, say you're a sales manager presenting this year's results to your team. At this moment in time you are positioned beside the screen, where you click the mouse and advance a new slide on the screen, revealing a bar graph. Rather than launching into a description from that same location, try showing the graphic and then pausing for three to five seconds, giving your viewers time to read and interpret the information. Then, take a couple of steps toward your listeners and elaborate on the data. Show another slide and elaborate. Stay there for a few moments. Then, as you black out the screen, move to the center of the room, look your listeners right in the eye, and say, "The results are not what we had hoped for. I'd like to hear your ideas for improvement. What do you think we need to do differently?"

Remember, too much movement is distracting to an audience. Excessive motion is a sign of nervousness. But then, so is a total absence of it. The key is a combination of purposeful movement to support and enhance your message.

CHAPTER 8: EXECUTIVE SUMMARY

➤ Create a strong visual bond with your audience through effective eye communication. It's the most important nonverbal tool you have.

➤ Evaluate your audience's body language to gauge the effectiveness of your presentation.

➤ Use honest and sincere facial expressions.

➤ Punctuate your message with meaningful gestures.

➤ Avoid distracting mannerisms.

➤ Practice good posture, which connotes leadership and authority.

➤ Plan purposeful movements into your presentations.

CHAPTER 9

Conveying a Professional Image Through Dress and Appearance

> A fair exterior is a silent recommendation.
> —PUBLILIUS SYRUS

A client of mine who provides software and services to the healthcare industry recently asked me to attend and evaluate one of their sales presentations, especially noting the presenters' caliber of professional image and executive presence. The hospital to whom they were presenting is known for their casual culture—in fact, they'll cut off your tie if you wear one to a meeting. The CIO was laid back and informal, and the team had met with him several times. When it finally came time to give the big presentation to the decision makers—the CEO and the hospital's board of directors—the sales team, to my surprise, arrived wearing business casual.

As I suspected, the CEO and the board of directors were all wearing suits. Even the CIO was wearing a suit. The members of the sales team, however, were wearing golf shirts and slacks.

To start the meeting, the CEO stood and addressed the group. "I would like to welcome you here today, and I'd just like to say that there is nothing causal about health care in this hospital." There was a long pause, which I thought was done with great effect. The sales team sank into their chairs. Finally, after what seemed like several minutes, the CEO continued. "As you can see by the way my colleagues and I are dressed, we are respectful of your message. I would just ask that you return the favor next time, if there is one."

Later, the CEO of the hospital called the chairman of the software company and told him what had happened. Though there were several product-related reasons the team did not land the business that day, the casual, relaxed wardrobe and laid-back demeanor certainly did not help matters. News travels fast. Needless to say, from that day forward, when anyone from this company presents at high-stakes executive-facing events, they dress appropriately. Dressing appropriately not only makes a great first impression, it also affects your credibility as a speaker and as a person. I recall another, more positive story about a woman who had worked her way up the corporate ladder, but she underrated the importance of her wardrobe. She would really take advantage of Casual Friday and often travel in sweats. Since she was a rising executive, I advised her to improve her image if she expected any further promotions. As an experiment, I encouraged her to wear a suit when traveling.

"Diane," I told her, "if you will just for one month travel like you are going to a job interview, just see what happens. At a minimum, you're likely to get more respect, better service, and possibly seat upgrades."

So, Diane did as I recommended and wore her best clothes while traveling on her next business trip. Because she had some extra time before her flight, she went into the airline's priority club lounge to relax. As she got a drink and sat down at a table, she glanced over and saw her company president.

"I must say," she told me, "that our eyes met and he recognized me, but he didn't know my name. If I had been wearing my normal sweat suit, I would have been mortified. I probably would have looked away quickly. But, because I felt like a million bucks, our eyes met, he nodded, and I went across the room and shook his hand. We talked for about thirty minutes until it was time for his flight. When he asked, 'How's business?' I told him about a particular customer issue and how my team and I were resolving it. The next time he was in Chicago visiting our office, he and the executive committee members invited me to join them for a meeting." That was the first of many.

Within eighteen months, Diane was promoted to VP. While many factors contributed to her advancement, I believe one of them was being prepared to meet opportunity face to face; to present herself proudly and extemporaneously to the president that day.

While fashion changes quickly, I would like to share some basic guidelines for men and women in regard to executive attire and grooming.

EXECUTIVE ATTIRE FOR WOMEN

I've really tried to learn the art of clothes, because you don't sell for what you're worth unless you look good.

—LADY BIRD JOHNSON

Suits

Wear a two-piece matched skirt suit or pantsuit. For the optimum executive image, choose a conservative color such as navy, dark gray, dark brown, or black. Other suit colors such as beige, blue, and green are professional yet convey a more informal look. Fabric may be wool, wool blend, or micro fibers, either with no pattern or a very subtle weave pattern. The suit jacket, pants, or skirt should be lined. Skirt hem should be no shorter than one inch above the knee. When you sit, if the skirt pulls up toward mid-thigh or restricts movement, it is not appropriate. Pants should be creased and tailored, not tight, with the hem at the middle of the shoe heel, not below it. If you step on your pants when you walk or stand, they are too long. Ensure that all garments are pressed properly and have a well-tailored fit. Check clothing for missing buttons, hanging threads, lint, dandruff, stray hairs, and stains. Remember to remove the tacking stitches and tags from new clothing.

Blouses

Underneath the suit jacket, wear a well-tailored silk or cotton blouse, or a quality knit or silk shell to complement the executive image. Choose a conservative cut with a non-revealing neckline. Ensure the blouse is long enough to tuck into your pants or skirt. Solid light colors work best. Pinstripes or subtle soft patterns are also acceptable. The blouse collar may be worn inside or outside the suit jacket.

Long sleeves are best for business. Avoid low-cut, see-through, tight, lacy, midriff-baring, or frilly tops. A tank-top style or sleeveless shell may be worn if the suit jacket remains on for the entire executive event. For professional business attire, camisoles should only be worn underneath a blouse and not as an outer garment.

Shoes

Shoes (ideally leather or fabric) should match your suit. Classic stylish pumps in colors such as black, brown, or navy with one- to two-inch heels convey the optimum executive image. Shoe styles that are inappropriate for professional attire include open-toed, open-heeled, sling-backs, mules, platforms, spike and stiletto heels, boots, athletic shoes, sandals, flip-flops, and clogs. Ensure your shoes are in good polished condition, free of nicks and scuffs.

Hosiery

Stockings add a necessary finished look. Go with neutral tones for business—and carry an extra pair in case of a run or snag. Avoid trendy designs such as dots, stripes, patterns, and opaque; they're not considered professional business attire. Nor are bare legs acceptable, despite outdoor temperatures.

Accessories

Jewelry should be minimal and not noisy. A subtle, simple style works best in business. Wear no more than one ring on each hand, a professional watch, and simple non-dangling earrings, such as pearl studs. Avoid charm bracelets, multiple bangle bracelets, loudly patterned scarves, or bright floral prints. The handbag, portfolio, and briefcase should be in leather. Use a high-quality gold, silver, or corporate writing pen.

Coats

Wear a classic business overcoat for cold weather. Avoid wearing fur coats, stadium jackets, or casual weekend wear.

EXECUTIVE GROOMING FOR WOMEN

Make sure your hairstyle is current, neat, and clean. Shoulder-length hair or shorter tests best in business and connotes an executive image. If your hair is longer than shoulder length, consider wearing it up in a neat twist or pulled back in a chignon—a low bun at the nape of the neck. Avoid ponytails, hair bows, large barrettes, or anything that glitters. Don't allow hair to cover your face or eyes. Remember to spray fly-away hair or loose ends for a polished look. Invest in a great hair stylist—he or she is worth it.

Nails and Hands

Nails should be neatly manicured. Avoid very long, patterned, or brightly polished nails. Stick to neutral shades and a short to medium length.

Makeup

Apply makeup sparingly, but do use it. Strive for a natural and subtle look. Be sure to blend your base makeup evenly, especially from the jaw line onto the neck. Avoid dark eye makeup such as heavy eyeliner and brightly colored eye shadow. Eye makeup and lipstick should complement your face and skin tone. Wear matte lipstick in a conservative color. Avoid lipsticks that are ultra shiny or frosty. Do not use a lip liner that is darker than your lipstick. This draws attention to your lips and not your professional image. Be sure to blot your lipstick so that it does not smudge on teeth. Use a blush that goes with your skin tone. Remove visible facial hair.

Eyeglasses

If you require glasses, be sure they are clean, stylish, and in good condition. Your pupils should be centered in the glass, and the top of the frame should be in line with the eyebrows. Request an anti-reflective coating to ensure your eyes may be seen. Don't wear sunglasses or tinted glasses indoors. To ensure your audience can see your eyes, avoid thick or darkly colored rims. Select a rimless style if possible.

Cologne or Perfume

Because of others' allergies and sensitivities to smells, business etiquette guidelines suggest not wearing any scent at all. This avoids the risk of offending your coworkers, customers, or prospects. If you use perfume, please do so sparingly.

Perspiration

Wear unscented antiperspirant or deodorant. To avoid excessive perspiring and/or body odor, bathe daily; wash or dry-clean clothes after one wearing; choose natural-fiber clothing and leather shoes so the body can breathe; and avoid foods with strong odors.

Smoking

If you smoke, avoid smoking while wearing your presentation attire. Cigarette odors cling to your clothes for several hours. Avoid smoking in the presence of nonsmokers.

Breath

Breath should smell fresh, but do not chew gum during a business meeting or presentation. Rinse with mouthwash or eat a breath mint prior to interaction with others. Remember to brush your tongue as well as your teeth, since many malodorous germs are harbored there. Also, try clinically proven all-natural products such as Mint Asure with Xylitol to eliminate bad breath. You can find such products at your local pharmacy.

Business Cards

Buy a small high-quality carrying case for your cards, ideally embossed with your name or initials. It imparts ceremony and importance to the exchange, and keeps your cards clean and wrinkle-free.

EXECUTIVE ATTIRE FOR MEN

The apparel oft proclaims the man.

—SHAKESPEARE, *HAMLET*

Suits

High-quality wool suits, well tailored in dark pin-striped or plain tones, test best in business. For a top-notch professional look, make sure your jacket is buttoned when you're standing or walking. For jackets with three buttons, button the top one, and sometimes the center one if you'd like, but do not close the bottom button. For two buttons, close the top one—not the bottom one. Make sure the pant cuff falls lightly over your shoes.

Ties

Do make sure that your tie is tasteful and, preferably, made of 100 percent silk. As a rule of thumb, do not wear a bow tie. The width of your tie should be between 2¾ and 3½ inches and should extend to the top of your belt. The size of the knot should be small (no ascots). For critical presentations or meetings with executive-level decision makers, avoid wearing ties with large or bold prints, cartoon characters, holiday motifs, or sports themes.

Shirts

The 100 percent cotton long-sleeved, pointed-collar business shirts in white and blue are traditional safe choices. Ensure the shirts are pressed, clean, and fit properly. Long-sleeved white shirts test best in business settings. Wear an undershirt, and avoid wearing short sleeves under a suit—even during the summer. The shirt cuffs should extend ½ inch below the jacket sleeves.

Shoes and Socks

Wear well-polished dark brown, black, or cordovan leather wing-tipped or lace-up shoes with socks that complement the suit. Avoid wearing casual shoes, penny loafers, or sports shoes with a suit. Socks should reach to mid-calf to avoid showing bare leg when your legs are crossed.

Coats

Wear a classic business overcoat for cold weather. Avoid sports or stadium jackets.

Belt

If your pants have belt loops, always wear a leather belt to match your shoes. Stick with a conservative buckle.

Accessories

Wear a simple professional watch in a classic style and avoid plastic bands. Don't wear a sports watch or anything that beeps. Simple cuff links, wedding band, or a college ring is suitable. Avoid earrings, gold chains, bulging wallets, and oversized briefcases. Wallet, credit cards, and other paraphernalia should be kept in the leather briefcase. Use a high-quality gold, silver, or corporate writing pen.

EXECUTIVE GROOMING FOR MEN

For business, a classic haircut is best. Keep it short, neat, clean, and current. As for facial hair, the clean-shaven look is most common among business executives and tends to create the best first impression. If wearing a beard and/or mustache, keep them short and neat.

Nails and Hands

Clean, well-manicured nails solidify respect. Avoid bitten or chewed nails, which convey anxiety. Make time for a monthly manicure. When they ask, "Buff or shiny?" choose buff.

Eyeglasses

Be sure glasses are clean, stylish, and in good condition. Your pupils should be centered in the glass, and the top of the frame should be in line with the eyebrows. Request an anti-reflective coating to ensure your eyes may be seen. Don't wear sunglasses or tinted glasses indoors. To ensure your audience can see your eyes, avoid thick or darkly colored rims. Select a rimless style if possible.

Cologne

Because some people have allergies and sensitivities to smells, business etiquette guidelines suggest not wearing any scent at all. This avoids the risk of offending your coworkers, customers, or prospects. If you use cologne, please do so sparingly.

Perspiration

Wear unscented antiperspirant or deodorant. To avoid excessive perspiring and/or body odor, bathe daily; wash or dry-clean clothes after one wearing; choose natural-fiber clothing and leather shoes so the body can breathe; and avoid foods with strong odors.

Smoking

If you smoke, avoid smoking in your presentation or meeting attire. Cigarette odors cling to your clothes for several hours. Avoid smoking in the presence of nonsmokers.

Breath

Breath should smell fresh, but do not chew gum during a business meeting or presentation. Rinse with mouthwash or eat a breath mint prior to interaction with others. Remember to brush your tongue as well as your teeth, since many malodorous germs are harbored there. Also, try clinically proven all-natural products such as Mint Asure with Xylitol to eliminate bad breath. You can find such products at your local pharmacy.

Business Cards

Buy a small high-quality carrying case for your cards, ideally embossed with your name or initials. It imparts ceremony and importance to the exchange, and keeps your cards clean and wrinkle-free.

CHAPTER 9: EXECUTIVE SUMMARY

➤ A professional appearance makes a great first impression and adds to your credibility.

➤ Executive attire shows respect to your audience and customers.

➤ Avoid potential distractions and embarrassment with proper grooming.

CHAPTER 10

Speaking with the Voice of Authority

The voice is a second face.

—GERARD BAUER

As the guest of the vice president of sales for a large equipment manufacturer, I was watching various members of his team make presentations during a staff meeting. The VP wanted me to evaluate the presenters and advise him on which individuals needed coaching.

One man in this group was an absolute expert in the field. But there was a problem: he used poor grammar and lots of slang when he spoke. Before he even finished his presentation, the VP interrupted him. "Hold it, hold it," he said. "Any customer who hears you speak with that kind of grammar is going to think you are ignorant. And it is going to reflect poorly on our company and our product. You are going to have to learn how to speak properly, and until you do, I don't want you making any presentations." Needless to say, this man became one of my first coaching clients from this group, and we worked long and hard to correct the way he talked.

While I would have preferred that the VP take a more tactful approach in providing feedback, he was right about the impact that the voice and words have on decision makers. Having poor grammar leaves a negative impression with the audience. This is because grammar is one of the basics. If you don't have the basics down, you've lost your credibility as a speaker.

My reason for sharing this story is that it emphasizes how your audience of decision makers is influenced by what they hear. If they are distracted by the way you talk, they will miss your message and fail to take the action you want.

USING YOUR VOICE TO INFLUENCE DECISION MAKERS

A powerful, persuasive presentation requires more than well-organized content and effective body language; it requires a good speaking voice that has a pleasant yet authoritative tone and conveys a sense of friendliness. A good speaking voice is natural and unforced, reflecting the true personality and sincerity of the presenter. It's loud enough to be heard and clear enough to be understood.

How do you feel about your voice? Do you like the sound of it? Do you believe it is pleasant to listen to? Ideally, you said yes to both, and you and your listeners enjoy hearing it. If not, rest assured; with a few simple techniques and some practice you can discover your *best* speaking voice.

The fact is you have a good speaking voice—most everyone does. Though it may be buried underneath a few layers of bad speech habits or childhood conditioning, your optimum speaking voice is in there waiting to emerge. Finding and developing it is important because you are more likely to take advantage of opportunities to speak up and speak out if you feel confident about the sound of your voice. What you have to say is important and deserves to be heard. So why not polish the instrument that heralds your message by adding strength, vitality, and rich qualities to your speaking voice?

A controlled, expressive, authoritative voice will help you persuade and influence your listeners; earn the respect of your boss and coworkers; make sales; gain promotions; and help capture the attention of every audience to whom you present.

People want to listen to and do business with those in whom they have confidence. Putting your best voice forward connects you to your listeners and helps build rapport.

THE SIX QUALITIES OF A GOOD SPEAKING VOICE

The key to discovering *your* best voice is cultivating six key vocal qualities:

1. Tone—the attitude and emotion conveyed by your voice
2. Pitch—the highness or lowness of your voice

3. Pace—the speed at which you speak

4. Volume—how loudly or softly you speak

5. Inflection—the way you emphasize or accentuate a word or phrase

6. Articulation—the distinct enunciation and pronunciation of syllables

Let's explore each of these important qualities one by one, along with vocal exercises to help develop the expressive and powerful voice within you.

Use a Listener-Friendly Tone of Voice

Tone is *how* you say something. Your tone is your most important voice attribute because it conveys your emotions and attitude. It is highly possible—in fact, a frequent occurrence—for a person to say *one* thing, but for the listener to interpret it as meaning something totally different.

How many times have you received a scowl from someone either at home or work and you ask, "What . . . what did I say?" The person replies, "It's not *what* you said, it's *how* you said it!" The culprit in this case is the tone of your voice.

Apply a concentrated effort to sound friendly and gracious to your listeners; let them know through your tone of voice you are glad to see them and are excited about your message. Review these tips to develop a tone of voice that invites, inspires, and influences others.

Tone tips

Review your presentation script or notes. For each major point in your presentation, assign an appropriate emotion or attitude to it. For example: excitement, sincerity, forcefulness, friendliness, urgency. Rehearse each point, making a concentrated effort to vocalize what you think the emotion sounds like. Keep these audio feelings in mind when presenting and be sure to express them through your voice to your listeners.

Take your best friend to the presentation with you—at least mentally. When you are presenting, imagine her sitting in the front row listening intently. Visualize that person and her qualities, and then make believe you are talking one-on-one with her. This reminds you to keep your tone of voice friendly, natural, and conversational.

Record your voice during normal phone conversations. Set a microcassette recorder beside your telephone and just click it on when you answer.

Afterward, play back the recording and listen for your tone of voice. What feelings and attitudes do you hear? Are they what you intended the listener to hear? You will be amazed how this simple technique improves *how* you say what you say.

Control Your Pitch

Pitch refers to the highness or lowness of your voice. You have a natural speaking range of high, low, and mid tones. The goal is to speak normally and conversationally, while exercising this range to express your message. Controlled pitch creates a voice that is interesting, accentuated, and pleasant to hear.

A lower-sounding voice is perceived by audience members to be stronger, confident, and more authoritative than a high-pitched voice. This is of particular importance to women who wish to be perceived as credible and confident, since the female voice is naturally higher pitched than the male voice. Consider that in every species that makes audible sounds—including humans—the young have higher-pitched voices than do the adults.

This implication transfers to the business presentation arena. An overly high-pitched voice suggests qualities of a young person—junior status, non-authoritative, possibly immature. You are taken more seriously as a presenter when the general range of your pitch is lowered. Speaking in the lower register of your voice range sends the message of credibility and command.

Because you never want your voice to sound phony or forced in any way, the goal is to be yourself and speak normally and conversationally. The point is to make the most of the voice you have. You have an inborn speaking range—you can go up several levels without sounding shrill, and you can go down several levels without sounding grumbly. The key is to experiment with your full range and get comfortable talking in the lower tones. The following exercises will help.

Pitch tips

Think of your voice as a musical instrument. Sing the *ah* sound at various pitch levels, traveling up and down your vocal scale. Go as high as you can until you sound like a lyric soprano; go as low as you can until you sound like a bass. Repeat this exercise over and over until you can hear the full range of your voice.

Recite the letters of the alphabet or days of the week—and then go on to reading or speaking a memorized passage—while ascending and descending within your range. This exercise builds awareness of your various pitch levels and builds confidence to use more of the lower tones available to you.

Calculate and Vary Your Pace

Pace, or rate, is how quickly or slowly you speak. In recording and analyzing thousands of speeches over the years, I've noted the average rate of speech for most presenters is 150–160 words per minute. Interestingly, publishers recommend books on tape to be voiced at the same rate. This seems to be the range in which people comfortably hear and vocalize words. It's a rate that is quick enough to keep the listener interested and avoid a boring drone, yet not so fast that it loses or frustrates the listener.

Here's an easy way to determine your rate of speech. Find a document you have stored in your computer in a word processing system such as Microsoft Word. With a timer in hand, read a "test" paragraph aloud for one minute. Try to pace yourself as if you are talking conversationally to a group of people at your normal rate. See how far you get in sixty seconds. Highlight the passage you read and perform a word count (or manually count the number of words you read). This is your presentation speech rate.

Polished pacing

If you tend to speak too quickly, try this exercise: During rehearsal, present an excerpt from your presentation script or notes using an exaggerated slow pace. First, try rehearsing five minutes of content and clap your hands or snap your fingers between each word. For example: *Good* (clap) *morning* (clap) *everyone* (clap) *and* (clap) *welcome.* (Clap) *Thank* (clap) *you* (clap) *for* (clap) *the* (clap) *opportunity* (clap) *to* (clap) *visit* (clap) *with* (clap) *you* (clap) *here* (clap) *at* (clap) *[XYZ]* (clap) *[organization]* (clap). Continue for five minutes. Next, practice the same section again, but this time clap at each punctuation mark. For example: *Good morning everyone and welcome.* (clap) *Thank you for the opportunity to visit with you here at [XYZ organization].* (clap) Continue this exercise for at least ten minutes. By clapping your hands between words or at punctuation, you force yourself to slow the pace. This deliberate act trains your brain to insert natural pauses and eliminates rushed speech.

When delivering technical information or fact-based material such as instructions, statistics, or analysis, speak at a pace that is 20–30 percent slower than usual. Mark your notes accordingly to remind you. Remember, *you* know the information but your audience is hearing the data for the first time. They'll need a few extra moments to process the information and take notes. Conversely, when delivering entertaining or emotion-based information such as stories, anecdotes, scenarios, humor, or examples, speed up to a conversation pace. The goal with pace is variety.

Use Volume to Speak Up and Speak Out

As an infant, you unhesitatingly filled the world with confident vocal sounds until someone said, "Shhh . . . Be quiet!" Then, if you are like some of us, you were taught as a child to hold in the sound—to remain silent unless spoken to. Many people carry this quiet conditioned response into the business world. Unfortunately, it conveys insecurity. A timid, weak, or inaudible voice is not persuasive.

Good voice projection begins with the right mental attitude. Get it straight in your mind that you are not only a grown adult, but you are an expert in your subject matter. You have a message and a purpose for presenting it, and you have earned the right to be heard. The best way for that exchange of information to happen is with a strong, clear voice. Give yourself permission to project your voice with confidence.

Volume refers to the degree of sound intensity your voice produces. Think of the volume control on your stereo and the purpose it serves. Your voice also has a volume control—and it's important to turn it up when your message needs to be heard. Varying your volume during your presentation is an excellent technique for adding emphasis and holding interest.

Next comes the physical aspect of good voice production. As you strive to improve your speaking voice, it's essential that you know how to produce quality voice sounds. The understanding and application of this process transforms bad speech habits into good ones.

Breathing

The foundation of a good speaking voice lies in the speaker's breathing. Breath produces voice. Strong voice projection and volume depend on deep, controlled breathing. A column of air supports your voice. The depth and control of that air determines your vocal quality. Think of the diaphragm as the foundation on which this air column rests. The diaphragm is a large muscle attached to the lower ribs; it separates the chest from the abdomen. This important muscle controls the air as it comes upward to meet the vocal organs.

When you inhale or breathe in, your dome-shaped diaphragm moves downward and flattens. At the same time, muscles attached to the ribs cause them to move outward. This outward movement of the rib cage coupled with the downward movement of the diaphragm expands the abdominal wall and creates a slight vacuum in the chest. This vacuum causes air to fill the lungs through the trachea (windpipe).

When you exhale, the diaphragm relaxes and the abdominal wall contracts. The diaphragm rises up into its relaxed dome shape, which pushes air out of the lungs and upward against the vocal cords. The vocal cords are two small folds of tissue that stretch across the larynx (voice box). One fold stretches on each side of an opening in the trachea. Muscles in the larynx stretch and relax the vocal cords.

When you breathe, your vocal cords relax into a V-shaped opening that lets air through. When you speak, the larynx muscles pull the vocal cords together, narrowing the opening. Then, as you exhale, you drive air from the lungs through the larynx. The air vibrates the tightened vocal cords. And the result is sound.

The vibration of the vocal cords creates sound in what's known as the resonators—the upper part of the throat, the mouth, and, at times, the nose. As sound waves bounce around within these resonators they are reinforced and amplified. Thus, deep, controlled breathing is the groundwork for improved voice volume.

Before presenting, assess the room, your surroundings, and the physical distance between you and your listeners. You want to speak loudly enough so that everyone in the room can easily hear you, but not so loudly that those in the front row are wincing. Feel free to ask your audience members if they can hear you. Based on their feedback, adjust your voice volume.

When possible, use a microphone—the mark of a confident, persuasive presenter. A microphone enables you to speak naturally in a conversational tone without having to strain your voice to reach the back row. You look and sound better, and the audience benefits because your voice is clearer and easier to hear.

Projection

Good volume's partner in effectiveness is good projection. Imagine a stereo speaker with the volume turned up, but the speaker is aimed in the wrong direction, or facing the floor. The volume is fine but the sound is not projected properly.

In the theater, projection refers to an actor using his voice and body forcefully enough to be understood by an entire audience. In the presentation arena, the meaning is the same. This requires speaking outward, toward your audience rather than down at your notes, the floor, or toward the screen behind you.

Your listeners want to see your face, hear your voice, and connect with your eyes. They want to experience *you*. Projecting your voice and delivering your talk directly toward them shows your strength and character as a presenter. It gives you more credibility with your audience and exhibits your confidence.

Volume and projection tips

Stand tall and straight with your chin level with the floor and imagine an audience in front of you. Slowly count to ten at the volume you use at sports events to cheer your team; that is, as loudly as possible without straining your voice. Next, count from eleven to twenty at a somewhat lower volume, as though you're speaking to a neighbor across the road. From twenty-one to thirty, speak at a normal conversational tone as though you're chatting with friends across the dinner table. Finally, at your quietest audible tone, as though you're reading a bedtime story to a child, count from thirty-one to forty.

You'll hear the wide range of volume that you're capable of speaking. Apply this variety to your presentation. For example, when you welcome the audience, or want to emphasize a point, use a loud, strong, steady voice. If you want to bring the audience closer and have them sitting on the edge of their seats, use a quieter volume. When you shift your volume, you add auditory variety that makes your presentation more interesting.

Use Inflection to Influence Decision Makers

According to my surveys of audience members over the years, a monotone voice is a listener's number one pet peeve. A monotone delivery can put an audience to sleep quicker than a prescription pill. The remedy is *inflection* — adding special emphasis to a word by modulating your tone, pace, or pitch.

Think of it as bending a word with your voice to communicate your message more effectively. Inflection is an effective technique used by skilled communicators to sustain audience attention and influence listeners' thinking.

Inflection exercises

Inflection allows you to alter the entire meaning of a sentence or word simply by the way you say it. Consider the word "Oh." In the following examples, say that word aloud, indicating how you would express the assigned emotion or situation.

- ► Express surprise—your boss tells you you're the substitute speaker for the noon meeting—and it's currently 11:55 AM: "Oh."

- ► Express joy—your colleague shows you a picture of his newborn baby: "Oh."

- ► Express disappointment—your customer informs you she just lost her job: "Oh."

- ► Awe—on your drive to work, you witness a beautiful sunrise: "Oh."

As you can hear in your voice, a simple shift in inflection gives completely different meanings to a single monosyllabic word.

Now let's apply this exercise to a few sentences in a sample presentation. First, practice reading aloud the following sentences in a monotone voice; do not change a single vocal quality as you recite it:

- ► Monotone read: "This laptop is the best-selling model on the market today. It's a full-featured business solution with smooth multitasking and lightning-fast performance."

- ► Now, following the markings, inflect your voice appropriately. For bolded words, use more volume. Where you see spaces between letters, slow down and elongate the word. For underlined words, raise the pitch of your voice. For italicized words, speed up the pace: "**This** laptop is the b e s t—s e l l i n g model on the market today. It's a <u>full-featured</u> **business** solution with s m o o t h multitasking and *lightning-fast* performance."

On your presentation script or notes, place inflection markings on particular words or phrases that deserve special emphasis. Also, remember to use the power of the pause. A brief period of silence is a powerful form of expression. It holds audience attention, separates or emphasizes a point, and conveys confidence.

Practice Articulation to Speak Clearly

Articulation is the skill of speaking clearly and distinctly. All words are pronounced correctly and each syllable is enunciated intelligibly. Inarticulate speech includes mumbling, muttering, swallowing words at the end of phrases, trailing off at the end of sentences, or failing to properly form words before they are spoken. The remedy for this negative habit is simple: good articulation.

Unintelligible speech robs the audience and the presenter. Listeners grow frustrated—even annoyed—when they cannot make out what the presenter is saying. They're likely to view him as lethargic, disinterested, or timid due to a lack of vocal vitality. And if you're a presenter, indistinct speech can jeopardize your image and prevent you from communicating your message with impact.

Articulation exercises

The following articulation exercises involve moving the mouth; relaxing the lips, tongue, and jaw muscles; and voicing all sounds, especially consonants, clearly and distinctly. Practice the following exercises daily to create distinct speech.

Warm up your mouth muscles by practicing a few tongue twisters. Begin by saying them slowly and deliberately. Gradually advance to a faster-than-normal rate.

- Peter Piper picked a peck of pickled peppers. If Peter Piper picked a peck of pickled peppers, how many peppers did Peter Piper pick?
- How much wood would a woodchuck chuck if a woodchuck could chuck wood?
- She sells sea shells by the seashore to seasick sailors and shy shivering soldiers.
- Rubber baby buggy bumpers.

Select an excerpt from your talk. Reading aloud slowly and deliberately, exaggerate the formation of each word. Over-enunciate. Then, after practicing this several times, repeat the excerpt normally and conversationally. You will immediately notice better-articulated speech.

Identify a speaker on television or radio whose voice you like. Record that person's voice and listen carefully. Study the articulation as well as the other qualities that make the voice pleasing to you—and practice emulating those traits.

Pronunciation

Good pronunciation is saying a word correctly according to its phonetic spelling. Enunciation—clearly articulating each syllable—makes accurate pronunciation possible. Consider the commonly mispronounced words listed in Figure 10-1. As an exercise, correctly pronounce each word or phrase by enunciating each syllable slowly and distinctly.

Figure 10-1

Word or phrase	How to pronounce	How not to pronounce
going	go-ing	gunna or goin
probably	prob-uh-blee	pra-lee or prob-lee
picture	pik-cher	pit-cher
would you	wood yoo	wood ja
orient	or-i-ent	orien-tate
library	li-brer-ee	li-bary
asked	askt	axed
similar	sim-i-lar	sim-yoo-lar
athlete	ath-leet	ath-a-leet
escape	es-cape	ex-cape

AVOID JEOPARDIZING SPEECH HABITS

In addition to cultivating these six key vocal qualities, an authoritative, persuasive speaking voice also requires that you avoid common language mistakes that can sabotage your credibility.

► *Up-Speak.* When you make a statement, does it sound more like a question because your voice gets higher at the end of the sentence? If so, you are practicing a speech pattern known as the high rising terminal (HRT), also called up-talk, rising inflection, or high rising intonation (HRI). Up-speak places an upward inflection on the final word or syllable in a phrase or sentence, making it sound inappropriately like a question. Imagine how odd it would sound for a presenter to open a presentation with up-speak: "Thank you for joining us today? The purpose of today's presentation (?) is to show you how this solution can save you time (?), reduce your costs (?), and improve your productivity?" Make sure you place a downward inflection at the end of your sentence to indicate a confident declaration, not a question that makes you sound tentative and insecure.

➤ *Fillers.* Non-words such as "Uh" and "Um," as well as the overuse of any word such as "So," "You know," "Okay," and "Actually," are known as filler words and phrases. They're often heard when the speaker's brain is searching for information, or when the speaker is unprepared. Excessive fillers can jeopardize a speaker's credibility and affect how the audience perceives him. The chief executive officer of a large insurance company was listening intently to one of his business unit presidents deliver a budget proposal presentation. Following the presentation, the CEO handed the man a note that read: "You had 28 ums in your first minute." Unfortunately, the president did not get the funding he was requesting. He believed that was partly due to the CEO's perception of him. After this incident, the man called me and we began working on eliminating this jeopardizing speech habit. Here are a few tips to limit fillers in your speech.

- ➤ First, become aware of your use of fillers. Record your speech and count the number of occurrences. Ask your colleagues with whom you regularly communicate to tell you when they notice them.
- ➤ Second, prepare content early and rehearse aloud. During rehearsal, ask a listening friend or coworker to give you an audible reminder—such as a tap on the table—every time you use a filler.
- ➤ Third, be mindful of your speech. The goal is to become alert and self-aware. Only then can you consciously substitute a pause for a filler.

➤ *Speed Talking.* People speak quickly for a variety of reasons ranging from geographic location to nerves to learned patterns. If you talk too fast, your audience might not understand you. Slowing down will increase both your credibility and clarity. The first step is self-awareness. Begin by taping yourself during a normal conversation or presentation. Play back the tape and ask yourself if you're talking too fast and whether or not you're speaking clearly. Also ask your friends and coworkers if they perceive your speech as too fast. If so, the second step is changing the behavior. To slow your rate of speech and increase clarity, insert a few pauses. It might not be so much about the speed at which you speak as allowing your audience a little time to process what you're saying. Use the one-second technique: During rehearsal, at the end of each sentence, count silently, "One thousand one." This will give your listeners time to process—and it will give you time to take a breath. You can also create reminders to slow your speech. Write the words Slow Down or Pause on note paper and post it in a prominent place to remind yourself to monitor your pace.

CHAPTER 10: EXECUTIVE SUMMARY

➤ The key to discovering *your* best voice is by cultivating the six key vocal qualities:

1. Tone—the attitude and intonation conveyed by your voice

2. Pitch—the highness or lowness of your voice

3. Pace—the speed at which you speak

4. Volume—how loudly or softly you speak

5. Inflection—the way you emphasize or accentuate a word or phrase

6. Articulation—the distinct enunciation and pronunciation of syllables

➤ Avoid jeopardizing speech habits such as up-speak, fillers, and speed talking

Leveraging the Language of Leadership

> The difference between the almost right word and the right word is really a large matter—'tis the difference between the lightning-bug and the lightning.
>
> —MARK TWAIN

Effective leaders use language that captivates, motivates, and persuades others. They take a position and state a point of view with words and phrases that strike at the very heart of an issue, shed light on the subject, and cause people to take notice.

Effective leaders translate situations into positions. They present evidence to back up their position, and then they propose a course of action. They speak simply, directly, and convincingly. They're likely to answer our objections before we can raise them. They believe, and as a result their listeners believe. That's why they're seen as leaders—their actions and words compel people to follow.

What are their techniques? Their deliberate choice of specific words and phrases is one of the key components of their persuasive communication. Regardless of the audience, topic, or industry, or whether the setting is a stand-up presentation, sit-down conversation, or online meeting, a leader attempts to influence someone's mind in order to achieve a certain result. Here are some tools to help you get the results you want by leveraging the language of leadership.

"YOU" AND "YOUR" VS. "I-ME-MY-MINE"

In my professional opinion, the three most compelling words in the language of persuasion are one's own name, "you," and "your." These words capture and hold attention more than any others because they refer directly to the listener. The frequent use of the word "you" answers the audience's unspoken question: "What's in this for me?"

When the goal is to influence, often the least persuasive words are first-person pronouns, such as "I," "Me," "My," and "Mine." In addition, the third-person pronouns "Us," "We," and "Our" are not persuasive unless they include the listener. For example, if I say "Our customer service is number one," that refers only to my colleagues, my company, and me. However, if I say "Our partnership can ensure you reach your goals," the pronoun refers to the listener and me. The point is, to optimize your influence, use pronouns that directly relate to and include the listener. Otherwise, you risk sounding self-centric versus customer-centric.

For example, imagine you're the decision maker for a large multi-hospital health system. You and four other chief officers are attending a presentation to decide which software vendor you will choose to replace your outdated system; it's a $5 million decision for your organization. Two vendors have made it to the finals. My client, Stephen, is one of them.

When Stephen and I met the first time to prepare for this big presentation, without any discussion or coaching, I asked him to stand and deliver his first five minutes, just to give me an idea of his style. Here's his opening sixty seconds, which is an actual transcript of the videotape. (Notice that the self-centric pronouns and names are in bold.)

Self-Centric Pronouns

"**I'm** glad to be here today representing **Acme Solutions**. **I** visited this facility six months ago when **my** colleagues asked **me** to join them for a walk-through of the IT department. **I** must say, **I'm** quite impressed with the growth since then. **I'm** glad to see the cardiac wing is finished. Let **me** get to **my** reason for attending today. As **I** understand from **my** team, **I'm** supposed to address patient safety, operational efficiency, and financial performance. But first, what **I** want to talk about is why **I** believe **Acme** is the right choice. **I'll** begin with **our** company overview. **I'm** happy to say, all the industry ratings rank **our** company as the proven leader in healthcare. **I'm** pleased to say **we** have topped the charts for four years in a row. Plus **our** customers say that **we** are the best at what **we** do. Let **me** show some of their quotes that recommend **our** solution."

In Stephen's opening sixty seconds, in just 156 words, he spoke twenty-seven self-centric pronouns and not a single listener-based audience-centric pronoun. When I shared this fact with him, he said, "No way!" We reviewed the video and he was shocked.

Stephen had no intention of sounding self-centered and unconcerned about his potential customer. He's a fine leader; however, his language jeopardized his ability to connect with and persuade his audience. After several rehearsals, he was a pro. Here's his new and improved opening, with the audience-centric pronouns and names in bold. (Fortunately, it's the version his prospect ended up hearing.)

Audience-Centric Pronouns

"Thank **you** for **your** time today and for the privilege of visiting with **you** here at **Martin General**. **Jim**, **you** and **your** colleagues gave us a beneficial and productive tour of **Martin** six months ago. Thank **you** again. **You've** certainly grown since then. Congratulations to all of **you** on completing the new cardiac wing plus **your** achievement of being ranked the number one hospital in the state. In fact, **your** continued success is the purpose of this presentation. **You've** told us **your** three main initiatives are to ensure patient safety, boost operational efficiency, and maximize financial performance. What **you'll** see today is a brief demonstration of how Acme, as the industry leader, can ensure **you** achieve your objectives. **You'll** discover how **you** can easily implement this solution faster, safer, and more economically than any solution on the market. Other hospitals, similar to **Martin's** shape and size, attest to the value. Here are some of their comments."

Stephen's revised one-minute opening is the same length, 156 words, but what a difference! This time he uses a whopping twenty audience-centric pronouns and proves he is focused on the prospect through his language.

It may help to think of a presentation as dining with a companion. If you talk about yourself the whole time and overuse the I-Me-My-Mine pronouns, your friend will likely become exhausted (if not bored and uninterested) because everything is all about the speaker, not the listener. Here are five quick tips to help you cultivate the habit of sounding listener focused.

Using audience-centric pronouns

Assess your "I" to "You" ratio. The first step is to become aware. Are you overusing first-person pronouns? Using a tape recorder or camera to record your words, rehearse your opening sixty seconds aloud. Then, as I did with Stephen, simply play back the recording and count the number of times you hear I-Me-My-Mine. Also count the use of "We-Us-Our" if the word refers solely to you, your colleagues, and your company. Then count the occurrences of "You-Your" plus the listeners' names (either personal or their company name).

Write down your opening minute and closing minute. Be listener-focused. Rephrase as many sentences as possible to have a "you" slant. This process will result in a rehearsal script, as it did for Stephen. Certainly, you won't read this script during the live presentation; you won't even follow it precisely. What counts is the process of training your mind and mouth to produce more listener-focused words and phrases, in a natural, conversational way.

Begin and end by saying "Thank you." At a minimum, if you begin your presentation with these two magic words, you've placed the opening focus on the audience. Similarly, if you close by saying, "Thank you for your time and attention," or "Thank you for the opportunity to work together," the closing emphasis is also on the audience.

Say their company name before yours. As seen in Stephen's two examples, it sounds both polite and persuasive to say the customer's or prospect's company name before your own. For example, "Thank you for your time today and for the privilege of visiting with you here at Martin General" versus "I'm glad to be here today representing Acme Solutions." Even for internal presentations within your own company, state the name of the executive listeners' department or committee. For example, "Thank you for the opportunity to address the executive leadership committee. My name is . . ."

Ask questions. Audience interaction is among the best ways to demonstrate genuine listener focus. Frequently invite your audience to speak and participate. For example: "What do you think about this feature?" "How would you describe your current process?" "What's your number one challenge in this area?"

ACTION VERBS AND CAUSE-AND-EFFECT PHRASES

To lead is to act. Achieving results requires some kind of action, some kind of doing. Therefore, when you speak with action verbs you connect the audience to your proposed outcome. Through your verbs you create momentum, drive, and energy; the audience can visualize and feel the thrust of your message. Notice in Stephen's revised opening, he uses three verbs to articulate the prospect's objectives: "You've told us your three main initiatives are to *ensure* patient safety, *boost* operational efficiency, and *maximize* financial performance." The next time you're creating a PowerPoint slide, try starting each bullet point with an action verb. Also, anytime you're communicating results, next steps, or outcomes, rely on verbs to tell your story. Here are my favorite fifty action verbs that cause decision makers to sit up and take notice. Also refer to Figure 11-1 for a more comprehensive list of action verbs.

Accelerate	Ensure	Leverage	Respond
Achieve	Expand	Manage	Save
Align	Find	Maximize	Simplify
Boost	Focus	Measure	Solve
Bridge	Foresee	Offer	Train
Build	Gain	Optimize	Transfer
Capture	Generate	Overcome	Transform
Commit	Grow	Plan	Understand
Control	Identify	Prepare	Unleash
Deliver	Increase	Produce	Use
Discover	Invest	Profit	Win
Drive	Lead	Raise	
Eliminate	Learn	Reduce	

Convince with Cause-and-Effect Phrases

In persuasive or argumentative speaking, we try to convince others to agree with our facts, believe our claim, share our values, accept our conclusions, buy our product, or adopt our way of thinking. One proven approach to convince your audience is cause-and-effect reasoning. It's a method that helps your listeners see why things have happened or will happen as they do. It shows the inevitable linkage between what happens first and what happens next as a result. Cause-and-effect reasoning makes a statement objective and

Figure 11-1
The Language of Leadership: Action Verbs

A
Abolish
Accelerate
Accomplish
Accumulate
Achieve
Acquire
Act
Adapt
Administer
Adopt
Advance
Align
Analyze
Anticipate
Apply
Approve
Ask
Assess
Assist
Attain
Augment
Avoid

B
Balance
Benefit
Better
Boost
Break
Bridge
Broaden
Budget
Build
Burn

C
Capture
Champion
Change
Choose
Clarify
Commit
Communicate
Complete
Comprehend
Conceive
Conduct
Confront
Connect
Conquer
Conserve
Contribute
Control
Convert
Convince
Coordinate
Correct
Create
Cross
Cultivate
Cut Down

D
Decide
Define
Defuse
Delegate
Deliver
Demonstrate
Deploy

Design
Develop
Diagnose
Discover
Direct
Drive

E
Earn
Economize
Effect
Elevate
Eliminate
Enhance
Enrich
Ensure
Escalate
Establish
Evaluate
Exceed
Excel
Expand
Expedite
Exploit
Explore

F
Facilitate
Feature
Filter
Finalize
Find
Focus
Foresee

G
Gain
Gather
Generate
Give
Grasp
Grow
Guide

H
Have
Harbor
Help
Honor

I
Identify
Ignite
Illuminate
Implement
Improve
Increase
Influence
Initiate
Innovate
Inspire
Intensify
Instruct
Interpret
Invest

J
Join
Jump
Justify

(continued)

141

Figure 11-1 (continued)

K
Keep
Know

L
Launch
Lead
Learn
Leverage
Listen

M
Maintain
Manage
Master
Maximize
Measure
Mobilize
Motivate
Multiply

N
Navigate
Negate
Negotiate
Neutralize
Notice
Nullify

O
Offer
Operate
Optimize
Organize
Originate
Outshine
Overcome

P
Participate
Penetrate
Perform
Persuade
Pinpoint
Pioneer
Plan
Position
Prefer
Prepare
Preserve
Prevail
Prevent
Prioritize
Produce
Profit
Promote
Propose
Protect
Provide

Q
Quicken
Qualify
Quantify

R
Raise
Realize
Recharge
Recommend
Reconsider
Recover
Recruit
Reduce
Refine

Refresh
Reinforce
Remember
Reorganize
Replace
Rescue
Resist
Resolve
Respond
Retain
Revamp
Review
Revise

S
Safeguard
Save
Scan
Schedule
Score
Segment
Serve
Set Up
Shatter
Shave Off
Sidestep
Simplify
Solve
Sow
Steer
Stimulate
Stop
Streamline
Stretch
Structure
Succeed
Supervise

Supplement
Supply
Support
Surpass

T
Take
Teach
Tell
Train
Transfer
Transform
Translate
Transparent

U
Understand
Unleash
Use
Utilize

V
Value
Verify

W
Wait
Whittle Down
Win
Work

Y
Yearn
Yield

rational rather than a blind assertion or empty hyperbole. Words to help craft *cause-and-effect reasoning* include:

Accordingly	Caused by	Hence	Thus
As a result	Consequently	On account of	
Because	Due to	Since	
Because of	For this reason	Therefore	

Notice how the following sentences express complete certainty:

- ► You can be assured you will receive the industry's best customer service <u>because</u> Acme has been rated number one in customer service for four years in a row.

- ► This product's consistent high rating is <u>caused by</u> faster implementation times, ease of use, and speed-to-value.

- ► You've heard five customers affirm that Acme software pays for itself in the first year. <u>Therefore</u>, we can help Martin General achieve *your* goal of maximizing financial performance.

- ► Our IT team has successfully implemented this solution in over 3,000 hospitals, on time and under budget. <u>As a result</u>, their experience ensures your installation will be fast, easy, and economical.

Employ Benefit Phrases to Answer "So What? Who Cares?"

Be sure to employ plenty of benefit words and phrases. The decision makers in your audience buy benefits, not features or functions. As the old saying goes, sell the sizzle, not the steak. Never assume that listeners will figure out for themselves what the benefit is. Oftentimes we think we're speaking in benefits; however, if you apply the following phrases, you can be sure of it.

What this means for you is . . .

Because of this, you'll be able to . . .

The bottom line for you is . . .

As a result, you can . . .

The benefits for you are . . .

For example, with Stephen's healthcare prospect, it would be a mistake to say, "This software features built-in coding intelligence."

This statement is factual; however, by itself it does not pass the "So what? Who cares?" test. We need to link the feature directly to the reward the listener receives.

"This software features built-in coding intelligence. Because of this, you'll be able to ensure proper reimbursement for your hospital, improve the efficiency of coders, and optimize revenue."

Broadly speaking, the short words are the best, and the old words best of all.

—WINSTON CHURCHILL

Craft and Repeat Power Phrases

A power phrase helps your customer visualize how they will feel when they own your product or use your service. The repeated use of an effective power phrase motivates your customer to convert that feeling into reality; therefore, these carefully selected words can actually trigger buying behavior. To craft your power phrase, start by listing some of the major benefits your customers gain when they buy from you. If applicable, use high-impact words to articulate the benefits:

Affordable	Low Cost	More Time	New
Best	Guarantee	Save	Proven
Fast	Enjoy	Reduce	Results
Easy	More Money	Discover	Safe
Free			

As a handy tip, use a series of three words or phrases to make the power phrase more memorable, dramatic, and rhythmic in the audience's mind. For example:

➤ Enjoy power, performance, and speed.

➤ You'll save time, save money, and get immediate results.

➤ It's fast, easy, and affordable.

➤ You can safely access your data anywhere, anytime, anyplace.

➤ Reduce hassle, reduce cost, reduce complaints.

➤ Enjoy it at home, in the office, or in your car.

LANGUAGE TO AVOID

Which of these two statements do you find to be more effective?

"I think you might like this new service we offer."

Or

"I believe you're really going to like this new service we offer."

The difference in wording is fairly subtle, but the influence communicated to your customer can be profound. Reread each sentence. The first one contains two weak words, "think" and "might." These words make the speaker sound unsure or insecure about the message, and subtly undermine his or her credibility. Notice how the second sentence is confident and strong. Replace the word "think" with "believe" and strike the tentative "might." That's a statement from someone who believes in what he's saying.

Eliminate Weak Words

In addition to "think" and "might," here are a few other "weak" words to strike from your vocabulary.

- ➤ Just: I was just calling to see if you want to serve on my committee.
- ➤ Wondering: I was wondering if you might want to present at next Monday's staff meeting.
- ➤ Hope: I sure hope we can accomplish this by Friday.
- ➤ If: If you close the deal, we'll celebrate at your favorite restaurant.

Instead, simply eliminate the weak word and transform the tentative sentence into a confident statement:

- ➤ I'm calling to see if you want to serve on my committee.
- ➤ Would you like to present at next Monday's staff meeting?
- ➤ I'm confident we can accomplish this by Friday.
- ➤ When you close the deal, we'll celebrate at your favorite restaurant. (Replace the word "if" with the word "when" to make it a positive affirmation.)

Avoid Validation Questions

Once you've made your statement or recommendation, simply stop. Avoid tacking on unnecessary words or an approval-seeking question. For example:

- ➤ I think that's acceptable, don't you?
- ➤ This is how we'll proceed, okay?
- ➤ That costs too much, doesn't it?

Instead, drop the unnecessary discrediting question. Don't ask permission or seek an approving nod; make the statement confidently. For example:

- ➤ Yes, I believe that's acceptable.
- ➤ This is how we'll proceed.
- ➤ That costs too much—it's not in the budget.

If you sincerely want to solicit the other person's opinion, use a distinct and separate question, such as:

- ➤ Yes, I believe that's acceptable. Tell me what you think.

Don't Hedge

Avoid the habit of evading the issue or seeming overly cautious.

- ➤ If it's okay with everyone, I sort of thought we might start the meeting now.
- ➤ I kind of wanted to work on that project.
- ➤ Hmmm, I have a little problem with your approach.

Instead, make confident, direct statements with no hedging. For example:

- ➤ Good morning everyone—it's time to begin the meeting.
- ➤ Bob, I'd like to work on that project. Here's what I can contribute . . .
- ➤ I don't understand this decision. Please help me understand the logic.

Stop Discounting

Eliminate any prefacing phrase that demeans or negates what you're about to say. For example:

- I may be wrong, but I think we're 10 percent over budget.
- I'm not sure about this, but I'm guessing we need one additional employee.
- This may be a silly idea, but why don't we conduct the quarterly meetings online instead.

Instead, simply drop the "but" and get rid of the phrase that belittles the conclusion. For example:

- Based on my data, we're 10 percent over budget.
- We need to hire one additional employee to meet our productivity goal for the year.
- To save on travel costs and optimize everyone's time, I recommend we conduct the quarterly meetings online instead.

Drop "Try"

Imagine your boss says to you, "I need your proposal by 10 AM tomorrow for the customer meeting." Your reply is, "Okay. I'll try to get it finished." The word "try" implies the possibility it may not get finished. It presupposes possible failure. Why not say, "I'll get it finished" or "I'll have it on your desk by 9 AM."

Replace "But" with "And"

The word "but" cancels anything that comes before it. Imagine if your significant other said to you, "Honey, I love you, but . . ." Similarly, imagine if Stephen, in the earlier example, had said, "Yes, our implementation process is fast, easy, and economical, but we don't have a time slot available until June." The "but" creates a negative that didn't exist before, offsetting the benefits of fast, easy, and economical. Replace the "but" with "and" and hear the difference: "Yes, our implementation process is fast, easy, and economical, *and* we have a time slot available for you in June." Most of the time, "and" can be easily substituted for "but," *and* with positive results!

Replace Negatives with Positives

Rather than announcing what you can't or won't do, why not create better collaboration and rapport with your listeners and state what you *can* do? Here are some examples of how to turn negatives into positives:

Negative: I'm sorry. We can't do that.

Positive: Here's an alternative we can try.

Negative: Our company policy won't allow that.

Positive: Let me check with the legal department to see what our options are.

Negative: You shouldn't have waited so long to tell me about this.

Positive: Next time, please feel free to call me right away. I'm here to help.

CHAPTER 11: EXECUTIVE SUMMARY

- ► Say "You" and "Your" more than "I-Me-My-Mine."
- ► Use action verbs.
- ► Convince with cause-and-effect phrases.
- ► Employ benefit phrases to answer "So what? Who cares?"
- ► Craft and repeat power phrases.
- ► Eliminate weak words.
- ► Avoid validation questions.
- ► Don't hedge.
- ► Stop discounting.
- ► Drop the word "try."
- ► Replace "but" with "and."
- ► Replace negatives with positives.

CHAPTER 12

Handling Q&A with Credibility and Finesse

> Before I refuse to take your questions,
> I have an opening statement.
>
> —RONALD REAGAN

You have just concluded your powerful, persuasive presentation. Feeling confident, you pause, and with a sparkle in your eye, you step forward and say, "I welcome any questions or comments you may have."

With all the preparation and hard work you put into your presentation, answering the questions should be easy. However, many of my clients tell me the Q&A session strikes fear and dread in their hearts, especially if tough, critical-minded decision makers are in the audience. Preparation is the key. By following these simple and proven techniques, you will be perceived by listeners as credible, confident, and in control.

TECHNIQUES FOR HANDLING QUESTIONS AND ANSWERS LIKE A PRO

Here are a few of my favorite tips on how to approach this critical and interactive aspect of your presentation.

Adopt and Convey a Positive Attitude

Take on a mindset that embraces interaction with an audience—including objections, feedback, and discussion. All of these are opportunities. When decision makers offer objections, they're telling you something that will help you better understand their problem. Therefore, objections *help* you.

Anticipate the Questions Your Audience Is Likely to Ask

As you prepare your presentation, ask yourself, "What objections or questions might this audience pose?" Take the time to predict and prepare for probable questions. Write down these questions and think about the answers. You may want to ask a few colleagues for input. When you predict and plan appropriately, you'll be able to craft well-thought-out answers, increase your own sense of self-confidence, and prevent an audience member catching you off guard.

Rehearse Your Replies Aloud

Get comfortable with your choice of words and tone of voice. Role-play with coworkers. Ask for coaching. Rehearsal will greatly reduce your nerves and help portray you as the expert you are.

Prepare Questions *You* Want to Answer

This is a tried-and-true technique used by masterful politicians. Besides predicting what the audience is likely to ask, make sure you use the Q&A session to reinforce key points that are critical to your message. This technique also comes in handy when no one asks a question and there is an awkward delay. To segue smoothly, you can say, "One question I am often asked is . . ." This helps break the ice and primes others to ask questions. You may also arrange to have a few "planted" questions in the audience to kick things off.

Give the Audience Guidelines

Let them know when you would like them to ask questions. Do you welcome questions throughout the presentation? Would you prefer them at the end? Are you comfortable with both? Direct your listeners accordingly. For example, you could say, "The purpose of this meeting is to address the topics most important to you. So, by all means, feel free to ask your questions throughout the presentation. I've also left twenty minutes at the conclusion for Q&A." Or, "Due to the amount of content we have to cover, if you don't mind, please hold your questions until the end. I've allotted twenty minutes at the conclusion to address your concerns." Caution: When presenting to senior leadership and high-level decision makers, my advice is to invite them to ask questions throughout your presentation. It's my experience that they will interrupt with questions regardless of your direction.

Display Confident, Open Body Language

When you take a question, be sure to turn toward the questioner. Extend an open palm forward to indicate you welcome their question. If possible, take a step or two toward the questioner. Square your shoulders and fully face the individual. This movement indicates you are giving your full attention to that person and their concern. Do not take a step back or move away from the questioner. This implies withdrawal or recoiling. Maintain eye contact with the questioner. Display neutral to pleasant facial expressions and avoid scowling or sending any negative cues. Stand tall with a confident posture. Keep your weight evenly balanced on both feet. Nod your head occasionally to indicate that you understand the questioner. Do not fold your arms across your body or cross your legs; both of these mannerisms convey a closed stance. Express openness and sincerity through natural, relaxed gestures and body movement. Avoid distracting mannerisms, such as clenching or clasping hands. The goal is to look calm, comfortable, and fully engaged.

Listen Carefully to the Entire Question

We've all seen speakers who interrupt and jump to the answer before the questioner is finished. Not waiting to hear the entire question results in at least two errors: First, you may provide a response that misses the mark and jeopardizes your credibility. Second, you may be viewed as being rude and impatient. So, give the questioner time to formulate their question. Be patient. Force yourself to listen to the entire question and make sure you understand it. Following this critical practice offers two rewards: First, it demonstrates courtesy, empathy, and understanding. Second, it gives you more time to think about your response and craft an intelligent answer.

Bonus tip: Watch your questioners' body language carefully. Does it reveal more about what they are thinking and feeling? It's always important to listen to what's being said. But sometimes it's even more important to listen to what's *not* being said.

Repeat the Question

This habit is the sign of a pro. By repeating or paraphrasing every question, you ensure that everyone in the room hears it. Plus, you give the questioner an opportunity to clarify his or her point in case you misunderstood. It also gives you more time to formulate your answer.

Ask Clarifying Questions if Necessary

If appropriate, ask the questioner a question to help define a term, or further explain the question. For example: "Don, when you say you'd like to hear more about our Business Continuity services, do you mean enterprise data backup, disaster recovery, or both?" By clarifying the question with a question, you keep your answer on target and concise.

Pause for One or Two Seconds Before Answering

Don't rush to answer. Always take time to think and gather your thoughts before you answer all questions. Do the same with those questions for which you readily know the answer. Pausing conveys confidence, composure, and consideration. It implies to the questioner that he asked a smart question (whether you think so or not). Responding too quickly implies the question has an easy answer. A quick answer also brings attention to the more difficult questions that actually do require a pause.

Remain Upbeat, Positive, and Courteous

Regardless of the attitude, tone of voice, or demeanor of the questioner, you should always be sure to remain in control and present a positive image. A key way to convey your composure is by speaking intentionally, in a pleasant, polite tone. I have known decision makers who play the "Stump the Expert" game. They try to throw you off guard and test your tolerance threshold. You can outsmart them by avoiding knee-jerk reactions that include an irritated or curt tone of voice. By pausing after each question, you're able to choose your attitude and respond in a thoughtful, controlled, and confident tone of voice.

Avoid Rating or Judging the Question

One of the most common errors I hear in Q&A sessions is when the presenter exclaims to one questioner, "Great question!" and then adds no editorial commentary to the next questioner. This can leave the second audience member wondering, "What was wrong with my question? Wasn't it great, too?" Rating the question carries another risk: it may seem patronizing or demeaning to the decision maker. I've heard senior leaders frequently respond to such judgments with retorts like, "I know it's a great question—that's why I asked it." Ideally, avoid any form of rating and just answer the question. Or, credit all questioners equally with variations such as, "Thank you for the question," "I appreciate that point," "That brings up a helpful insight," or "Thanks for making that connection."

Follow the K.I.S.S. Formula

Keep your answers short and simple. Especially with time-conscious, results-oriented decision makers, be concise. I once heard a CEO ask his finance director, "Are our cash equivalents truly liquid?" He wanted a yes or a no. The director said yes, and then launched into a detailed down-in-the-weeds analysis of why. The CEO interrupted him. "You answered my question five minutes ago. Let's move on."

To optimize Q&A sessions with decision makers, get to the bottom line quickly and say only what you *must* say. Ideally, strive for crisp answers that take one minute or less. If a longer explanation is required, ask the audience if they want to hear more, or offer to follow up after the presentation. Get to the point and avoid repeating yourself or belaboring the point.

Answer Only the Question That Was Asked.

I've seen many presenters dig a hole for themselves by bringing up information that was not requested. Steve, a sales manager for a large software company, spent several weeks searching for the right vendor for his annual sales-training conference. He was thrilled with his selection and had worked out all the details. His boss, the senior vice president of marketing, asked Bob during a presentation, "Have you found a vendor to provide your sales training?" Bob said, "Yes we have. The vendor is ABC Associates. I've audited their course and the curriculum is right on target to meet our goals." That would have been enough. Bob, however, went on to volunteer everything from the session outline to the trainers' credentials and finally (much to his regret) the cost. The vice president interrupted and said, "There's no room in the budget for an increase over last year's amount. Find another vendor who's less expensive." If Bob had answered only the question that was asked, he'd have been able to move ahead with his preferred vendor, and not launch the search process all over again!

Deliver Your Answer to the Entire Audience

As discussed earlier, begin each answer by looking intently at the questioner before delivering the rest of the answer to the entire audience. However, as you begin to repeat the question and respond with an answer, be sure to include and address the rest of the audience. Turn your answer into a mini-presentation delivered to the entire group. Otherwise, you and the questioner enter into a private dialogue and other listeners may feel alienated.

Don't Guess at the Answer

If you don't know the answer, admit it. Don't guess. Say, "I don't know the answer to that—I'll be glad to find out and get the answer to you by this afternoon." Your candor will mean more to your audience than guessing, rambling, or trying to fake it. Be sure to have pen and paper ready, or assign a scribe to record these questions. Also, leverage the intelligence of the group. It often works very well to ask the audience—including your colleagues—if they know the answer. And be sure to thank anyone who provides input. Some audience members may not necessarily have questions. Instead they want to participate by providing their input, ideas, experience, stories, or advice. Show appreciation any time an audience member speaks up to contribute a point, whether you agree with their opinion or not.

Once you've answered the question, confirm that you've answered it. Ask the questioner, "Does that answer your question?" "Is that helpful?" or "Was that the information you were looking for?" This gives questioners an opportunity to say, "No, not quite. Could you elaborate more on . . ."

Manage Your Time Wisely

As you move through the Q&A session, be aware of the time—and manage it appropriately. Depending on whether you invite questions throughout the presentation, take them at the end, or do both, be sure to watch the clock and stay on time. Say, "I see we have a couple of minutes remaining—there's time for one more question." Invite audience members to either write down their remaining questions and leave them on the table or e-mail them to you for follow-up. Be sure to end the meeting on time.

Handle the Over-Talker with Tact

What about the persistent, long-winded audience member who asks dozens of questions and belabors a point? Remain polite, but don't allow the person to ramble on, hijack your agenda, and frustrate others. Take control. Start with patience. Remain calm and polite—the audience will admire you for this. Avoid saying anything that may be perceived as rude or curt. On the other hand, you can't let the person monopolize the meeting; it's unfair to the rest of the audience. I call this technique "Interrupting with a Compliment." When you're ready to cut him off and move on, literally interject praise or a kind word, then redirect. Say, "Chris, you're raising some interesting points and I appreciate your insights. In respect of everyone's time, let's discuss these issues further after the presentation." Then step away from Chris, look at another part of the audience, and say, "Does anyone else have a point to contribute or a question?" By politely taking control, you're sending a strong signal to Chris that his time is over and it's someone else's turn.

Invite the Audience to Write Down Their Questions

To ensure you engage everyone in the Q&A session, have pen and paper available for people to write down their questions during your presentation. They might not want to interrupt you during a point. Unless they're reminded to write down their questions, they could forget what they were going to ask earlier. Also, particularly in large group settings, some audience members may be hesitant to ask questions in public. Say, "If any of you would prefer to write your questions and pass them forward, I'll be happy to address your points."

Conclude with a Rehearsed Summary

Don't end your presentation with the Q&A session. As the presenter, *you* get the last word. After you conclude the Q&A session and thank everyone for their input, provide a second summary. Deliver an abbreviated recap emphasizing your key points. Make sure your last words are your most important ones—actionable and memorable.

DEALING WITH DIFFICULT DECISION MAKERS AND TOUGH QUESTIONS

You cannot shake hands with a clenched fist.

—INDIRA GANDHI

Let's face it. Difficult audience members are a fact of life. They blame, attack, complain, whine, sabotage, vent, nitpick, and even try to stump you. At best, these individuals add a level of adrenaline that keeps you on your toes. At worst, they can derail you and keep you from delivering a powerful, persuasive message. It is fully within your power to control and optimize these difficult situations. By practicing the following techniques, you can smoothly overcome obstacles posed by the toughest decision maker, and emerge as the confident, credible, and composed professional you are.

Most important: Don't take it personally. Whatever questions a person asks, in whatever tone of voice, strive to de-personalize it. It's not about you. Separate the content of the question (which may be logical) from the questioner's attitude and tone of voice (which are emotional). A person's anger, hostility, or rudeness reveals more about him than about you. Maintain your emotional composure. Say to yourself: "This is not about me."

Empathize with such questioners. Try to feel what they're feeling. Within yourself, become curious as to why they're having this emotional reaction. Rather than becoming defensive and trying to prove you're right and they're wrong (which rarely ends well), seek first to understand them. Sometimes, someone who is upset just wants to be heard. For example:

- ➤ "Donna, I appreciate your conviction on this issue. It's a critically important concern."
- ➤ "Ralph, you make an interesting point. Please say more about why you believe . . ."
- ➤ "I can understand why you're upset."
- ➤ "Yes, I see your point."

Acknowledge that you hear the person's viewpoint. Recognize that he has a right to share his opinion, whether you agree with it or not. After listening patiently, validate that you hear and understand him. For example, "Thank you, Frank. I hear your point." Or, "Your point is clear. I appreciate your sharing your perspective."

Find agreement and establish common ground. Find something that allows you to see eye-to-eye with this person. If there's anything relevant to the discussion you agree on, highlight it to help diffuse hostility. For example:

➤ "Ted, we both agree that expenses are too high . . ."

➤ "We both share a common goal to improve customer service . . ."

➤ "You're right, Tom. Research has proven . . ."

➤ "Yes, I see what you mean. My own experience tells me that . . ."

➤ "Rhonda, I see your point. The data here supports your recommendation."

Put the question in neutral. When faced with confrontational or hostile questions, pause and look for the legitimate reasoning within it. Emotional intelligence gives you the ability to separate the attitude of the questioner from the content of the question. If the question is emotionally charged, rephrase it so that it sounds unbiased and noncombative. Restate the attack in the form of a logical, valid question. For example: "I agree with you, Bill. Timely delivery is a key aspect of customer service. What I believe I hear you asking is, 'Will this type of delay happen again?' The answer is no, it won't."

Don't ignore a question. It could be taken as a sign of hostility on your part. Even if you deem questions inappropriate, ill timed, or off topic, acknowledge them.

Always remain courteous and polite. As Will Rogers once said, "When you fly off the handle, you usually make a bad landing." Never, ever lose your cool. If you display negative emotions such as anger, sarcasm, or scorn you lose credibility and integrity. Separate the content from the person's tone and attitude. Realize it's not about you. Pause. Remain neutral. Restate calmly.

Ultimately, do not indulge another's disrespectful behavior. After you make two or three respectful attempts to resolve and neutralize the issue, politely offer to continue the discussion after the meeting. Disengage and move on. "Sue, as I've said, I hear you and agree that this is an important issue. In respect of everyone's time and our agreed-upon agenda, I'm not going to continue this discussion in this setting. I'll be happy to meet with you after the meeting."

OBJECTION-HANDLING TECHNIQUES

The more technique you have, the less you have to worry about it.

—PABLO PICASSO

If you're in the sales profession, you know that a key factor in gaining the prospects' business is the ability to effectively handle their objections. An objection is first and foremost a sign that at some level the prospect is interested in buying. To the best of your ability, welcome objections. Think of them as harbingers of good news because they indicate you have a potential buyer—and therefore a good chance of selling. Use the following techniques to expertly prepare for and handle objections. The more times you deal with a particular objection, the better you will become.

Feel, Felt, Found: The Customer Testimonial

This technique provides the most powerful form of marketing: third-party testimonial. You empathize with how the person *feels*, then associate him with a group that once *felt* the same way (or experienced the same issue). Since the group *found* your solution to be successful, the person usually wants to follow.

> Example: "Bob, thank you for that question. I understand how you <u>feel</u> about risk mitigation and quality outcomes. Other customers, such as XYZ Corporation, have <u>felt</u> the same way. What they have <u>found</u> after implementing our solutions is a 30 percent savings in . . .

Checklist

Begin by asking for the audience's questions, concerns, and objections. Write them on a flip chart. Verify that if you successfully address each one, the next step toward partnership may be taken. Then, as you handle each one, place a green check mark next to it.

> Example: "Sally, have we addressed your main concerns regarding more accurate coding and reduced transcription costs? [Sally says yes.] Great, I'll check that one off the list."

Then in the closing and call to action, you can confidently say, "As you can see from these check marks, our proposed solution successfully achieves 95 percent of your initiatives. We at Acme would value the opportunity to partner with Martin General to ensure you achieve this list of stated goals. Is there anything standing in the way of your moving forward with our solution? Let's open the floor for discussion and next steps."

Parking Lot

You may want to write or "park" an objection or question on the flip chart when:

- ➤ You don't have the answer to an objection;

- ➤ You have the answer, but don't want to give it at the moment because doing so would be unwise; or

- ➤ The objection is out of sequence with your presentation and you'll cover it later.

In all cases, listen to the objection and show understanding.

> Example: "Thank you, Ray. I'll write that down and we can come back to it later. The next section addresses that very issue . . ."
>
> Or, "Thanks, Sue. John Brown would have the most up-to-date figures on that. Let me write it down so I don't forget, and I'll get back to you first thing tomorrow."
>
> Or, "I appreciate that question, Lisa. Our legal department would need to answer that. I'll ask Jane Davis, our chief counsel, to contact you tomorrow."

Preempting

What main objection is this particular audience sure to have? Rather than letting them ask it and drive a stake in the ground on the issue, be sure to preempt the question by bringing it up first. Preempting addresses the objection right away and prevents the audience from "losing face" or being proven wrong. Offer a brief customer testimonial of someone who had the same objection, but experienced success after resolving it. Here's an example of preempting a prospect's concern about changing software in their hospital:

> "If you're like most of our clients, the fear of change is often a common objection to physician solutions. Change can be scary—it feels uncomfortable, it's unpopular, and seems costly. Another hospital that is similar in size to you, Memorial Mission, objected to change at first. But within three months, 100 percent of their Emergency Department physicians had adopted the tool and was using it daily. This yielded a 15 percent increase in billable charges for the hospital, plus they had zero chart deficiencies. In the words of their chief medical officer, "The change was definitely worth it."

Big Picture

If the objection concerns a detailed feature of the product, you elevate the discussion by offering the "Big Picture" view. Remind the questioner of their larger vision: their overall goal, mission, target, or objective. Emphasize how your solution addresses their main concerns and solves their primary issues. A higher, broader perspective can make the small, specific issues seem insignificant.

> "You're right, Mark. The current version of this software does not currently perform that particular alert function. However, that feature will not affect the overall success of our plan. When we look at your major goals of improved financial performance, improved patient safety, and rapid adoption, this solution guarantees results faster and more cost-effectively than any other tool on the market."

Justification

Rather than fight the objection, justify why it is reasonable. In fact, turn the objection into a benefit. Tell the audience member the supporting reason behind her complaint.

> "Yes, you're right, Lynn. Our solution does cost more than the competition. That slight differential is necessary because it allows us to provide you with 100 percent more value. For example, with Acme's solution you get A, B, and C, whereas with other vendors you don't."

Reprioritizing

When the decision maker has a priority that is stopping him from buying from you, find ways of changing the order of his priorities. Appeal to the company's core values, mission statement, reputation, and financial performance. Recognize and validate the decision maker's current priority and lower its hierarchy. Show him how another priority is really more important and emphasize how your solution delivers it.

> "Dan, you've mentioned that loyalty is a key value. You're devoted to your current supplier and that's admirable. You and the chief officers have also mentioned that financial performance is a top priority. If I could show you how we as a new vendor would save you 30 percent

more than the current supplier and add $_____ to your bottom line in the first year, would you consider a change?"

Pushback

If the questioner is wrong, push back respectfully and assertively. Object to the objection. Avoid blaming or shaming the person, pointing fingers, or getting defensive; simply state the truth about your solution in a positive and courteous manner. For example:

Questioner: If the software in our emergency department isn't fully integrated, it greatly impacts patient safety. The word on the street is that your solution has zero integration and that it doesn't connect well to the rest of the platform.

Answer: Thank you, Randy. I appreciate your bringing up the critical points of integration and patient safety. Those are both hallmarks of our solution. Unfortunately, you've received some false information. The Acme solution *is* indeed fully integrated. Rest assured, this solution definitely delivers the quality clinical outcomes you're looking for. May I arrange a visit with one of our reference sites where you can see this integration in action? Would you be available later this month?

CHAPTER 12: EXECUTIVE SUMMARY

Techniques for Handling Questions, Objections, and Answers Like a Pro

- ➤ Adopt and convey a positive attitude.
- ➤ Anticipate questions and rehearse your replies aloud ahead of time.
- ➤ Prepare questions *you* to want answer and ensure these points are covered.
- ➤ Display confident open body language and speak with a pleasant tone of voice.
- ➤ Listen carefully to the entire question. Repeat it and ask clarifying questions if necessary.
- ➤ Pause before answering the question.
- ➤ Avoid rating or judging the question, and be sure to keep your answer short and simple.
- ➤ Deliver your answer to the entire audience, not just the questioner.

- Don't guess at the answer.
- Confirm you've answered the audience members' questions and thank them.
- Manage the time and stay in control.
- Encourage audience members to write down their questions.
- Don't end your presentation with the Q&A session. Provide a second short summary to reinforce key points.
- When dealing with difficult people and hostile questions, don't take it personally.
- Empathize with the questioner and acknowledge that you hear the person's viewpoint.
- Find agreement and establish common ground.
- Put the question in neutral.
- Don't ignore a question, and always remain courteous and polite.

Seizing Every Opportunity to Persuade Decision Makers

CHAPTER 13

Planning and Conducting Powerful Conversations

> **Seek first to understand, then to be understood.**
>
> —STEPHEN R. COVEY

During my one-on-one private coaching sessions, I often ask the business leader with whom I'm working, "What exactly do you get paid to do?" The answers vary from person to person: Set the strategy and vision for my company or division; build culture; coach and lead others; create teams; allocate resources; form alliances; grow the business; secure clients; identify innovations, find new markets; hire and develop talent, and so on.

I then ask, "If I videotaped you on the job performing these tasks, and then we sat down and watched the tape, what would we actually see you doing?" This time every person gives a similar answer: *listening and talking*. In other words, leaders get paid to conduct conversations—ideally, conversations that get results.

When you think about it, your most basic responsibility as a leader is to connect with those around you. Whether it's in a conference room or over the phone, in the elevator or hallway, giving a performance review or meeting with customers, you are listening and talking with people; you are having conversations. Ideally, those conversations are powerful, influential, and meaningful.

Are your conversations creating the outcomes you desire? Does everyone involved feel heard and understood? Do you rely on a process that ensures a results-oriented conversation? Ultimately, a leader's success depends on the quality of his conversations. The purpose of this chapter is to provide you with some best practices on how to plan, conduct, and measure powerful conversations.

WHAT IS A POWERFUL CONVERSATION?

A powerful conversation is different from an ordinary conversation. It's not a friendly chat over lunch, or bantering with colleagues in a meeting, or interacting socially at a party, or catching up with a friend. Those interactions don't necessarily produce results. For our purposes here, the term "powerful conversation" implies intention, objectives, and results. It's a discussion between two or more people that includes an agenda, the open exchange of thoughts and desired outcomes, and an agreement regarding action steps and mutual commitments.

When Do You Need a Powerful Conversation?

I've asked many of my clients, "On what occasions do you conduct powerful conversations?" One of the most memorable replies came from Carolyn, a chief officer in a multibillion-dollar bank holding company: "Every time I need someone to help me." Paraphrasing the seventeenth-century English poet John Donne, Carolyn continued, "No man or woman is an island." Her reference to Donne's 1624 prose work, *Devotions upon Emergent Occasions*, was striking to me. It indicates why Carolyn is one of the most admired leaders in her field. In the meditation, Donne is comparing all of humanity to a continent and therefore each person is a piece of the continent, not an island. Donne goes on to say that if a clod breaks off from a continent, the continent is less than it was before.

That's how Carolyn feels about her team. Replace the word "continent" with "corporation," and you have Carolyn's management style and leadership philosophy. As one of Carolyn's long-time colleagues told me in an interview, "She has thousands of people working for her, and somehow she makes them all feel valued." I heard the legendary story of how Carolyn dropped what she was doing, boarded a plane, and flew halfway around the globe to meet with Adam, one of the firm's stellar global analysts. He had announced his sudden resignation the day before, after being wooed by the competition. Carolyn's colleague shrugged her shoulders, shook her head, and summed it up: "Carolyn met with him; they talked; he stayed." How did she do it?

CONDUCTING POWERFUL CONVERSATIONS: A FOUR-STEP PROCESS

Later, as I listened to Carolyn describe the details of the meeting, it became apparent that she had conducted a powerful conversation with Adam. You can learn to achieve the same kind of results by following four basic but important steps.

Step One: Establish Mutual Objectives and Purpose

Carolyn began the conversation with Adam by briefly setting up her own agenda and explaining why she was there. First and foremost, she said she wanted to hear Adam's side of the story and understand why he resigned. She spoke honestly and openly about her feelings and beliefs regarding his resignation. She was not afraid to express sincere vulnerability by telling Adam she wanted him to remain on her team, that she needed his talent, that the company was exposed to risk without him, and that she believed the company and the role were right for him. She also shared genuine appreciation for his years of service and contributions to the company.

Next, Carolyn asked Adam what *he* would like to accomplish in the conversation and invited him to share his objectives. He said he was frustrated, confused, and angry. Since she had come so far, he would be willing to tell Carolyn why he had decided to leave the company.

In this initial step, an effective leader goes first and gets the ball rolling, especially if the topic is emotionally charged or laced with conflict. The critical success factor in this step is *sincerity*. Be open, approachable, and transparent. Don't shy away from expressing what you need from the person and the conversation. Your candor and authenticity create an emotional connection with the other person that in turn gives him the green light to open up and express what he wants to accomplish.

Step Two: Express Mutual Needs and Wants

After this brief introduction of establishing goals and purpose, Carolyn quickly moved into the main body of the conversation, which is built on asking good questions and facilitating meaningful dialogue. Carolyn realized

Adam's agenda was as important as hers—she knew in order to fulfill her own wants and needs, she must likewise do her best to fulfill Adam's. Doing this requires gaining clarity by asking good questions, listening actively, and facilitating meaningful dialogue. Carolyn began to probe for Adam's thoughts, feelings, wants, and needs. During the dialogue, she interspersed plenty of thoughtful open-ended questions that gave Adam the opportunity to speak his mind.

- "Adam, please help me understand—Why have you decided to leave the company? What were the key events or issues responsible for your resignation?"
- "What do you feel your new employer offers you that we don't?"
- "You've spent over a decade with our team. What do you value about our company? About your job?"
- "What are your views about our firm's management and leadership?"
- "How was your relationship with your manager?"
- "What would you recommend to help us create a better workplace?"

By asking critical questions and actively listening, Carolyn was able to confirm her understanding and gain agreement with Adam on the basic reasons for his resignation:

- *Anger.* He felt he deserved more recognition for a high-profile, profitable deal that he'd led.
- *Frustration.* He believed the executive committee was not listening to him or following his recommendations.
- *Lack of Direction.* He needed guidance from management.
- *Need for Change.* He was bored and wanted more challenging projects.
- *Feeling Unappreciated.* He was 4,000 miles from corporate headquarters and rarely had face-to-face meetings with senior executives; he felt ignored and out of the loop.

During the powerful conversation, Carolyn's eyes were opened. Finally, she understood Adam's perspective. She gained clarity and discovered important facts and assumptions. Carolyn admitted to Adam she had no idea he'd been so unhappy, and she expressed her deep regret for his discontent.

Carolyn also knew that a powerful conversation has two sides. Once she had gained clarity on Adam's issues, it was time for her to elaborate in more detail on her needs and wants; that is, to express her side of the story and tell Adam why she needed him to stay on board.

- ➤ She needed Adam's highly specialized expertise to successfully spearhead the company's largest merger and acquisition to date.

- ➤ She wanted him to complete several significant outstanding deals that would likely be jeopardized by his leaving.

- ➤ She needed him to mentor a new analyst in the region who'd be starting in a month.

- ➤ She reminded Adam that the company had recently funded his MBA and advanced certification training with the expectation he would invest that education into the company.

- ➤ She also expressed her disappointment that he resigned abruptly, without ever communicating his dissatisfaction directly to her.

The second step—the critical success factor—is *seeking understanding*. An effective leader seeks to understand the other person; to gain clarity by probing for his or her wants and needs, ultimately for the good of all involved. Contrary to the autocratic style of management where the leader has all the answers, a participative style employs the powerful conversation to consider the needs and opinions of others, to bring out the group's best thinking, and to direct those conversations toward a positive outcome. In this setting, the leader creates a safe environment where people can say things they might not say under ordinary circumstances. It's critical, however, that when people say something controversial or contrary to the status quo, or when they ask tough questions, the effective leader affirms them in real time and incorporates their comments into the larger conversation. Be sure to ask questions like Carolyn did in order to uncover assumptions and discover the real facts behind the issue. Along the way, validate the other's contributions (whether you agree or not) and avoid making the other person wrong (which implies you're right). Ideally, both parties participate in a powerful conversation with equal enthusiasm and effort in a genuine attempt to take understanding to the next level.

As you can imagine, your partners in a powerful conversation may be reserved and not forthcoming at first. Often, employees are afraid that if they say what they are actually thinking, they will get into trouble. My clients tell me that gradually, when they see that no one has been fired, or even reprimanded, for speaking their mind, the gateway of candor opens. In fact, this safe, open environment creates more energetic discussion and makes people feel that they're playing a role in shaping the future. More important, it actually accelerates the rate of change. The sooner you get real issues on the table, the sooner you can address them and find solutions.

The second part of step two is clearly stating your own wants and needs. Once you have sought to understand the other person, it's time for *you* to be understood. This is where planning the powerful conversation is critical. In advance of meeting with the person or group, clearly define your own desired outcome in your own mind. Of course, you'll remain flexible and adaptable once you've listened to the needs of others. Understanding your own wants and needs is as important as understanding other people's wants and needs. Carolyn's ultimate need was to persuade Adam to withdraw his resignation and remain employed. Additionally, she clearly planned and delivered five supporting points to aid her argument.

Step Three: Explore New Possibilities

Because Carolyn and Adam shared their thoughts, feelings, and beliefs openly and honestly, thereby gaining clarity on each other's specific needs and wants, they were able to create new options. Again, Carolyn relied on questions to open the door of dialogue. She said, "Adam, I need your help. Would you be willing to stay? What are the possibilities?"

Adam confessed there was a time when he loved his job and the company. He began to reminisce about time in the trenches, lessons learned, and success stories. Then came the big promotion, the move abroad, differences with new management, and physical distance from headquarters. There was a long pause. He confessed to being sad and disappointed about leaving the company, but he hoped the competitor's offer would provide more satisfaction. Carolyn asked, "What needs to happen to keep you on our team, Adam? How can we work together to restore this relationship?"

The tables began to turn. Before long, both Adam and Carolyn were fully engaged in a brainstorming session about the new possibilities. What could Carolyn and other management members do differently to optimize Adam's employment? What could Adam do differently? What processes needed to change? According to Carolyn, they both built off each other's ideas, perspectives, and logic. There was note-taking, rapport, synergy, hope, and a renewed trust.

The key success factor in step three is *curiosity*. English author Samuel Johnson asserted in the late 1700s, "Curiosity is one of the most permanent and certain characteristics of a vigorous intellect." The same is true today, especially when it comes to conducting a powerful conversation. All too often, leaders skip this critical stage. Their results-oriented personality urges them to jump directly into an action plan. It's critically important, however, to invest some extra time to imagine all the possible options and alternatives. Ask "What if?" "What's doable?" "What's possible?" A great leader challenges his or her team to stretch their thinking and go beyond textbook answers; to explore new boundaries and enter a space of curiosity where new possibilities emerge. Once all participants have clearly shared their needs and wants—and fully explored what's possible in meeting those goals—you'll have a solid foundation for the final step: shared responsibility.

Step Four: Commit to Mutual Action

Carolyn asked, "Now that I understand your side of the story and you understand mine, if I agree to correct the issues that are within my control, will you agree to stay?"

Adam agreed to remain with the company. At Carolyn's urging, he also committed to speaking up, communicating his issues at the appropriate levels, and dealing with conflict more effectively. He agreed to schedule quarterly visits to headquarters to meet with senior leaders face-to-face to communicate his strategies. He consented to work with a communication coach to help improve his presentation skills. (As it turned out, the executive committee had been listening, but they didn't understand many of his recommendations due to his laborious delivery style and overly complex content.)

In turn, Carolyn agreed to a biweekly meeting with Adam for the next six months to ensure he had a clear sense of direction and purpose. In addition to the large merger and acquisition project that she promised Adam, she also agreed to place him on a plum project in a new market under a different manager. And to ensure he felt properly recognized for the large, headline-making deal in which he had to this point gone unnoticed, she committed to make a concentrated effort with their public relations department to get personal coverage for him in several trade publications.

Together they confirmed the commitments each had made and agreed to follow up the conversation in writing. Carolyn thanked Adam for his consideration and for agreeing to remain on the team. In closing she asked,

"Adam, I've certainly received what I needed out of this conversation and I'm thrilled you've decided to stay. Did you get what you needed out of the conversation? How do you feel about the outcome?"

Adam concurred. He said it was very helpful to hear Carolyn's side of the story and gain a better understanding of management's perspective; he appreciated her flying sixteen hours round-trip to invite him to stay; and he felt the conversation had laid the groundwork for a stronger working relationship. They shook hands and Carolyn flew home.

Having the knowledge and courage to conduct a powerful conversation enabled Carolyn to save a very important piece of her "continent" from falling away. She knew that neither she nor Adam was an island. They needed each other to create new opportunities and optimize outcomes.

The key differentiator between powerful conversations versus the ordinary run-of-the-mill variety is measurable outcomes. As Shakespeare wrote in his play *Coriolanus*, "Action is eloquence." *Action* is the critical success factor in the fourth step of this process.

According to a survey I conducted with more than 100 senior leaders in corporate America, the number one reason for nonproductive conversations and meetings is *non-action*. Some of the responses include the failure to:

➤ Take charge of an issue
➤ Allow both parties to walk away believing their own agenda was advanced
➤ Gain the person's commitment
➤ Clearly articulate action steps
➤ Hold people accountable for their duties and responsibilities
➤ Implement agreed-upon outcomes
➤ Achieve alignment, shared understanding, and next steps with decision makers
➤ Reach a mutual agreement on action

It's critical that all action items are clear and explicit and that each person commits to his or her to-do list. Clear mutual commitment is crucial. It provides everyone involved with pride of ownership and a sense of shared responsibility; it provides measureable results; it helps achieve the participants' goals; and it helps prevent non-action due to misunderstandings or unclear expectations.

RELATE TO CREATE POWERFUL CONVERSATIONS

What about you? How can you conduct powerful conversations that get results? As a leader, you have the opportunity every day to create powerful conversations. Whatever your title, company, or industry, the best way to communicate your vision, strengthen relationships, and gain commitment is through powerful conversation.

Sales conversations motivate teams to find new business and provide better account management. Negotiation conversations produce agreements and preserve partnerships. Recruitment conversations inspire people to sign up and lend support. Strategy conversations define the vision and chart the course. Relationship conversations show respect for others and build trust. Performance conversations set clear expectations and clarify job duties. Accountability conversations confront inappropriate behavior and gain commitment on change.

The list of types and occasions for powerful conversations is endless. What matters most is that you use the four-step process presented in this chapter—adapted to your needs:

Step One: Establish mutual objectives and purpose.

Step Two: Express mutual needs and wants.

Step Three: Explore new possibilities.

Step Four: Commit to mutual action.

Now that you have a process to follow, it's critical to practice five key interpersonal communication skills necessary for effective relationship building. To make the points easy to remember, I've arranged them to form the acronym RELATE:

Reach out

Engage with questions

Listen

Align through empathy

Teach and be teachable

Enjoy

Reach Out

Like Carolyn, initiate contact with the people who are important to you, whose help and support you need. Get in touch with them and schedule a conversation. Fly halfway around the world if that's what it takes to optimize outcomes. This level of effort immediately sets you apart from the average leader. Contact, ideally face-to-face, is where it all begins. Avoid sitting in your office, held hostage to e-mail, spreadsheets, and paperwork. Reach out and go meet with people.

Engage with Questions

Showing interest in others is the cardinal rule of building rapport and cultivating a strong relationship. Most people would rather talk about themselves than hear about you. That's why it's so memorable and meaningful when you take the time to ask thoughtful questions about them and listen. Try the 80/20 rule and watch your relational skills skyrocket: Ask thoughtful questions and actively listen 80 percent of the time, and talk the other 20 percent.

Legend has it that Dale Carnegie once sat beside a famous New York gossip columnist at a fancy dinner party. To stay out of trouble and ensure his comments didn't end up in the paper the following morning, he decided he would be quiet. His only interaction with her the entire evening was to ask her questions and listen. Much to his surprise, he did end up on the front page of the social section. The columnist wrote, "Mr. Dale Carnegie is by far the best conversationalist I have ever met!"

Contrary to popular belief, the person who has the most influence is usually the one asking the most questions. This begs the question, "What types of questions are best to ask?" There are two types: open-ended and closed-ended.

Closed-ended questions

Closed-ended questions can be answered with a one- or two-word response. They are often yes-or-no questions with little room for elaborating on ideas, interpretations, or opinions: "Do you like the new strategy?" "Is your team performing well?" As you can see, the respondent could simply say "Yes" and be off the hook for further discussion. At times, closed-ended questions are certainly necessary, mainly when you need to elicit specific facts or data ("Did you say a 30 percent reduction?") or to confirm your understanding

("Did I hear you correctly—you won't be attending the meeting?"). Closed-ended questions often begin with the following words:

Do	Is	Haven't
Does	Isn't	Will
Doesn't	Can	Won't
Did	Can't	Would
Didn't	Could	Wouldn't
Are	Couldn't	
Aren't	Have	

Open-ended questions

Open-ended questions cannot be answered with one-word responses. They require some thought and detail on the part of the responder; they ask for further information, opinions, and feedback. For example, compare the difference between these two questions:

"Do you like the new strategy?" (closed-ended)

"What do you think about the new strategy?" (open-ended)

Here's another example:

"Is your team performing well?" (closed-ended)

"How would you describe the performance of your team?" (open-ended)

You may also phrase open-ended questions in the form of a statement that invites a response. Again, compare the difference:

"Aren't you ready to move forward?" (closed-ended)

"Help me understand how you would like to proceed." (open-ended)

The first question may sound defensive, even interrogative. The second is an invitation to share ideas. As you can see, open-ended questions and statements are designed to stimulate dialogue, encourage discussion, share feelings, elicit feedback, spark ideas, and invite opinions. They begin with these words and phrases:

What	Elaborate on that
How	Under what conditions
Help me understand why	Give some examples
Tell me about	What might happen if
Describe	In what areas could we

Open-ended questions ensure that you give others a chance to talk more than you do. This practice shows you have genuine interest in them and care enough to want to take the time to listen. Not only will this provide you with helpful information about them, you may also gain insight into crucial issues. Perhaps most important, this caliber of communication creates more meaningful, engaging conversations; fosters trust; and strengthens the relationship.

Listen

Ever notice that if you rearrange the letters in "listen" you get the word "silent"? In the context of a powerful conversation, to listen well is as influential a means of communication as is the ability to speak well. The following are a few guidelines to ensure you practice active listening during your powerful conversations.

Demonstrate attentiveness

When interacting with others, don't multitask. Stop what you're doing, face them fully, and make eye contact. Give them your undivided attention and tune out distractions. Even if you are capable of performing multiple activities while simultaneously listening intently to the other person, it won't appear as though you're listening. It's as important to visibly demonstrate good listening as it is to actually engage in it. Square your shoulders to the speaker to show open body language. Lean forward and nod your head from time to time to indicate engagement and understanding. Take notes if appropriate. Align your facial expressions and voice tone to reflect the feelings and emotions of the speaker. As U.S. President Woodrow Wilson once said, "The ear of the leader must ring with the voices of the people." The first duty of leadership is to listen.

Be open-minded

A fundamental cause of failure in interpersonal communication occurs when people listen so they can reply or retort rather than listening so they can understand. Too often, they want to prove themselves right and the other person wrong. This attitude poisons the potential for building rapport and trust. What most people really want in a conversation is to feel heard and understood; to be listened to, respected, and valued. Therefore, as the listener, it's critical to suspend assumptions, expectations, and prejudices. Think about what the speaker is saying, not how you're going to respond. Allow the person to express thoughts and feelings without your passing judgment, verbally or nonverbally. Remain neutral and avoid showing any sign of defensiveness. When the goal is to seek understanding and build rapport, effective leaders offer an open mind.

Practice patience

Wait for the speaker to complete her thoughts before adding yours. Avoid interrupting the other person and refrain from completing her sentences or filling in the blanks. When you rush to conclusions you remove your own incentive to listen. Even if the speaker is launching a complaint against you, don't respond until you've heard what she has to say—and be sure she knows you've heard it. Consequently, she won't feel the need to repeat herself and you'll know the whole argument before you answer. As Isaac Newton wrote, "If I have ever made any valuable discoveries, it has been owing more to patient attention, than to any other talent." There are valuable discoveries to be made in powerful conversations, and patience will help you mine them.

Verify your perceptions

Check with the speaker to be sure you heard the intended message. Occasionally restate her main points. When doing so, you're not necessarily agreeing with the speaker—you're simply paraphrasing what was said. For example, "Sue, if I understand you correctly, you're recommending that we . . . Is that accurate?" This practice not only ensures you've heard the correct message, but also confirms with the speaker that you've been actively listening; that you've heard and understood. In addition to verifying the verbal message, you may also want to verify your nonverbal perception. For example, as an active, attentive listener, you may notice body language signals or a voice tone that indicates certain feelings the speaker is experiencing. Rather than merely repeating the words the speaker has said, you might also verify the underlying emotion you perceive. For example, "I sense that you may be frustrated. How do you feel about this change in policy?"

Align Through Empathy

Empathy literally means "in feeling" as translated from its ancient Greek equivalent, *empatheia*. To show empathy is to be in alignment with another person's feelings—to appreciate, understand, and accept his or her emotions.

After hearing Carolyn's story earlier in this chapter, it may come as no surprise that she has a pair of leather moccasins hanging on a wall in her office to remind her of the Native American proverb, "Never criticize a man until you've walked a mile in his moccasins." Empathy begins with awareness of another person's feelings, often unspoken. Sometimes, the most important thing in communication is hearing what *isn't* being said. It would be easier to be aware of other people's emotions if they would simply tell us how they feel, but because many people do not, we must rely on asking questions, listening actively, reading between the lines, and trying to interpret nonverbal cues. Here are a few tips on how to create rapport and build stronger relationships by aligning through empathy.

Reflect on what the other person is saying

Think about the word *reflect*: it means to show an image of; to mirror. By actively listening and staying in the moment with the speaker, you truly hear what is being said. In turn, you can honestly mirror what you've seen and heard. For example, you may say something like, "I see this is upsetting to you," or "I sense you are uncomfortable about this," or "I can understand why you would be upset." Reflecting helps show that you understand what the other person is saying to you. It demonstrates that you are concerned.

Validate the other's emotions

Validating the other person's feelings helps to convey your acceptance and respect for another's emotional state. For example: "I can understand why you would be angry under these circumstances." "Anyone would find this difficult." Validating others' emotions doesn't necessarily mean you agree with their arguments or support their viewpoints. It simply means you acknowledge what they are feeling.

Show respect and admiration

Though empathy is usually used in reference to sensing someone else's painful feelings, it can also apply to someone's positive feelings of success, achievement, and pride. On the positive side, take the time to celebrate others' accomplishments. It's just as important to recognize and align with their positive emotions as their negative ones. When a colleague gets a promotion, an employee completes a stellar project, or a friend wins the lottery, you can show empathy and build rapport by aligning with that person's joy, excitement, and surprise. For example, you might say, "I'm so happy for you! I can see you are thrilled." Or, "Congratulations! I can understand why this is an emotional moment for you." And if your conversation partner is persisting in the face of adversity, or going through tough times, show your respect for the person's tenacity and fortitude. For example: "Despite these challenges, you seem to be coping so well." "That is quite an accomplishment. I am very impressed by how well you are adjusting to all the change."

Share a similar experience

When you are actively listening and showing empathy, it's all about the other person. However, there are times when it may help to share an experience from your life that relates to the situation, if you believe doing so would foster rapport and understanding. You might say something like, "I can empathize with what you're feeling. Last year the same thing happened to me . . ." Be brief—and use this technique sparingly to avoid dominating the conversation or turning the focus on yourself.

Offer personal support or partnership

When appropriate, you may want to go beyond words and extend an offer to help. This gesture enhances rapport by letting the other person know that you want to assist. For example: "I want to help in any way I can; please let me know what I can do." "If it would be helpful, I'll be glad to . . ." Empathic leaders have developed a mindset that asks, "When I communicate, am I delivering the message in such a way that others will want to listen to me?" They are skilled at placing themselves in the shoes of another person and seeing the world through that person's eyes.

Teach and Be Teachable

A chief officer in one of the largest electronics companies in the world once said to me, "If I'm meeting with someone and they don't teach me something new about our business, I wonder why I'm paying them." Clearly, this leader wants his conversation partners to enlighten him with the latest intelligence about his company and industry. Part of a powerful conversation is the transfer of relevant information and valuable knowledge. As stated earlier in this chapter, effective leaders spend most of their time asking questions, probing, listening, learning, reflecting, and showing empathy. As an effective leader, when it comes time for you to speak—to share your wisdom, expertise, experience, and intelligence—be sure you've planned appropriately. It's a critical opportunity. Ask yourself in advance, "What can I say that will be most helpful? What do they need to know? What can I share that would make them more successful? What information or knowledge do I have that they may need?"

There are a variety of ways to teach or coach somebody, regardless of their title. You can tell a personal story, share a customer experience, report the results of a study, impart an insight, speak from experience, quote an article, inspire with an anecdote, use a prop, educate on best practices, demo a product, or employ a metaphor or analogy. The list goes on. As the proverb goes, "If you have knowledge, let others light their candles at it."

Shared learning is a key result of a powerful conversation. Just as important, an effective leader not only teaches but is teachable. As legendary basketball coach John Wooden once said, "It's what you learn after you know it all that counts." Thinking we have little to learn from others is perhaps the most deadly impediment to cultivating rapport and building strong relationships. Self-important, know-it-all leaders leave little room for input from others. Being teachable requires us to lay aside our pride and admit we don't know everything. Other people, in fact, should and do know more than we do in certain areas. Sometimes we mistakenly believe this situation can make us look weak or foolish; however, looking at it from the others' viewpoint, we see that welcoming their input and allowing them to teach us makes them look good and feel smart. When you value other people's intelligence, they'll typically enjoy your company and want to be around you. Before you know it, you've cultivated the enviable quality of charisma—the ability to draw people to you.

Enjoy

Speaking of charisma, "enjoy" literally means "to give joy, rejoice, take delight in," from the Anglo-French word *enjoir*. People who enjoy themselves—at whatever they're doing—are magnetic. How would you describe the people you want to spend time with? Grouchy? Angry? Pessimistic? Of course not! Most likely, you enjoy people who are easygoing, cheerful, and optimistic. Most important, you probably enjoy people who express genuine enjoyment in being with you! The stresses and strains of work life can affect a leader's demeanor. One CEO who called me for help reported that his leadership assessment ratings were at an all-time low. For example, one employee wrote, "He always acts hurried and worried." Indeed, the most visible signs of workplace pressures manifest themselves in a leader's body language. Leaders frequently walk hastily to and from meetings, eyes cast downward, holding a pensive scowl, passing dozens of unnoticed employees along the way. They enter a meeting room to conduct a powerful conversation, yet their body language is anything but warm, open, and friendly. They don't intend to send negative signals to their team members, but perception is reality. A client who is the general manager of a major international hotel chain displays this proverb on his desk: "Everyone smiles in the same language."

Relax, smile at people, and be pleasant. Approach what you're doing with a positive attitude and tell yourself you're going to enjoy it. Try this: for just one day, wear a cheerful countenance and give a smile to every living creature you meet. Talk health, happiness, and prosperity to others and notice the difference in your own outlook and those around you. You'll quickly discover that attitude determines altitude. The positive energy you radiate will foster rapport, strengthen relationships, and draw others to you like metal to a magnet.

CHAPTER 13: EXECUTIVE SUMMARY

Conduct a powerful conversation using these four steps:

Step One: Establish mutual objectives and purpose.

Step Two: Express mutual needs and wants.

Step Three: Explore new possibilities.

Step Four: Commit to mutual action.

Practice these five relational skills to create rapport and build stronger relationships:

Reach out

Engage with questions

Listen

Align through empathy

Teach and be teachable

Enjoy

CHAPTER 14

Writing E-Mails That Get Results

"The most valuable of all talents is that of never using two words when one will do."

—THOMAS JEFFERSON

How many business e-mails do you receive per day? I posed this question to 200 of my U.S.-based clients who hold titles of vice president and above. The average was eighty-nine per day. They reported that 25 percent (roughly twenty-two per day) was spam or junk mail. According to the survey, that leaves a whopping sixty-seven e-mails that they are required to read and respond to every day.

BEST PRACTICES FOR EFFECTIVE E-MAILS

The goal of this chapter is to ensure that your e-mails get the attention and response they deserve.

Make the Subject Line Clear and Meaningful

When decision makers receive your e-mail message, they should be able to immediately see three things:

1. How the message relates to them
2. Why it's important
3. Whether action is required on their part

The best way to accomplish this is by providing them with a clear subject line. Most decision makers with whom I work report this technique as the number one best practice for getting a reply. If your subject line is confusing, vague, irrelevant, or blank, your e-mail will likely be ignored or deleted. Also, capitalize your subject line like a title—it adds an air of importance and declaration. Here are some examples of what can be included in the subject line to make sure decision makers read your mail:

- If you need them to take action, announce it in the subject line:

  "Action Requested: Please Sign/Return Attached P.O. by 5pm Today to Ensure Vendor Discount"

- If you are sending information they have requested, avoid a vague subject line such as "Here's the file." Chances are they will receive many files that day from various people. Instead make sure they know they requested it, plus state the exact topic of the file:

  "Per Your Request: Budget Proposal for Systems and Technology Group"

- Rather than inappropriately marking your e-mail urgent, or brashly typing "Important! Read Immediately!!" craft a subject line that actually communicates the urgency and consequences:

  "Emergency: Approval Needed Today on Attached Compliance Form to Avoid $2K Gov't Penalty"

- Avoid writing "Quick Question." Instead just write the question:

  "Will You Be Able to Attend the Smith Client Dinner Tonight at 6PM?"

Keep Your Message Short

There is no standard protocol for the "right" length of an e-mail. The rule of thumb is "The shorter the better." Out of curiosity, I've combed through hundreds of archived e-mails sent to me by senior leaders in various corporations. Over 90 percent of the e-mails are under 200 words, require no scrolling, and take less than one minute to read. That isn't to say every e-mail you send must be 200 words or less. It does say that high-level decision makers communicate using a particular pattern that honors succinctness and time management. Of course, the length of your e-mails depends on the recipient, subject matter, and purpose. The key is to make sure you send clear, concise, well-organized e-mails that get to the point quickly. An effective e-mail targets the subject, allows the reader to grasp the message quickly, and en-sures a prompt reply.

Communicate First Things First

Prioritize your text using the most-important-to-least-important method. As you may recall from Chapter 6 regarding effective slide design, the three-tiered pyramid approach ensures that we deliver content in the order of importance: *Must say; need to say; want to say.* Effective e-mails follow the same format. Write what you "must say" in the first two or three sen-tences. If the recipient reads nothing else, she will get the gist of the mes-sage and know what action (if any) you want her to take by reading the first several sentences. In the second paragraph, write what you feel you "need to say" to provide support, explanation, or critical details. Finally, include additional paragraphs (made up of what you "want to say") only if necessary. Label this section with a heading such as "Background," "De-tails," or "Rationale."

Tell Recipients What Action You Want Them to Take

State the action items first. Be clear, concise, and immediate. To get even faster responses, tie the action to a benefit and talk about how the action relates to the recipient's objectives. Give due dates. If appropriate you may even mention a consequence of not replying promptly—just be care-ful to avoid sounding like you're issuing a threat. For example: "Hi Lou, Please sign and return the attached contract by 5pm tomorrow to ensure we get the June 1st implementation time slot you requested. Securing this slot is critical in order to meet your goal of a January 15th product launch."

Number Your Points

When you have multiple items on the same topic, organize your points us-ing bullets or a numbered list. If an e-mail is not well organized, many fast-paced decision makers will scan the message and quickly reply to the first item that requires attention. If action items are in the second, third, and fourth paragraph, they'll likely go unread. This often leaves you with an incomplete response. Instead, add an introductory preview line that tells the reader how many items you wish her to address. Then number your items.

Here's an example:

Subject: "Action Required: Please Provide Exec Briefing Details by 5pm Today"

Hi Samantha. To ensure a successful executive briefing with your client on Friday, please reply to these five details by 5pm today.

1. What are your audiovisual requirements?
2. Would you like classroom style or U-shaped setup?
3. Please send a final roster of attendee names to ensure your requested name tents are printed on time.
4. Are you going to kick off the meeting, or shall I give the introduction?
5. What is the dress code for internal attendees—business or business casual? I'll inform the team accordingly.

Thanks for your replies and I look forward to a great meeting on Friday.

This format sets clear expectations and provides an easy-to-read structure for the decision maker. Usually, the recipient will respond, "See replies below." Then under each numbered point, he or she will insert the answer to that issue. If the points are stand-alone topics and require a substantial reply, you may want to split them into separate e-mail messages so that the decision maker can respond, file, or forward each item appropriately.

Make Sure Your Intent Is Clear

Start with your conclusion, and then explain. For example, if you are replying to an e-mail, give your answer in the first sentence. Then, if necessary, briefly provide the details of your reasoning. If you have a question to ask, do so in the first sentence. As I mentioned earlier, if you are requesting action from someone, say what you want in the first couple of sentences—don't bury it in the third paragraph. This approach gets to the point, doesn't waste time, and ensures your request is noticed right away. If you are providing an information e-mail or update, summarize the situation in a short three- to five-sentence paragraph, then provide details in the second and third paragraphs. Remember, attention diminishes with length. The longer it takes to get to your point, the less likely it is that the reader will take action. Therefore, state your intention up front.

Use Proper "Netiquette" and E-Mail Formatting

The basic rule of etiquette in any situation is to show thoughtful consideration for the other person. When you stop to think how the other person is likely to receive your communication, or how you would feel receiving the same communication, you almost always make the smartest choice. This simple step will go a long way toward crafting clear, concise, convincing e-mails. It will also help prevent misunderstandings and hurt feelings.

NETIQUETTE GUIDELINES

When you write a business e-mail, especially to senior leaders and decision makers, imagine you're writing it on company letterhead. Use the same protocols as you would in a written letter, such as salutations, well-organized text body, and a complimentary close. Use standard English and good punctuation. Even though an e-mail is digital, immediate, and sometimes more personable, avoid becoming too casual and informal. A certain degree of formality is required in all business communication, including e-mail. The following tips on using proper e-mail formatting and netiquette will help ensure that your messages get noticed, read, and acted upon.

Proper Salutation

Start your e-mail with a courteous personal greeting: "Hi Jim," or "Dear Bob," or "Good morning, Sally." This helps ensure your e-mail does not seem curt or demanding. Be sure to address your contact with the appropriate level of formality and make sure you spell the name correctly. And end your e-mail with a courteous close. For example, "Sincerely, Elizabeth" or "Best regards, Bill."

Under your name, add your contact information. For formal or external e-mails, include your full contact information: name, title, company name, address, phone and fax numbers, e-mail address, and website address. For casual and informal communications, you can sign off with just your name; however, include enough contact information for your colleagues to reach you (don't assume they have your number or extension memorized).

Matters of Style

Before you send, proofread and check for correct spelling. I suggest reading the e-mail aloud. It's a great way to catch typos and other errors. Your computer's spell-checker can be a big help, but do not rely on it! For example, if you're replying to someone and intend to say, "I can't attend" but accidentally write "I can attend," the spell-checker will not catch the error.

Use standard capitalization of upper- and lowercase lettering. Avoid ALL CAPS, which implies that you're shouting. Conversely, avoid using all lowercase with no caps, as this connotes a style that's too informal and casual.

Skip lines between paragraphs. White space adds a visual transition between key points. The reader's eyes need to skim and scan, alternating between focusing and resting. But a dense screen full of solid black text does not allow this freedom of eye movement. In fact, it may be perceived as daunting, time-consuming, and labor intensive, and therefore will get skipped (if not deleted). Alternating text with white space speeds things up for readers, holds their attention, and aids better reading. Similarly, avoid fancy typefaces or nonstandard fonts. Use a common sans serif font such as Arial.

Another key to good netiquette: Identify yourself clearly, if necessary. If there is any chance the decision maker might not remember you or recognize your name, be sure to identify yourself in the first sentence of the e-mail. For example, if you are following up on a face-to-face contact, drop casual hints to jog his memory: "Hi Bob, I enjoyed talking with you in the elevator this morning about the on-boarding process for new hires. Please find attached . . ."

When contacting someone cold, such as a prospect, always include your name, title, company, and any other important identification information in the first few sentences. In addition, try to get an introduction to the recipient by someone who already knows her. For example: "Dear Meredith: Your Vice President of Supply Chain, Alan Gold, recommended I contact you. My name is Jane Doe . . ."

Limit the e-mail to one subject. Avoid discussing or requesting action on separate topics. For example, in the e-mail labeled "Action Requested: Please Sign/Return Attached P.O. by 5pm Today to Ensure Vendor Discount," don't include requests regarding the Budget Proposal or the Smith Client Dinner. Each is an individual topic deserving of its own e-mail and may need to be filed separately by the recipient.

Mark a message as "urgent" or "high priority" only when absolutely necessary. Never cry wolf with your e-mail by getting in the habit of marking all your messages "urgent." In fact, when you have an urgent message to send, you may consider telephoning instead of (or in addition to) sending an e-mail.

In the body of the e-mail, use gender-neutral language. For example, write "salesperson," not "salesman." Also, use standard English: avoid the use of emoticons (smiley faces and other facial expressions), undefined acronyms, abbreviations, texting shorthand, and over-exclamation such as "!!!" or "???," which may be perceived as rude or condescending. Business e-mail is not a chat room or a text message. To avoid appearing too casual or making your reader guess at your message, use standard spelling, punctuation, and capitalization. When you are writing to a friend or a close colleague, you may bend the rules a bit if you're sure they know the shorthand (e.g., IIRC for "if I recall correctly," LOL for "laughing out loud," etc.) These linguistic shortcuts are generally signs of friendly intimacy, like sharing cold pizza with a friend. If you tried to share that same cold pizza with a first date, a visiting dignitary, or your company's CEO, you risk hinting that you don't value the encounter or care about the meeting. By the same token, don't use informal language when your reader expects a more formal approach. Always know your audience. Think about the situation, and write accordingly.

In addition to sticking with standard English, avoid fancy vocabulary. "Laconic" is a great word, but "concise" or "succinct" may work better in a business e-mail context. The goal is not to impress your readers with an extravagant vocabulary; it's to get the message across as clearly and concisely as possible.

Responding, Forwarding, Attachments, and CC

When responding to an e-mail, provide context by including a copy of the previous message or use a few lines as a quote. Considering how many e-mails business professionals receive in a day, don't assume the reader will instantly recall the particular situation about which you're writing. As a courtesy to readers and an aid to understanding, jog the recipient's memory by including pertinent context and background.

When sending an attachment, explain what the attachment is within the e-mail message. However, be aware of the size of the files you are sending. As a general rule, think twice before e-mailing a file bigger than one megabyte (1MB). For people who may use a dial-up connection to collect their e-mail, an attachment of this size can take between five and ten minutes to download. Only send very large attachments (over 1MB) to the recipients after gaining their permission. Consider using compression software such as WinZip to compress large files before sending them. This can reduce the size of files by up to 80 percent, but make sure the recipient(s) can handle that format. If you have large files to make available to a number of people, consider placing them on your company's File Transfer Protocol (FTP) servers or a synchronization service such as Dropbox.

This should go without saying, but when you present by e-mail, be sure to provide the proper data and documents. Before you send, review the e-mail and the attachments. Do your recipients have all the information required for them to complete an action or respond successfully to your request?

When you are out of the office for longer than one business day and will not be able to respond to your e-mails, use an out-of-office notice that automatically responds to your e-mails. An auto-respond message can be set up in your e-mail program. It will automatically send a message to anyone who sends you a message while you are away. Your auto-respond message can inform the senders that you are away and will respond to their e-mails at a specific time when you return.

Target the appropriate audience; send your e-mail only to the appropriate people. If, in the subject line, you highlight an action to be taken, only those who are to take that action should be on the "To:" line of your e-mail. Be thoughtful and respectful when you enter names on that line. Here are two simple questions to help you filter the "To:" line recipients:

1. Does this e-mail relate to the recipient's objectives?
2. Is the recipient responsible for the action in the subject line?

Use the CC line wisely. It's tempting to put loads of people on the CC line to cover your bases, but doing so is one of the fastest ways to create an unproductive environment. Here are some things to consider when using the CC line:

➤ No action or response should be expected of individuals listed on the CC line. The recipient only needs to read or file the message.

➤ Only those individuals whose meaningful objectives are affected by the e-mail should be included on the message. (If you are not sure that the information is related to a coworker's objectives, check with that person to see if he or she wants to receive your e-mail on that topic.)

With just a few exceptions, refrain from using the "Reply To All" feature. In most cases replying to the sender alone is your best course of action.

Reply To All is best used when the content of your reply affects everyone on the list and they need to know its content in order to do their job. Otherwise, avoid cluttering inboxes with unnecessary e-mail.

Think before you click "Send." Be professional. Do not flame (sending messages that contain harsh, insulting, or derogatory language). If you find yourself writing while you're angry or highly frustrated, save a draft, go get a cup of coffee, and imagine that tomorrow morning someone has published your e-mail on the front page of the company newsletter. Would you feel remorse and embarrassment, or would you be proud of your professionalism, tact, and courtesy? The immediate gratification of "flaming" someone is no comparison to the long-term damage it can do your reputation and possibly your career. If you need to express strong feelings of frustration or disapproval to someone, do so face-to-face, or pick up the phone and call.

One of the quickest ways to get onto your recipients' "delete" radar is to forward meaningless chain e-mails, jokes, urban legends, cartoons, the latest virus scare, fundraising pitches, recipes, a slide show of nature photos, and assorted spam that clutters their inboxes. At a minimum, ask the recipient if you may send such an e-mail; gain their permission first. Serial forwarders often don't realize they're damaging their own reputation, wasting other people's time, and using business e-mail inappropriately. A good policy is "business only."

In fact, don't forward any message without the author's approval. There may be many reasons why someone wouldn't want his or her message forwarded. The message may be for you only, the tone might not be appropriate for others, or the sender might not want to share his or her e-mail address with others.

If you don't want a message you send to someone to be forwarded, how should you let the recipient know? Make it clear that the message is for that person's eyes only, and request that he or she not forward it. Before forwarding a message that contains a history of replies, check to make sure that everything in the message is appropriate for all readers before you forward. Remove any unnecessary or sensitive content. And regardless of your request not to forward, you may assume that it will nonetheless be forwarded to someone. Not everyone follows the correct protocols.

Is it necessary to reply to forwarded messages? The answer is usually no, unless you find that there is something in the message that specifically applies to you or one of your responsibilities.

International E-Mails

There are special guidelines that apply to international business e-mails. To be on the safe side, start by addressing the recipient as Mr. or Ms. and his or her surname. Do not use the recipient's first name. Keep the tone of your e-mail formal, and avoid humor that might be misunderstood. Convert your measurements to metric, and be careful about calendar dates. To be clear, always write out the month, day, and year. For example, in the United States the date 12/6/14 means December 6, 2014; in Europe it means June 12, 2014. If your message concerns money, be specific about which currency you are talking about. If you ask the international recipient to call you, provide him or her with the appropriate telephone country code. Also watch out for time zone confusion. To be on the safe side and considerate of the other person, list both time zones for meetings. For example, if you schedule a meeting with a customer in Munich, Germany, confirm the date and correct times as follows: November 22 at 3:00 PM CET (Central European Time), 9:00 AM EST (Eastern Standard Time).

A Note on Privacy

Remember, your e-mail is not private. If you're an employee, you are sending communications from your employer's equipment, which usually provides justification for the company to search through your e-mails. Even if you delete an e-mail from your inbox, it will still exist on the recipient's computer, at your Internet Service Provider, and on multiple servers in multiple locations. A good rule of thumb is to imagine that every e-mail you send will be read by everyone, including your boss—and maybe even broadcast on your local news.

CHAPTER 14: EXECUTIVE SUMMARY

Follow These Tips for Writing E-Mails That Get Results

- ➤ Write a clear, meaningful subject line.
- ➤ Keep your message short.
- ➤ Organize content from most important to least important.
- ➤ Tell recipients what action you want them to take.
- ➤ Number your points.
- ➤ Make sure your intent is clear.

➤ Start your e-mail with a courteous personal greeting.

➤ End your e-mail with a courteous close.

➤ Under your close, include your contact information.

➤ Proofread, check for correct spelling, and read the e-mail aloud.

➤ Use standard capitalization of upper- and lowercase lettering.

➤ Skip lines between paragraphs to provide white space.

➤ Avoid fancy typefaces or nonstandard fonts.

➤ Identify yourself clearly, if necessary.

➤ Limit the e-mail to one subject.

➤ Mark a message as "urgent" or "high priority" only when absolutely necessary.

➤ Use gender-neutral language.

➤ Avoid the use of emoticons, acronyms, abbreviations, and shorthand.

➤ Avoid fancy vocabulary.

➤ When replying, include a copy of the previous message.

➤ Avoid sending long documents as e-mail messages—use attachments instead.

➤ Provide the proper data and documents when you present by e-mail.

➤ Use an out-of-office auto-respond notice.

➤ Send the message only to relevant recipients.

➤ Use the CC line wisely.

➤ Refrain from using the Reply To All feature.

➤ Be professional—don't flame.

➤ Don't send junk e-mail.

➤ Don't forward messages without the author's approval.

➤ Use best practices for international e-mails.

➤ Realize your e-mail is not private.

Facilitating Effective Meetings In Person and via the Telephone

> Meetings are indispensable when you don't want to do anything.
>
> —JOHN KENNETH GALBRAITH

Are meetings the bane of your existence? That's what some of my clients tell me. They consider these gatherings to be a waste of time and rate them as unproductive, unstructured, and uninspiring. One CEO with whom I work likes to say, "A meeting is an event at which the minutes are kept and the hours are lost."

To her point, I recall seeing a cartoon that showed several business professionals sitting around a conference table while the leader of the meeting glumly announced, "There's not really a specific agenda for this meeting. As usual, we'll just make unrelated emotional statements about things that bother us . . ."

On the other hand, for some companies, meetings are highly valued and considered to be vital vehicles of critical information. Stan, the chief operating officer for an auto manufacturer, conducts between sixty and seventy meetings each week. His office is the last stop before directors, managers, and engineers send the product to market. In his words, "I have to make sure my teams understand the company's strategic direction, remain accountable to specific action steps, and stay on time."

The following tips and techniques will help you run effective, efficient meetings, whether in person, by phone, or by videoconference.

TIPS FOR RUNNING EFFECTIVE, EFFICIENT MEETINGS

First of all, don't meet if you can avoid it. Ask yourself, "Is a meeting absolutely necessary?" If not, save everyone the time and money. Don't just have a meeting because it's Monday morning, or because you haven't met in a while and feel as though you should. Phone calls, e-mails, and one-on-one conversations can be valuable, productive replacements for unnecessary larger group meetings. If you must meet, try the following tips to optimize outcomes and ensure a good use of time.

Determine Your Objective and Agenda

Define a clear-cut objective or purpose. Make sure there's an important reason for scheduling the meeting. Complete this phrase and you'll have your objective: "At the end of this meeting, I want this group to: _____." Start the objective with an action verb, such as decide, achieve, select, vote, brainstorm, prioritize, generate, or solve. Refer to Chapter 11 for a comprehensive list of business-oriented action verbs. A meaningful meeting begins with defining the purpose: What are the measurable outcomes you want to accomplish as a result of this meeting?

In addition to setting a clear objective, craft a clearly focused agenda. To assist your efforts, please see the sample template in Figure 15-1. *Set a firm agenda.* To optimize engagement and participation from your attendees, *be sure to send the agenda to everyone ahead of time, ideally at least three business days before the event.* Advanced review gives everyone time to think about the topics and prepare questions, comments, and research. *For each topic, list the name of the assigned leader; the time allotment; and the objective.* A well-crafted agenda is the road map to a good meeting and serves as a tool to oblige attendees to think about meeting structure and outcomes. Use the agenda to set clear expectations and communicate accountability. Strive to stick to the agenda. At the same time, keep in mind that it must also remain flexible due to changes in the business, disruptions in the industry, staff changes, scheduling changes—even weather and travel conditions!

Figure 15-1

MEETING AGENDA

Date:	Time/Length:		Place:	
Meeting Objective/Purpose:				
Attendees:				

Topic/Item	Time Allocated	Topic Leader	Objective/ Desired Outcome	Task/Timeline Person Responsible
Topic 1: Key Points:			Discussion Information Decision Other:	
Topic 2: Key Points:			Discussion Information Decision Other:	
Topic 3: Key Points:			Discussion Information Decision Other:	

Invite the Right People

Another requirement for productive meetings is to make sure the right people are there. You need no more attendees than that. Do you need multiple representatives from the marketing department, or can one of them serve as the spokesperson and report back to the team? If you have an attendee who never contributes, that person is either too shy or does not need to be there. It's perfectly appropriate to be selective and invite only those people who can significantly contribute to the outcome.

On the same note, confirm the attendance of key decision makers. If your meeting objective is contingent on a particular decision maker's presence and participation, make sure he or she is going to be there. Otherwise, your objective cannot be accomplished and the meeting may need to be rescheduled.

Limit and Prioritize Topics

Another best practice is to limit the number of topics. If your meeting is scheduled for one hour, deduct ten minutes off the top: five for the opening and five for the closing. That leaves fifty minutes. If you know each topic will take at least fifteen minutes on average, including discussion, you have time for three, maybe four topics. Avoid scheduling five, six, or seven topics in a one-hour time frame. Cramming too much content into a meeting dilutes the impact of each topic and also prevents participants from quality discussion and feedback.

In addition to limiting the number of topics, be sure to prioritize the ones you select. Rank the topics from most important to least important on the agenda and cover them in that order. This ensures you cover the most important content while everyone's minds are fresh and before anyone leaves early.

Encourage Involvement

In the opening and throughout the meeting, encourage all attendees to participate and contribute. Invite people to speak. If a person is attending, that person is responsible for contributing; therefore, it's highly appropriate to call on them. For example, "Fred, you have years of experience in encryption. What do you think the security risks are in this project?"

These open-ended questions help facilitate dialogue and discussion.

Consistently, my clients tell me the highest-rated meetings are the ones with the most interaction. Discussion and dialogue are critical. The meetings also need to be controlled and well facilitated (more on that in the next section of this chapter).

To ensure that all meeting attendees are involved contributors, consider assigning everyone a task prior to the meeting. For example, in advance of the meeting, send all attendees a notice that reads: "Please be prepared to offer your top three ideas for . . ." Or, "Please survey three people on X and bring the replies to the meeting." The information will be helpful to you, and it also sets a precedent that everyone is accountable and responsible for contributing to the meeting's outcomes.

A great way to ensure involvement is to solicit input and suggestions prior to the meeting. Let the attendees co-create the agenda. In the spirit of making every meeting beneficial to its attendees, survey participants ahead of time. Ask them what they would like to learn regarding X topic.

An effective meeting also needs a great note-taker. Be sure to assign a scribe to this role. As the meeting leader, your job is to facilitate discussion, manage the agenda, and keep everything on track. Your scribe will keep a record of tasks, timelines, responsible individuals, and action items—and will then prepare a meeting summary. This meeting summary may be distributed afterward as effective follow-up. Anyone who missed the meeting can receive a copy. The summary also serves as an official set of notes that can be critical to ensuring that inaccuracies and inconsistencies are caught immediately. The notes will prove to be invaluable when people are trying to remember what decisions were made, what strategies were discussed, and what actions need to be taken; they can simply go back and review the notes.

Prepare a Strong Opening

As you open the meeting, be sure to offer the group a warm welcome. Review the purpose, agenda, guidelines, and ground rules. Craft a well-planned opening, as you would for a formal presentation. Ensure that everyone understands the purpose and objectives of the agenda along with their responsibilities during the meeting. Briefly cover housekeeping details and logistics.

As a leader, you need to convey enthusiasm. If the topic is important enough to call people away from their jobs and sit in a room for an hour, it's important enough to get excited about. A friend once told me that the last letters of enthusiasm—IASM—stand for "I Am Sold Myself!" Enthusiasm is contagious. It shows you are sold on the topic, your purpose, and the measurable outcomes. I guarantee if you show some enthusiasm, your attendees will too.

Manage the Time

The true sign of a professional is to start and end the meeting on time. This practice sets an important precedent, establishing you as a punctual leader who respects other people's time. And it reinforces good behavior: by starting on time, you reward on-time attendees while training the tardy ones to be prompt next time.

And what about those who are late for the meeting? Clients often ask me if they should stop the proceedings and bring the tardy ones up to speed. The answer is no. Do not spend time recapping for latecomers. Feel free to welcome them. For example, "Hi Jim, welcome. There's a chair right over here." However, refrain from summarizing what you've covered so far. Jim can read about it in the meeting summary. The only exception to this guideline is when a senior executive or key stakeholder arrives late. If you feel he or she needs to know what you've covered in order to make a decision, take a minute to recap.

To assist with punctuality and time management, display a clock. One of my clients takes this to the limit. To add a little pressure and accountability, she uses her computer to project a six-foot-high timer on the wall, counting down the remaining minutes for a particular meeting or topic. The timer sets the expectation to keep meetings running on schedule. She often announces to attendees before they speak, "Okay Jim, you have ten minutes on the clock to bring us up to date on the government compliance issues." Jim (and everyone else) can plainly see the countdown. My client reports that, sure enough, the speakers time their delivery accordingly and almost always finish before the buzzer goes off.

If a countdown doesn't work, you'll still need to control the time. No matter how detailed your agenda, attendees will exceed their time limits if left to their own devices. As a leader you're faced with deciding whether you should allow more time for a topic or table it for another time.

Always have a system in place to deal with "derailers." For example, when a meeting participant talks too much, or there's a sidebar conversation, or an unforeseen disruption, it's up to you as the meeting leader to say something like, "It looks like we've drifted a bit off topic. So, in respect of time, let's return to point number three . . ." On the other hand, if the prolonged discussion is necessary and useful, but time is running out, quickly assign a smaller group to schedule another meeting. Don't allow the agenda to be derailed. The group looks to you to accomplish the meeting objective and also start and end on time.

Bring the Meeting to a Close

An effective meeting has a strong closing. As you carefully watch the clock, leave three to five minutes for the summary. Briefly recap each topic. Gain agreement upon tasks, timelines, and responsible individuals. If needed, schedule a next meeting with specific follow-up tasks and assignments.

Follow Up Promptly

Either at the end of the meeting or in a follow-up conversation, ask attendees what they thought of the meeting. Solicit feedback regarding the meeting's purpose, topics, process, and outcomes. Consider sending a questionnaire or survey for the participants to complete. The best way to find out if you had a successful meeting is to ask those who attended. Find out what worked and what could be better next time.

Prepare and distribute a meeting summary that notes all of the essential elements of the meeting. As described earlier in this chapter, the assigned note taker prepares the meeting summary. Again, see Figure 15-1 as a guide. Include the type of meeting; name of the organization and department; date and time; name of the leader, chair, or facilitator; the main topics with key discussion points; adjournment time; action steps; and names of responsible individuals.

Finally, be sure to follow up as required. If you promised to send attendees copies of the slides, meeting summary, handouts, or other materials, strive to do so within twenty-four hours of the meeting time. Include a thank-you message for the attendees' time, attention, and contributions.

HOW TO FACILITATE MEETINGS EFFECTIVELY

Leading a meeting may or may not involve facilitation. You can do a fine job running a meeting simply by following the agenda, sticking to the topics, and ensuring good time management. Facilitation, however, goes a few steps further.

The root word of "facilitator" comes from the French word *facile*, which means "easily accomplished." A good facilitator makes it easy for the group to have a successful meeting. Useful facilitation skills include planning targeted agendas, creating the appropriate group environment, encouraging participation, leading the group to reach its objectives, and guiding the group toward consensus. The main focus of facilitation is to optimize the engagement process and manage group dynamics in order to accomplish the meeting objectives. Here are my top ten techniques to help you facilitate meetings more effectively and ensure the results you want are easily accomplished.

1. *Focus on the task.* As the facilitator in charge of the meeting, your main role is to help ensure a successful, productive outcome by guiding group processes effectively; therefore, purposeful direction is necessary. Prior to the meeting, thoroughly define the What, When, Where, Why, How, and Who of the meeting. "Good morning everyone, and thank you for joining us today. The purpose of our meeting is to share best practices from each of your agencies in order to improve care management. To make the most of your time, let's take a look at the agenda and make sure we all agree on the focus of the session. Are there other objectives or topics you would like to add? Does everyone agree on the proposed agenda? In addition, a few ground rules may help: no cell phones; be punctual; all ideas are valid; no interrupting; everyone contributes. Are there others you would like to add? Do we agree on these five?"

2. *Ask questions.* An effective facilitator asks a combination of open- and closed-ended questions to elicit the most helpful information from group members. "Our first topic is 'best practices in the area of managing clinical costs.' What are some best practices that have helped you expose cost inefficiencies? Thank you, Bob. Would anyone like to add to that or contribute a question? Let's hear some more success stories. What are other ways you've found to manage clinical costs effectively?"

3. *Collect all data.* As the facilitator, make sure that everyone hears, sees, and understands what the group members present during the meeting. Keep all suggestions, comments, ideas, agreements, votes, etc., visible by writing them on flip charts, boards, or via an electronic medium. Summarize what the speaker has said without changing her essential words. Consider using a colleague or group member to serve as a scribe/recorder. "So far,

we've listed seven best practices in the area of managing costs. Joe and Susan have raised some helpful points and suggestions in other areas that we've listed in the 'parallel agenda.' We'll come back to those before the end of the meeting."

4. *Introduce and involve all audience members.* If time permits and the group isn't too large, ask everyone to introduce themselves when you open the meeting. Use name tags or tents if appropriate. As the facilitator, introduce yourself first; this helps others decide what they will say and how long to speak. Keep everyone involved. "We haven't heard from some of you yet, and we value your input. So I encourage you to share your ideas, questions, and suggestions." If necessary, call on them: "Sally, I know you and your team had great success at ABC Agency with cost projection. Please tell us how you did it."

5. *Listen actively.* Pay attention. Strive to hear and understand everything that is said. Repeat and paraphrase when necessary. Be attentive to what's happening at all times. Listen for common themes and connect the dots. "Allow me to repeat Frank's question for those who may not have heard it. 'How does aggregate cost per visit compare to using actual labor cost per visit?' Who has some experience they would like to share with Frank? Thank you, Susan. Frank, your question reminds me of what Sally said earlier. There may be a key connection between her success with cost projection and your challenge. What do you or other members of the group think?"

6. *Intervene if necessary.* As a facilitator, your goal is to support the participants in achieving their desired outcomes. Therefore, key responsibilities include controlling and managing sidebar conversations, laborious discussions, conflict among members, and punctuality. "Emma, sorry to interrupt but in respect of time and our agreed-upon agenda, let's move on. Thank you for your comments. We've recorded them here for future discussion."

7. *Track time, topic, and task.* Keep the meeting moving along. Remind people of the time and appoint a timekeeper if necessary. If the designated time for a topic runs out, ask the group if they want to spend more time on the issue, or postpone it for later discussion. Also, be sure to end on time and summarize the main ideas, takeaways, and action steps. "According to our agenda, our task is to cover all four topics by two o'clock. We're out of time for this issue. Is there agreement to spend another ten minutes to get a few more ideas on the table, or would you like to move on to the second topic?"

8. *Assess the group dynamics.* Watch the composite body language of participants and respond accordingly. Note how they relate to one another and to you. If they are fully engaged in productive discussion, avoid interrupting. If they seem lethargic, bored, or withdrawn, consider using interaction techniques, increasing your own energy level, or taking a break. "I see a few people resting their eyes. By show of hands, who would like to take a five-minute break to stretch and get some fresh air? OK, let's agree to be back in our seats at 1:15."

9. *Talk neutrally.* Try to keep yourself and your personal opinions out of the dynamics of the process. Rather, be a good observer and see yourself as an interested but detached instrument in the communication process. It may help to focus on issues rather than personalities. If disagreement arises, do not take sides. Instead, ask the group to resolve the issue. At all times, remain upbeat, positive, respectful, and nonpartisan. "I can see this is a critical topic for many of you. There's a lot at stake. Remembering our agreed-upon ground rule that all ideas are welcome, let's brainstorm some solutions. Who would like to begin?"

10. *Ensure a safe, comfortable environment.* Groups work best when individuals are made to feel comfortable expressing their ideas. Encourage all participants to listen to what others are saying. As the facilitator, you lead best by example. Also, ensure a conducive and functional working space with proper lighting, comfortable seating, appropriate temperature, minimal outside disturbances, and properly working equipment. Tend to physical needs such as directions to the restrooms, room temperature, and refreshments. Schedule at least a five-minute break every hour or a ten- to fifteen-minute break every ninety minutes. "Your comfort is very important to the success of our meeting, so if you have questions or special requests, please let me know and we'll do our best to accommodate your needs."

BEST PRACTICES FOR TELECONFERENCE CALLS AND SPEAKING OVER THE PHONE

As a general rule, conference calls and telephone conversations cannot fully replace the impact of a face-to-face meeting or facilitation; however, they are a necessary communication tool in a world of limited travel budgets and fast-paced projects. It takes a few simple techniques to turn a conference call into a productive meeting with tangible results and measurable outcomes.

Here's an easy-to-follow guide to ensure proper telephone etiquette and maximum participation.

➤ For starters, as with any meeting, state the specific purpose of the call. A top pet peeve of decision makers is having their time wasted. Put them at ease by kicking off the meeting with a clear purpose statement. State the reason for the call, the objectives, and a brief preview of the points to be covered. This provides focus and direction. It also shows you're prepared, in charge, and committed to a successful meeting.

➤ When you're on the phone, a pleasant tone of voice is key. It's always a good idea to record your side of a telephone conversation. Afterward, listen to the recording and evaluate your voice. Do you sound happy or annoyed? Enthusiastic or bored? Helpful or impatient? Self-assured or timid? Smile when you dial. You'll have a warm and friendly tone regardless of your current mood or circumstances. To make sure you're smiling, keep a mirror by your phone and occasionally check your facial expression. Also, place photos of friends and loved ones by the phone and look at them as you speak. You'll most likely sound more warm and friendly.

➤ Avoid speakerphones whenever possible. Ideally, speak directly into the telephone receiver or use a high-quality headset. Use the speakerphone only when absolutely necessary, such as when multiple people are in the room. When using the speakerphone, make sure you place it as close as possible to the speaker(s) and urge everyone to speak up so the callers can hear all comments. If speaking directly into the telephone receiver, avoid cradling the receiver between your ear and shoulder. This usually gives a muffled sound and strains your neck. The main point is to ensure good sound quality. A poorly placed receiver, too much distance from the speakerphone, or a bad connection can ruin a call. At the start of the call, confirm with listeners that you have a good connection and that everyone can hear clearly.

➤ Good posture is a big part of clear speech and confident volume. Sit up straight as if you were actually face-to-face with the person you are calling. Also try standing up when you speak to project an even more commanding, confident voice tone. Gesture as you would in conversation and imagine you are making eye contact with the callers.

➤ Avoid discrediting speech habits such as filler words and phrases: "um," "uh," "er," "like," "sort of," "you know." Other jeopardizing habits include talking too much, speed talking, not listening, and not asking enough questions. As a self-coaching practice, record and play back a day's worth of phone calls (your side of the conversation only). At the end of the day, listen to the recording. You will immediately hear your strengths and areas of opportunity. Count the filler words and phrases. After being as mortified as I was the first few times I listened to myself, you will become acutely aware of how disruptive this habit can be—and more likely to replace fillers with pauses in future calls. For more information on avoiding jeopardizing speech habits, refer to Chapter 10.

➤ While on the phone, avoid multitasking, such as checking e-mail, filing, or doing paperwork. Concentrate on the other speaker. No matter how hard you try to camouflage your activities, your voice will give you away. The listener can hear a tone of distraction in your voice. Give your callers the full attention you would if you were face-to-face with them. Use good manners. Do not eat, chew, sip, slurp, tap, type, or multitask in any way while on the phone. Avoid sidebar conversations with others. Focus on the listener and tune out all other distractions and activities.

➤ In addition to keen concentration, listen actively. Tune out distractions. Focus only on the speaker's voice and the meaning of the message. Take notes. Keep track of who says what. For example, "Mike, you said earlier the differential is 10 percent. Please help us understand the impact of that number."

➤ Remember that the listener can't see you, so be sure to prove you're listening by giving occasional *verbal nods*. Verbal nods are words and phrases that tell others you are paying attention. They include "That's interesting," "Oh, really," "Uh-huh," "Good," "I see," "Please go on," "Yes, I understand," "Could you please say more about . . ."

➤ Good listening requires patience; don't interrupt or jump to conclusions. Wait for the person to finish. Then, make reflective statements to verify and clarify what you hear. For example: "Don, what I hear you saying is . . . Is that correct?"

➤ The ability to concentrate and listen actively is greatly aided by ensuring a quiet setting. Close your door or use a phone in a quiet area. Turn off your radio and any external music. Avoid shuffling papers or making any noise in the background. And try not to have wireless handheld devices on your desk that vibrate, ring, or otherwise distract. If possible, keep these devices turned to silent mode during the call. Noises from pagers, cell phones, and other devices hinder your ability to concentrate and may be annoying to the listener.

► Rehearse your opening remarks prior to the call. Your listeners form their impression of you in the first few seconds, much as they do at the opening of a presentation. Give extra preparation to your opening. Rehearse and practice aloud the tone and content of your first two minutes. One positive aspect of telephone communications is that you can have plenty of good notes and scripting in front of you to help prompt your comments. These cue cards help ensure that you cover all the important points and use your desired wording.

► Another sign of courtesy is thoughtful language, such as "Thank you for that question." "I'll be glad to address that point." "I appreciate your insight on this issue." By all means, avoid the use of blaming language or an unfriendly tone of voice. I've actually heard presenters respond to their audiences using an irritated tone of voice, saying "I've already covered that point" and "You must not be listening." Keep your words and tone positive and upbeat. Also, don't use the thoughtless phrase "I'll be honest with you." If you think about it, this phrase implies you have previously been dishonest. Instead, say "May I be perfectly candid with you . . ." or "Allow me to be blunt . . . ," or just state your point without the conditional preface.

► In addition to thoughtful language, use positive words. Instead of saying "Can't," "Won't," or "That's impossible," soften the tone (if appropriate) and say, "That's an interesting idea—I'll see what I can do." Or "I appreciate that point. It may not be feasible due to our budget constraints. Let's explore all the options." When you're speaking over the phone instead of in person, words themselves carry a greater impact because the listener does not have your nonverbal cues to provide meaning. That's why it's especially important to keep the language and tone positive, inviting, and upbeat.

► Be caller-centric. Avoid making the conversation all about you and your interests; focus on the listener. As we learned in Chapter 11, be careful not to overuse the "I, me, my" pronouns. Consider this example: "What I hope to accomplish here are next steps that I believe are important to my company's growth. Based on my data, I think . . ." Do you see how many times the words "I" and "my" are used? Instead, employ one of the most persuasive words in the English language: "You." For example: "Thank you for your time. With your approval, this agenda presents next steps that will help us accomplish your primary goal, which is to ensure you receive a quality implementation on time and on budget. As you review the agenda, do you have any questions before we address topic number one?"

➤ Share control with those to whom you're talking. Avoid telling your conversation partner(s) what they should do, must do, or need to do. Instead, try the following: "May I make a suggestion?" "With your permission . . ." "Another option is . . ." "Here's an idea for your consideration." "What additional ideas do you have?" By using a participative leadership approach, you wisely "pull" information from attendees rather than "pushing" it on them. This keeps them involved and also shares ownership of the outcomes.

➤ During the call, if you must place someone on hold, be sure to do two things: ask for permission and explain the reason. It's impolite to place someone on hold abruptly without telling them why. Also, never leave someone holding for more than twenty seconds without offering to call them back.

➤ If you're not the leader of the call, be sure to assign someone the task. Put a qualified candidate in charge of the call. Every meeting needs a leader, whether you're talking via phone or in person. The leader opens the call, facilitates discussion, manages the topics and time, fields Q&A, clarifies next steps, and closes the call on time.

➤ Identify yourself before you speak and instruct others to do the same. Avoid guessing games. Don't assume that everyone will recognize your voice. Even if they know you, the speakerphone or conference bridge often distorts the voice. Therefore, establish the habit of identifying yourself every time you speak—or at least the first three or four times until your voice is established and easily recognized. Say, "This is Darlene. I recommend that we . . ." Likewise, encourage all callers to identify themselves by saying, "To ensure we have accurate minutes, may I remind everyone to please state your name before contributing a point." If someone speaks without identifying himself, repeat the point by asking, "Who's the speaker, please?"

➤ Another critical practice for conference calls: Always direct questions and comments to others by name. When you're face-to-face, you can use your eyes and body language to cue a specific person to respond to your question or comment. But when you're on a conference call, you should address that person by name: "Sarah, you've had a lot of experience in that area. What do you think?" Also, if you want a response to the last thing you've said, avoid asking, "Are there any comments?" Instead, direct certain individuals to respond in sequence: "Jeff and Alice, I know you have a lot of experience in this area. Jeff, let's start with your ideas."

► Be patient and don't interrupt speakers. Even though you may eagerly want to say something, or finish the speaker's sentence, or chime in with a profound thought, please wait your turn. Let the other person finish her thought. There are two reasons for this. First, it's polite, shows good manners, and is proper business decorum in a meeting. Second, some conference bridges or speakerphones will only allow one person to talk at a time. If you jump in and start talking while someone else has the floor, you may unintentionally cut her off in mid-sentence.

► Finally, let the other callers hang up first. Before I conclude a telephone meeting, I usually say something like this: "It's two o'clock and that concludes our call today. I'll be glad to stay on the line if anyone has additional questions. Otherwise thanks, everyone, for your participation, and have a great weekend! Goodbye." As I stay on the line, I hear lots of beeps indicating people have left the call. Then, a few seconds later, there's one lone voice in the distance: "Darlene, I did have a question. Are you still there?" By adjourning the meeting on time with a polite farewell, yet still remaining on the line, you ensure all your participants' questions are answered.

CHAPTER 15: EXECUTIVE SUMMARY

Tips for Running Effective, Efficient Meetings

- ► Unless absolutely necessary, don't meet.
- ► If a meeting is necessary, define your clear-cut objective and know exactly what you want to accomplish.
- ► Craft a clearly focused agenda and distribute it to attendees ahead of time.
- ► Invite the right attendees and confirm the attendance of key decision makers.
- ► Limit the number of topics and prioritize them from most important to least important.
- ► Assign tasks to the attendees prior to the meeting to help ensure everyone will contribute during the meeting.

- ► If appropriate, send a survey to attendees in advance to ensure you meet their needs.
- ► Recruit a proficient note-taker and prepare a meeting summary.
- ► Craft a well-planned opening and closing. Rehearse them ahead of time.
- ► Convey enthusiasm for the topic and encourage all attendees to participate.
- ► Start and end the meeting on time.
- ► Don't spend time recapping for latecomers.
- ► Display a clock in the room.
- ► After the meeting, solicit feedback and follow up as required.

How to Facilitate Meetings Effectively

- ► Focus on the task to ensure a productive meeting outcome.
- ► Ask questions to engage your audience and gain valuable information.
- ► Collect all data contributed by audience attendees.
- ► Introduce and involve all audience members.
- ► Listen actively.
- ► Intervene if necessary to manage time and control sidebar conversations.
- ► Track the time, topic, and task to ensure you accomplish the goal and end on time.
- ► Assess group dynamics and respond appropriately.
- ► Talk neutrally and avoid taking sides or becoming defensive.
- ► Ensure a safe, comfortable environment

Best Practices for Teleconference Calls and Speaking over the Phone

- ► State the specific purpose of the call.
- ► Use a pleasant tone of voice with plenty of volume.
- ► Avoid speakerphones whenever possible.
- ► Sit up straight (or stand up) as if you were actually face-to-face with the person you are calling.
- ► Avoid discrediting speech habits.
- ► Focus on the caller and the message; avoid multitasking and tune out distractions.
- ► Listen actively; indicate your attentiveness by using verbal nods.

- ➤ Be patient. Don't interrupt or jump to conclusions.
- ➤ Ensure a quiet environment to optimize concentration and minimize disruptions.
- ➤ Rehearse your opening remarks prior to the call.
- ➤ Keep your words and voice tone courteous, positive, and upbeat.
- ➤ Be caller-centric. Use the pronouns "you, your" more than "I, me, my."
- ➤ If you must place someone on hold, ask for permission and explain the reason.
- ➤ With multiple attendees, identify yourself before you speak and instruct others to do the same.
- ➤ Direct questions and comments to others by name.
- ➤ When you adjourn the call, let the other callers hang up first.

CHAPTER 16

Delivering Winning Webinars

> **Any sufficiently advanced technology is indistinguishable from magic.**
>
> —ARTHUR C. CLARKE

Most of us are accustomed to delivering our presentations and conversations in person, where we can communicate face-to-face, gauge our audience's responses, and connect with them visually. To build on Arthur Clarke's quote, delivering an effective presentation online using Cisco WebEx, Microsoft Office Live Meeting, or other available webinar services can seem shrouded in mystique.

PLAN, PREPARE, AND REHEARSE

In a virtual environment, just like magic, presto!—your audience is invisible. Therefore, effective webinar presenters must rely more heavily on voice and visual aids as the primary communicators. The following guidelines are designed to help you improve your ability to present powerfully and persuasively in the virtual presentation environment.

Webinar Logistics

First, be sure to choose your webinar hosting vendor wisely. Not all are alike. Choose a vendor that works with a variety of operating systems and is reliable and scalable. Also, consider vendors experienced in the latest techniques in application sharing, polling, chat, and recording features.

My clients tell me that webinars scheduled on Tuesdays and Wednesdays consistently receive the highest attendance. Avoid Mondays and Fridays (unless absolutely necessary, of course) so you're not competing with long weekends. And, if possible, plan to host the webinar at least twice to accommodate different time zones and schedules. This maximizes attendance and ensures the greatest distribution of learning.

Ideally, schedule the webinar to begin at fifteen minutes past the hour; e.g., from 2:15 until 3:15 PM. Most business meetings end on the hour; the extra fifteen minutes gives your participants time to get back to their desks, decompress, and dial in. Times such as 10:15 AM and 2:15 PM are optimal to ensure participants' availability before or after lunch. Keep your presentation relatively short—typically no more than an hour if possible.

If the webinar is scheduled on the hour, begin two minutes past the hour. This gives people time to call in, but won't make the punctual attendees wait too long. Starting on time sets a professional precedent and encourages people to be on time for the next webinar.

Leading up to the webinar, send at least two reminder e-mails: one the day before, and another one an hour before the webinar. Be sure to make the registration process easy for attendees. After registration, provide a confirmation e-mail with a link that adds the event to their calendar for their time zone. Include the dial-in number and a link to the webinar as well as the pass code, software requirements (if relevant), and the phone number for technical support. Also include the meeting agenda in the e-mails.

For technical assistance, appoint a colleague (preferably one with some web conference experience) to act as "tech support" during the webinar. This person will attend to technical issues that arise. This frees the presenter(s) to focus solely on delivering the content and connecting effectively with attendees. You may also consider hiring a meeting consultant or IT specialist provided by the web-hosting vendor. These experts will be present and on hand during the webinar to assist with technical issues.

If technical assistance is not possible, be prepared to answer at least a question or two from attendees about setting up the webinar. If the participants are required to install software plug-ins, make sure you can point them to the download location; if there are particular browser requirements, make sure you know what they are. Your vendor will give you a technical support number. Have it ready—not filed away—in case you encounter any significant issues. Your primary focus is delivering an effective presentation, not solving technical problems.

Webinar Rehearsal

Be sure to do a "trial run" practice session of your presentation prior to the actual webinar. Include all team members and guests who will be presenting. This webinar dress rehearsal helps you discover and resolve any kinks in the technology prior to the live webinar. You'll also be able to practice with the presentation tools.

Conduct your own personal rehearsal with your content to ensure proper timing. If possible, ask one or two colleagues who work in remote locations to dial in and serve as the audience. This dry run should be conducted as if it were the live webinar.

Prior to the webinar starting, have someone on your team dial in to make sure the number and link are working properly for participants. Have this person send you a question using the webinar software, just as the attendees may do, so you know the system's working properly.

Webinar Presentation and Slides

When it's time for the live webinar, request that the host, presenters, and moderators arrive early, ideally thirty minutes before the meeting starts. The early arrival allows one last chance to verify that the webinar is set up properly, slides are uploaded, and all the links are working. In addition, it shows that you're prepared and professional. By the time attendees virtually "arrive," the welcome slides should be on display and all technical discussions completed. Freed up and relaxed, you can welcome attendees as they call in.

For the welcome slides, I recommend using a looping series. This technique is a great way to keep attendees entertained while they're waiting for your presentation to begin. The looping slides can contain important information, such as the title of the webinar along with the presenter's photo; inspirational quotes that apply to the topic; interesting "Did you know?" industry facts; the conference dial-in number and technical assistance phone number; quiz questions; and also announcements such as "The webinar will begin in 10 minutes." Be creative!

If the group is small (fewer than twelve people), consider requesting attendees' photos ahead of time and incorporating their names and pictures into the opening. When you start your webinar, remember to open with an attention-getting grabber slide, such as a photo, shocking statistic, or question. Refer to Chapter 4 for more ideas on attention-getters.

To avoid interruptions and background noise, find a quiet conference room from which you can conduct the webinar. Be sure to place a "Meeting in Progress" or "Do Not Disturb" sign on the door to discourage people from entering the room unexpectedly. Also, turn off any devices such as cell phones, alarms, and fax machines that could interrupt you or make noise during the program.

For your own comfort and care, have a glass of water at your desk to keep your voice clear throughout the program. Add lemon to your water, or sip clear grapefruit juice without the pulp. This helps avoid a dry throat and keeps your mouth moist and throat clear.

Just as you would in a live presentation, follow the presentation development guidelines discussed in Chapter 4. First, create a compelling opening that includes an introduction, attention-getter/hook, and brief executive preview. In the preview, be sure to emphasize benefits to the audience, key points you're going to cover, logistics, and instructions for asking questions. Second, be sure the main body includes your key points with supporting material, clear transition statements, and audience interaction. Finally, design a close that summarizes your key points, issues a call to action, and thanks the audience.

Use more slides for a webinar than you would in a face-to-face presentation. Because the screen is the primary visual aid (versus your physical presence) it's important to keep the attendees' eyes engaged. An easy way to do this is to reveal bullet points one at a time as you discuss them, rather than all at once. Incorporate lots of relevant photos and eye-catching graphics.

The Presentation Computer

Be sure to close all unused applications on the presentation computer. Turn off instant messaging or automatic e-mail notifications. You do not want any personal or confidential information displayed, and you don't want pop-ups to interrupt the webinar.

Make sure your desktop doesn't display anything unprofessional or contain anything that might be offensive to your audience. Please don't use a computer with outdated software—one that prominently displays icons showing you haven't installed your latest software patches or anti-virus updates. Have a backup computer powered up and on standby in case of technical mishaps.

EFFECTIVE PRESENTATION AND FACILITATION

After you're prepared and well rehearsed, let the magic begin. It's show time! Here are a few tips to ensure that you, as the presenter, deliver a dynamic, engaging webinar.

- ► If possible, stand up to present. This aligns your body for better vocalization, adds energy to your delivery style, and helps avoid a tone that's too laid-back or casual. You want to convey the same level of energy and enthusiasm you would if you were in a live face-to-face environment.

- ► Remember that as the presenter, you are always on a full interactive line to the listeners for the duration of the program. Minimize noise from your location, such as ruffling through papers, tapping the table with a pen or finger, or noisily sipping a beverage.

- ► Do not host your conference from a speakerphone or cell phone. These devices undermine vocal effectiveness and diminish sound quality. Use a high-quality headset or your standard telephone handset. If you must use a speakerphone, be sure to position it as close as possible to you and other speakers.

- ► Once under way, provide a quick review of logistics. For example, if the web hosting software allows participants to queue up questions, explain how that works. Let attendees know how you'll handle Q&A (during the session, at the end, or both). You could even allow participants to fax or e-mail their questions to you or the host before or during the call.

- ► Next, instruct attendees to identify themselves when speaking. (If during the webinar a speaker does not do so, simply say "Thanks for that point. Who was the speaker? Great, Barry! I appreciate your insight.")

- ► Finally, ask attendees to mute their phone to avoid background activities and noise. Also request that they avoid placing their phone on "hold" during the webinar. Many phones have an "on hold" recording or music. This is highly distracting when it broadcasts to all the callers.

- ► Before you dive into the main content, let attendees know if they will receive or have access to the slides. If so, let them know you'll send them following the presentation, or provide instructions for accessing the file.

- ► As you would with any other meeting, be sure to start and end on time. Don't make punctual attendees wait because you expect more people to log in. Create a schedule and stick to it. Whether your webinar participants are customers, employees, partners, or some other mix of people, make every effort to respect their time. As the host or presenter, it's your responsibility to keep the meeting on track.

➤ Confirm that the attendees can see your screen or slide when you start. It also helps to have a dialed-in "spotter" in the audience who can alert you to audio problems, desktop resolution issues, or other glitches that come up.

Keys to Creating Compelling Content

It's most important for you to develop compelling, high-quality content for the webinar. As you would in a face-to-face presentation, know your audience and tailor the material to meet their needs. To provide supporting materials, invite an industry expert, customer, or partner to participate. This will stimulate more interest, drive participation, and create synergy. A well-known key opinion leader or company executive can add cachet and even double or triple your attendance.

Even though the forum is a webinar and people are closer to the screen, honor best practices for slide design: Don't cram too much text or information onto your slides. Keep them simple and leave plenty of white space and a clean background.

The most captivating presentations tend to be multimedia. In other words, avoid using PowerPoint only. Include animation, video, photos, web demos, or other visual aids to make your presentation more interesting. When doing a demo or showing software, try not to move too fast or scroll up and down a web page too quickly. Often, a refresh takes some time to complete based on the user's bandwidth. Every time you change your screen, allow three to five seconds for everyone to see the change.

Engage your audience and keep their attention. For example, include polling questions at key points in your presentation. (You can also survey attendees prior to the webinar, which can help you tailor the content and know your audience better.) Here are a few tips to follow when using polling/voting features:

➤ Display polling questions in your web presentation so that attendees can both see and hear each question.

➤ Make the questions and answers short and clear. Long, multifaceted questions and answers are hard to follow and are the most common problem for listeners.

- ➤ Have a colleague review the questions and answers for clarity.
- ➤ Use the polling feature throughout the program, rather than presenting the questions all at once.
- ➤ Limit your total number of polling questions to no more than five.
- ➤ Decide ahead of time how you wish to share polling results. You may wish to display or announce them in real time or wait to disclose the results later in the program.

Regardless of which method you choose, make sure to have a plan for how to incorporate audience feedback into the flow of the event.

When moving between slides or screens during the webinar, periodically read aloud the slide number or slide title to help participants know they are in the right place and seeing the same thing you are. For example, "Now let's move to slide number 10 and discuss 'Five Steps to Selling.'"

I've learned many presentation lessons the hard way. Here's one: Prepare a hard copy of your slides, URLs, or any other visual elements to keep on hand for your own reference during the webinar. This way, in the unfortunate event of a power outage, disconnection, or unexpected technology glitch on your end, you can continue the webinar without interruption. Years ago in one of my first webinars I was alone in my office, miles away from the 200 attendees who had dialed in from all over the country. My computer crashed in the middle of the webinar. Because I couldn't see the slides and had no hard copy, I had no choice but to apologize profusely and end the meeting.

After that, I was more prepared. A year or so later, I conducted a webinar for seventy-five pharmacists who had called in from multiple locations around the world. We were reviewing best practices for presenting a new drug to the FDA. Five minutes into the webinar, lo and behold, I heard a loud bang outside my window. The transformer in the office complex exploded and the power went out. Seconds later sirens screamed in the distance. Of course, my office was dark and the desktop displaying the slides went black. I felt like the sky was falling. Meanwhile, an expectant group of audience members awaited my next slide. Fortunately, this time I had a hard-copy printout of the slides with all my notes. I took a deep breath and I told the client host on the line, "Sandy, I've just experienced a power outage and can't see my desktop. If you don't mind, please use your desktop to take over as the presenter and advance the slides on my cue." Within a few seconds we were back on track as though nothing had happened. Because I had the printout of the slides, their numbers, and my notes, I was able to continue the webinar for the remainder of the hour as planned.

As described in Chapter 6, one of my favorite tricks in PowerPoint is the ability to seamlessly navigate to any slide during the presentation. Suppose you're displaying slide 27, but an audience member asks a question related to a different slide, let's say number 14. Wouldn't it be great to access that slide instantly, without having to click backward for thirteen slides, or hitting the Escape key to locate the right slide in the thumbnail view? All you need is a printout showing numbered slides. Here's how to create it: After you've finalized the order of the slides, set the print options to "Handouts." Opt for nine slides per page with a horizontal orientation. Be sure to check "Print hidden slides." Then click "OK" to print. On the printout, manually write the slide numbers horizontally, left to right, underneath the slides.

Using the preceding example, you would then be able to simply glance at the printout, see that the slide you need is number 14, and type "14" on the keyboard. Press the Enter key and voila!—the slide will appear on demand. When you are finished discussing slide 14, you can return to slide 27 by right-clicking on the screen and then selecting Last Viewed. You're right back where you started. To jump to any slide, just enter the slide number on the keyboard and press the Enter key. This will move you directly to that slide.

In the webinar setting, it's a good idea to change slides (or a visual element of the slide) approximately every thirty seconds. This provides consistent new information at a smooth pace to keep attendees engaged. The easiest way to accomplish this is to reveal your bullet points one at a time versus all at once in a large block of text.

Avoid using slides that you only want to show for a few seconds. Because there is a slight time lag between the presenter clicking and the attendees seeing the slide, some attendees may only see such slides for a microsecond. In the same vein, don't build a sequence of slides that is reliant on exact synchronization between the slides and what you say. The timing may be off for viewers.

To guide the viewer's eye appropriately, highlight what you want people to look at on the slides. In a face-to-face presentation, you can physically point to the item on a slide or use the laser pointer. Similarly, most webinar software has handy tools available that allow you to draw or highlight items on the screen. Familiarize yourself with them and use them frequently to help keep viewers engaged. You can also emphasize items on a slide during the design phase by building in an animation or special effect.

Keeping the Audience Engaged

By all means, build in frequent interaction points for the audience. For example, involve your listeners through discussion questions. Show the question(s) on the slide and ask for volunteers to reply; if appropriate, call on members by name. Interact with the audience when it's most logical, given the technology you use and the tools that are available. A simple method is to stop between key points and ask, "So that wraps up point number one. Before moving on to point two, what questions or comments do you have?"

Use memorable stories. Your attendees will not remember your exact words, but they *will* remember the mental images that your words and slides inspire. Support your key points with relevant stories and vivid experiences. Create a "theater of the mind" by using memorable characters, exciting situations, interactive dialogue, authentic humor, and graphic illustrations or photos.

Speak clearly, at a comfortable pace. By taking your time and not rushing, you make it easier for the audience to comprehend your presentation's content and scope. Part of good pacing is the ability to use effective pauses frequently. Give your listeners an opportunity to absorb the content. Stop talking from time to time. Check in between key points to see if anyone has a question. If you rush along from slide to slide at full speed, you'll lose the audience's attention and likely frustrate them. An energetic pace is okay, but don't try to cram in too much information. And when you deliver a complex concept, describe a tedious process, or say something of particular impact, be sure to slow the pace a bit. Pause afterward to allow the audience to ponder your words.

As with phone calls and live meetings, avoid filler words and phrases. Pay extra-careful attention to eliminating the usual suspects: "uh," "um," "er," and "you know." In a webinar, these unnecessary fillers sound even more prominent than in person. Replace them with a pause. And be sure to record a run-through. It will give you a chance to monitor the occurrence of these fillers and work to eliminate them.

Record your seminar. If appropriate, post the webinar on your website for future viewing. Build a reference library of past webinars for your colleagues, customers, and prospects to peruse at their leisure. Recorded webinars and their Q&A sessions can also be helpful in training new employees or reviewing customer input prior to a new product launch, selling event, or internal business strategy session.

Create a schedule and stick to it. Whether your webinar participants are customers, employees, partners, or some other mix of people, make every effort to respect their time. As the host or presenter, it's your responsibility to keep the meeting on track.

If you have provided handouts or written materials to the participants, and you're referring to them during the webinar, be sure to reference your location in the materials. Allow plenty of time for instructions and directions. For example: "Now we're going to move from the slide to the handout. (Pause). Does everyone have the handout in front of you? Please turn to page four of the handout. (Pause). Notice the green column on the far right. Allow me to explain these expenses line by line, beginning with row one." This level of guidance keeps people on track and allows them to visually follow along.

Concluding the Webinar and Handling Q&A

Inform attendees when you've reached the end of the core material within the scheduled time allotment. This way, attendees who must leave on time won't be irritated by the fact that they're missing core content. It's fine to extend beyond the end time as long as the "officially scheduled program" has a clean end and those who need to leave may do so without feeling deprived of critical content. For example, when I'm conducting a webinar, after the summary and next steps, I usually adjourn by saying, "I see that it's 9:58 and almost time to adjourn. This concludes the content on the agenda. I'm happy to remain on the line if anyone has additional questions or comments. Otherwise thanks again, everyone, for your time and attention this morning, and have a great week!" Inevitably, many people hang up to run to their next meeting; however, one or more will still be on the line and will ask, "Darlene, can we go back to slide number five? I have a question." This technique makes you a meeting hero and gives you the best of both worlds. The majority of attendees will admire your punctual dismissal, value your ability to cover all the promised content in the allotted time period, and appreciate the fact that you respect their time. The other attendees will be grateful you were willing to spend a few extra minutes with them on the line to resolve their issues.

During the Q&A session, be sure to repeat each question so that the entire group can hear it and also to ensure that you understand it correctly. As obvious as the question may sound to you, others on the line may have a poor connection and be unable to hear the question clearly. If the questioner does not identify himself, ask for his name. For example: "Thank you for that question. May I ask your name? Thanks Ben. Ben's question is, 'What's the process of certification?'" This adds a personal touch and also allows you to return a minute later and say, "Ben, did that answer your question?"

Keep answers as short as possible, ideally under a minute. Then ask if you have answered the question to the participant's satisfaction. Avoid over-answering or belaboring the point. You want to address as many questions as possible.

Regardless of the questioner's tone of voice, remain upbeat, positive, and courteous. Remember, if someone sounds angry, frustrated, or annoyed, it's usually not directed at you. Avoid taking it personally. Simply rephrase the question, thank the questioner for the input, and respond in a courteous tone.

After concluding the Q&A session and before you adjourn, provide a summary of key points and issue a call to action. What do you want the listeners to do as a result of the information you've just shared? Invite attendees to take an action and tell them what you want them to do next. Be clear and specific on next steps and mutual commitments. Send them off energized, focused, and ready to act on your message.

End on a positive note. Based on a communication principle known as "the recency effect," your last words will be among the most memorable. Make sure you close with a powerful, unforgettable impact statement supported by a visually compelling slide.

WEBINAR FOLLOW-UP

If you want to improve your presentations, ask for feedback. Send attendees an evaluation form afterward with a few simple questions, such as:

- ➤ What did you like most about this presentation?
- ➤ What did you like least?
- ➤ On a scale of one to ten, with ten as the highest, how valuable was the content?
- ➤ How could future webinars be improved?

You may also want to use this survey to gather attendees' unanswered questions. Be sure to provide an avenue for attendees to submit questions that were not resolved during the allotted time. Follow up promptly with answers.

Send a follow-up e-mail telling participants where the presentation has been posted and how to access it. If the webinar is not posted, send out a recording and the slides within twenty-four hours. Based on my experience, about half of your attendees will request the information anyway. Be proactive and send it out as a courtesy. Fast follow-up motivates attendees to take action on your message while the webinar content is still on their minds.

Good etiquette is good etiquette—online or off. Be sure to also send a follow-up e-mail to participants thanking them for their attendance. Include additional relevant information. Invite them to the next webinar. Send a "sorry we missed you" e-mail to registrants who did not attend. Nurture these prospects to encourage them to attend your next event. If your webinar is a sales presentation, pass all the registrants and participants to the sales department for follow-up. Include survey and qualifying information.

Evaluate all feedback gathered from the webinar. Consider making improvements to the registration process, your content, delivery style, and the Q&A session to determine what could make your next webinar even more engaging and beneficial.

Watch your archived presentation and experience it just as your audience did. You'll get a sense of how they perceived you and your content, which may be much different from how you experienced the webinar as the presenter!

CHAPTER 16: EXECUTIVE SUMMARY

- ➤ Before the webinar, plan, prepare, and rehearse.
- ➤ To optimize attendance, schedule webinars on Tuesdays and Wednesdays if possible.
- ➤ Schedule your webinar to start at fifteen minutes past the hour, rather than on the hour (e.g., 2:15–3:15 PM).
- ➤ Arrive thirty minutes early to ensure proper technical setup.
- ➤ Use a series of looping slides to entertain and inform attendees as they call in.
- ➤ Open with a captivating attention-getter.
- ➤ Provide structure with a well-organized opening, body, and close.
- ➤ Design and use more slides for a webinar than you would in a face-to-face presentation.

➤ During the webinar, present and facilitate effectively.

➤ Stand up to present; exude enthusiasm and use an upbeat tone of voice.

➤ Use a high-quality headset or handset; avoid the speakerphone.

➤ Start and end on time.

➤ Navigate seamlessly to any slide using a printout of numbered slides.

➤ Interact with your audience frequently and change a visual element every thirty seconds.

➤ Close with a compelling summary and call to action.

➤ After the webinar, follow up appropriately.

➤ Ask for feedback or conduct a survey to improve your next webinar.

➤ Follow up with attendees within twenty-four hours and send promised materials.

➤ Send an e-mail thanking attendees for their participation.

➤ Review the recorded webinar to refine and improve it.

CHAPTER 17

Leading Team Presentations

> I not only use all the brains I have, but all I can borrow.
>
> —WOODROW WILSON

Sometimes for large accounts, multiple-solution presentations, and big-ticket items, a team will work together to deliver a message. Each team member brings his or her expertise to the meeting and presents a particular topic. In addition to several presenters, one or two subject matter experts may attend to answer questions during the presentation.

In the lessons-learned category, I'd like to share one team presentation story that didn't work out the way my client planned. Steering committee members for the Olympics invited my client, a major nationally known event-planning company, to bid on a large contract involving the Games. Luckily, this company made it into the top three vendors. As they were preparing for the final presentation to the committee, my client—in the eleventh hour—decided no one on their team wanted to present. Apparently, they felt so much was riding on the contract that they wanted to hire a "professional" to deliver the presentation. I stressed to them they were the experts and encouraged them to present.

Despite my coaxing, they declined and I reluctantly accepted. They assured me they would be available to "chime in and answer questions," but they didn't want the pressure of a speaking role. Over a twenty-four-hour period I studied all the materials I could get my hands on. The following day, the team and I delivered the big presentation. Everything was going pretty well, until the end. The head decision maker for the Olympics looked at me and all the members of my client's team and asked, "I want to know one thing: Who can I call at two o'clock in the morning when something isn't going right?" There was a long, awkward silence. Jim looked at Bob. Bob glanced at Karen. Karen eyed Tom. Tom stared at me. And I finally said, "Mr. Smith, to ensure we understand your question, are you asking for the name of your on-call coordinator—your 24/7 point person?"

"That's right," he replied. There was still no answer.

Finally, Bob spoke up. "Uh, er, um . . . that would be you, Jim, wouldn't it?"

"No," replied Jim. "I thought that would be Karen."

"That's okay," said the decision maker. "You've answered my question."

Needless to say, the Olympic committee did not award the hefty contract to the event-planning company. Despite my client's impressive collateral material, slick mock-ups, expensive multimedia, and "professional" presenter, the group did not appear as a confident, cohesive, and well-organized team. As the saying goes, hindsight is 20/20. In retrospect, the team did not have a leader; they lacked the confidence to present the message themselves; and they failed to anticipate and rehearse answers to questions they were likely to face.

GUIDELINES FOR PRESENTING WELL WITH OTHERS

If you and your team want to avoid this type of scenario, use the following guidelines for planning, rehearsing, and delivering winning team presentations.

Appoint a Strong Leader or Captain

The team leader is responsible for total project management from concept development through the final presentation. He or she has the leadership ability and authority to make on-the-spot decisions. Whether it's content, structure, presenters, or logistics, the captain takes full responsibility for the overall outcome of the presentation. The leader or captain's tasks include setting deadlines, overseeing the production schedule, arranging for rehearsals, ensuring proper room setup and supplies, providing detailed customer information to fellow team members, and keeping everything on track and well organized. The team leader also decides on the specific outcome to be achieved. Most important, the team leader should guide, not dictate. The leader's job really is to facilitate the process of deciding objectives and key messages. What response does the team want from its audience? If the team is successful, what will happen?

Decide on Three Clearly Defined Goals

Make a list of goals, then narrow it down to those that are most important. A good rule of thumb is to focus on the three most essential goals you as a team want to achieve with this specific audience. Everything in the presentation should point to these goals and work toward achieving them.

Prepare, Prepare, Prepare

Know your audience. Make sure every team member understands the audience's key pain points, issues, challenges, expectations, and facility specifications. As you prepare, organize your individual presentations as if they each were part of one continuous presentation delivered by several people. It may help to think of these as chapters in a book, with a story line running through it that leads to a specific end. Think of each team member's segment as a mini-presentation module.

Deciding who should present which topics depends on your overall objectives and the command of the content each person has. Your team preparation must include a careful analysis of your audience. What you don't know can hurt you. Obviously, team members must never contradict or criticize one another.

If possible, assign one person to be in charge of all the visual aids. This will ensure a consistent look. You might want to use a single template, with everyone following the same design guidelines. Use the same color-coding and consistent font style and size for each person's presentation. And of course, stick with the same graphics software. This integrated approach prevents inconsistencies and avoids a haphazard, piecemeal appearance to the presentation.

For a unified look and higher quality, I strongly recommend using a designer to prepare the visuals.

Optimize Individual Strengths

Consider the special knowledge and job experience of each team member and how that fits into the overall picture. That's more important than picking team members based on rank alone. Assign each team member specific responsibilities regarding content, delivery, visual aids, research, handouts, and deadlines—based on each person's strengths and expertise. If one is a great storyteller or has a knack for captivating an audience instantly, she may be the one to kick off the presentation and deliver the opening. Each "module" should contain the elements of a presentation—a strong opening, body, and close. Practice smooth transitions between the segments. Make sure everyone understands the overall presentation objectives as well as their roles in the development of the final presentation.

Set and Meet Deadlines

Work backward from your presentation deadline. Build multiple deadlines along the way for creative development, content generation, handouts, visual aids, and rehearsals.

Give Good Introductions

Introduce all members of your team to the audience. In the beginning, proudly announce the correct full names and titles of your fellow presenters. Recite a few credentials such as number of years in the industry or with your company. State each person's role in the presentation. For example, "In addition to Ned and Cathy, it's also a pleasure to introduce Jerry Andrews, Acme's senior vice president of operations. Jerry has served the industry for twenty-five years and the Acme team for twelve years. He's a certified Six Sigma Black Belt and has spearheaded more than 200 software implementations. Jerry's role today is to present to you Acme's recommended installation process, which ensures an on-time, on-budget outcome with minimal downtime."

Stick to the Game Plan (As Best You Can)

If you drift or attempt to "wing it," you risk repeating yourself, stealing your associate's thunder, or even worse, exceeding the allotted time. Strive to stay on schedule and on track. Assign a timekeeper and work out the signals for fifteen minutes, ten minutes, five minutes, and two minutes remaining.

Listen Actively During the Presentation

Show your support. Establish and maintain eye contact with your fellow members as they present. The audience may take their cues from you. When you listen actively, you won't repeat what your partner has already said. Be fully present and available to support your team members at any moment.

Individuals play the game, but teams win championships.

—SOURCE UNKNOWN

Ask the Lead Presenter to Facilitate Q&A

The team leader also serves as the lead presenter and may act as an emcee of the event. The team leader makes the introductions, keeps everyone on schedule, controls the flow, and facilitates questions and answers. During the Q&A period, after an audience member asks a question, it's important for the presentation team to avoid long pauses and confused expressions. The leader should respond immediately with a brief answer and then direct the question to the member who is best equipped to elaborate. Or the person who feels he or she is best equipped to answer the question may immediately speak up and say, "I'll be glad to answer that question."

Keep a Friendly Tone

Avoid a stiff, over-rehearsed delivery. Be warm, attentive, and responsive to the audience. Most important, be yourself.

Organize Content Development

Attempting to collectively "write" a presentation is a challenging task. Ask all team members to write down their own ideas and the key topics they wish to cover—one per sticky note. When it comes time to "write" the presentation, meet in a room with a large blank wall and use this flat surface as a clean slate. Organize the presentation content (aka sticky notes) on the wall, moving the topics as desired into a logical flow. Once the content is organized, the group can determine the order of presenters, what types of visual aids are needed, and where to place them.

Include Clear Transitions

Transitions are the all-important bridging elements that conclude one presentation and lead to the next one. As each presenter wraps up a module, he or she should establish a link to the next presenter. Wherever appropriate, each presenter should include brief references to the key points made by the other speakers. This reinforces key messages and helps your audience retain information, an important consideration given that your listeners are receiving much more input than they would from a solo presentation.

Be Sure to Rehearse as a Team

When pulling together a team presentation, it's important that everyone become familiar with presentation content, visual aids, and transitions between presenters. Because everyone presents in a unique way, it's critical that the team practice together. It's the best way to ensure a high level of comfort with the presentation and each other. A full dress rehearsal with visual aids is a must for a successful team presentation! Get used to one another's speaking styles, especially strengths and weaknesses. Run through all the mini-presentations. Focus on how each one is structured. Review visuals. Clearly establish everyone's role and how the presentations link to one another. Is there too much content? Too little? Is there overlap? Do the modules complement and support one another? Do they flow logically? Are they aligned with your objectives?

The team should also prepare for Q&A as a group. That means anticipating questions that are likely to come up and agreeing on the answers. Also agree in advance on the team member or members who are best suited to respond to a given question. Include both introductions and transitions as part of your preparation and rehearsal. The team leader may choose to act as host rather than as one of the presenters. In any case, the team leader should be ready with a brief introduction of what's to come. State the overall theme. State the topic each presenter will cover. Ask each presenter for a concise—repeat, *concise*—description of his or her presentation. In a few words, what does each presenter think is most relevant? Include that as you mention each topic in your introduction. Also find the most relevant things to say about each presenter other than simply his or her name and title. It doesn't help much to say, "Bob here in sales will talk about our sales results." Instead you might say, "Bob Smith, Acme's vice president of sales, will now discuss our award-winning customer satisfaction strategy and how it saves you time and money."

Finally, when you think everyone's ready, do a final run-through. Assemble a small live audience to serve as a sounding board. Think of this as a dress rehearsal before opening night. It's likely you'll still find things to improve upon.

Perform an On-Site Dress Rehearsal

The team should arrive early at the meeting site. Ideally, everyone should run through their segment at least once, in the order in which they'll speak. They should click through their visuals and get comfortable with the equipment and physical setting. Practice with a microphone if you're going to be using one. Know where to find technical help, just in case. This on-site test run is important in any case. It's even more important when the presentation is taking place before a large audience.

Remember, You Are Always On

In a team presentation, everyone is being watched, even when they're not presenting. Stay alert. Listen. Show interest in what's being said. Remember that your body language can convey a positive or negative message. Stifle that yawn. Don't slouch or look bored. And unless it's absolutely necessary, do not whisper an aside to another team member. Finally, pay attention to the audience. You may pick up signals that help you gauge audience response and then tailor your comments and presentation accordingly.

CHAPTER 17: EXECUTIVE SUMMARY

- ➤ Appoint a strong team leader or captain.
- ➤ Decide on three clearly defined goals.
- ➤ Prepare, prepare, prepare.
- ➤ Ensure consistency with visual aids.
- ➤ Optimize individual strengths.
- ➤ Set and meet deadlines.
- ➤ Give good introductions.
- ➤ Stick to the game plan (as best you can).
- ➤ Listen actively during the presentation.
- ➤ Ask the lead presenter to facilitate Q&A.
- ➤ Keep a friendly tone.
- ➤ Organize content development.
- ➤ Include clear transitions.
- ➤ Be sure to rehearse as a team.
- ➤ Perform an on-site dress rehearsal.
- ➤ Remember, you are always on.

Afterword

Among life's most satisfying experiences is knowing that you have influenced others for the good, whether it's to buy your product, adopt your proposal, approve your budget, follow your recommendation, or change the course of their lives. Perhaps that's why Ralph Waldo Emerson said "Speech is power." At work, at home, in the community, and in the world, please speak up and speak out. Claim your power, find your voice, and present yourself. Present your message, services, products, company, and convictions to the world around you.

Effective presentation and communication skills will not only get you noticed, remembered, and promoted more often and more quickly than any other skill set; they also help ensure that you get more of what you want and deserve in life. By acquiring these abilities, you can be certain that you possess the number one skill in business today and will begin enjoying a whole new level of success, personally and professionally. Thank you for reading my book. Please accept my sincerest and best wishes for your continued success.

Index